Steve Bartram began working at Manchester United in 2003. He is now Contributing Editor to *Inside United*, *United Review* and manutd.com, as well as being the author of eleven previous books on the club. Steve lives in Manchester with his wife, Leanne, and two young children, Emily and Charlie, and is a Stretford End season ticket holder.

Paul Davies has been editor of Manchester United's official match programme, *United Review*, since March 2006. He began working at Old Trafford in January 2000, first for the official magazine and has since worked on numerous other official publications. Paul lives in Altrincham with his wife, Ninka, and still attends home matches with his dad.

Ben Hibbs joined Manchester United's media department in 2002 and later became deputy editor of manutd.com and *United Review*. After a brief spell away from the club in 2011 to travel, he returned in 2012. He lives in south Manchester with his girlfriend, Suzanne.

THE
IMPOSSIBLE
TREBLE

THE OFFICIAL STORY OF UNITED'S
GREATEST SEASON

STEVE BARTRAM, PAUL DAVIES AND **BEN HIBBS**

SIMON &
SCHUSTER

London · New York · Sydney · Toronto · New Delhi

A CBS COMPANY

First published in Great Britain by Simon & Schuster UK Ltd, 2013
This paperback edition published by Simon & Schuster UK Ltd, 2014

A CBS COMPANY

1 3 5 7 9 10 8 6 4 2

Simon & Schuster UK Ltd
1st Floor
222 Gray's Inn Road
London WC1X 8HB

www.simonandschuster.co.uk

Simon & Schuster Australia, Sydney
Simon & Schuster India, New Delhi

A CIP catalogue record for this book is available from the British Library

ISBN: 978-1-47113-060-1

Typeset in the UK by M Rules
Printed and bound by CPI Group (UK) Ltd, Croydon, CR0 4YY

Contents

Foreword
by Sir Alex Ferguson

I count myself fortunate to have managed so many wonderful players during my time as Manchester United manager and, within that, to have worked with several great teams.

A regular question I faced throughout my career was the age-old debate of which was my greatest United team. While it is hard to elevate one bunch of players above another – especially when they all have such great and varied attributes – it is fair to say that the Treble winners of 1999 had something special about them.

As a manager, you hope your personality and character eventually seeps into the pores of the players you work with, and I think in that squad we had quite a few players who, in their own way, developed some of the characteristics I saw in myself.

The unbreakable spirit and technical resolve they demonstrated on the most unforgiving of stages, such as the FA Cup semi-final replay against Arsenal and the Champions League semi-final against Juventus in Turin, were quite incredible.

I suppose it was demonstrated most memorably in the final game of the season, when we entered injury-time of the Champions League final losing to Bayern Munich, only to emerge victorious three minutes later. Amazing.

They were a group of players who, as well as being hugely talented and incredibly entertaining to watch, just never knew when they were beaten. They embodied the resolve so inherent in Manchester United as a club, and showed the spirit to keep fighting to the very last second of the greatest season English football has ever known.

Chapter 1

August – Rebuild and Go Again

Alex Ferguson, his players and 35,000 Manchester United supporters inside Wembley didn't need to hear the mocking words of the chanting Arsenal fans as they made their way across the Wembley turf ahead of the 1998 Charity Shield. 'You're not champions any more!' It was a reality they knew all too well.

The bitter blow of missing out on the 1997-98 Premiership crown was still painful. Memories of how Arsène Wenger's side, trailing by a dozen points entering March, had sprinted past them in the final straight to eventually take the title at the tape had hung over the club all summer. Defender David May summed up the feelings of United's dressing room when, in the aftermath of title despair, he said: 'I don't think we bottled it, but I do think that we lost it rather than Arsenal winning it. To be twelve points clear and not win it is losing.'

The Reds' appearance at the Twin Towers had come about only because of the Gunners lifting the FA Cup 13 days after claiming the league – their second ever Double, equalling United's record. Given a choice, Ferguson's men would probably rather not have suffered this afternoon of Cockney crowing in the capital, but as league runners-up they had a duty to play and so approached it as a new start, a clean slate, and a warm-up for the season proper.

As such, they could also have done without the 3-0 mauling that ground more salt into the wounds of the campaign past and did little to lift the gloom of a disappointing summer. Eight Manchester United players had been at the France '98 World Cup, while Jaap Stam, who helped the Netherlands to fourth place, became a Red three days before the semi-final. David Beckham, Gary Neville, Paul Scholes and Teddy Sheringham were part of the England squad that exited the Round of 16. Henning Berg, Ronny Johnsen and Ole Gunnar Solskjaer went out at the same stage with Norway. Peter Schmeichel's Denmark went a stage further, only to lose 3-2 to Brazil.

By contrast, two Arsenal players had become world champions in the FIFA showpiece: Frenchmen Patrick Vieira and Emmanuel Petit. While they were feted in France, back in the UK there was only one United player making post-tournament headlines: David Beckham. In under a week, the Reds' No.7 had gone from England hero to hate figure. His stunning free-kick to seal a 2-0 victory against Colombia for progress from Group G had seen his popularity hit new heights. But five days later, in the last-16 tie against Argentina, Beckham aimed a petulant but tame flick at Diego Simeone and so began a chain of events that were to make him public enemy number one. Simeone rolled around seemingly maimed, referee Kim Milton Nielsen produced a red card, and when England exited on penalties (how else?) the finger of blame was jabbed angrily at the United man.

'Ten heroic lions, one stupid boy,' screamed the *Daily Mirror*'s headline. The *Daily Star*'s 'What an idiot!' being harsher still. Even Beckham's emotional, heartfelt apology for his ill-advised kick did little to calm the outcry. His effigy was hung outside a London pub, the message 'God forgives even David Beckham' was displayed at a church, and former players formed a queue to have their say on the vilified midfielder.

'David Beckham has quite simply got to go and play abroad now,' wrote England legend Jimmy Greaves in a newspaper column. 'If he stays here it could destroy him.'

Sports psychologist Carole Seheult, who had worked with Aston Villa and the British Olympic team, agreed. 'Playing in Europe would give him space away from all the people who are questioning his attitude and temperament,' she told the *Daily Mirror*. 'The biggest problem he will face is how other people, especially the fans, react to him now.'

Others, like our own George Best, could see the potential positives for Becks. 'I used to love it when punters had a go. I got awful stick, with vile abuse being thrown at me, but I got a buzz out of it. It gave me the incentive to really turn it on. And, if David's like me, he'll react the same way,' suggested Best.

Alex Ferguson had no intention of allowing one of the club's prized assets to be driven out of the English game and, just three weeks after Beckham's World Cup dismissal, he was back for pre-season. United had played a first warm-up match against Birmingham City at St Andrew's without their World Cup stars, meaning the 4-3 defeat – they were also missing Roy Keane because of what the Reds' boss described as a 'wee knock' – was no real cause for alarm.

A few days later Beckham and Keane were back for the opening game of a three-match pre-season trip to Scandinavia (two games in Norway, one in Denmark). Against Valerengen in Oslo, a 2-2 draw, the man still being pilloried back home was greeted with 'Welcome Beckham' banners and presented with the 1998 Player of the Year award by members of United's Scandinavian Supporters' Club.

'It was always going to be a case of David getting back to what he does best,' said Ferguson, increasingly keen to draw a line under his player's World Cup trauma. 'I was also pleased for Roy, who gave me forty-five minutes,' he added, swiftly shifting attention to his other returnee, who was back after an 11-month lay-off. 'There was never any hesitation about him. He played as he always does – seriously.'

Keane figured in only 11 matches in 1997-98 before damaging his knee ligaments, and his absence had been sorely felt. 'The games we lost last season we would never have lost with Keane playing,' asserted the Reds' boss. 'If he had been on the field, I think there would have been something different about the place. There was a lack of leadership because of the youthfulness of the team.'

Ryan Giggs, whose own season had been interrupted by injury, summed up the feelings of the United players at having their skipper back. 'It's great to have our ears bashed again. We all missed the rollickings. It's like having another signing, and we missed him last year,' said the Welshman.

Two actual signings had been made by the time the Reds arrived in Norway – before heading on to Denmark. A deal for Stam had been finalised in May, and he joined up with the squad in time for the 6-0 thrashing of Brondby in Copenhagen. Jesper Blomqvist – signed for £4.4 million from Parma in late July – was recovering from a pre-existing injury and missed the tour entirely.

Another of those absent was back-up goalkeeper Raimond van der Gouw, unavailable due to illness. 'I had pneumonia. I have no idea how I got it, but I spent a week in hospital,' recalls the Dutchman. 'I was on a boat when I went to England and I had a bad cough. I'd been watching the World Cup on the boat to England, and when we got back it was worse. So I went to get checked over and have a scan and they saw that there was a big spot on my lung so they just said: "Raimond, go home and get your stuff."

'I was on a drip and had treatment for a week in hospital. Then I needed another week to recover after I left the hospital, so I went to Holland to be with the family and missed the pre-season tour. It wasn't the best of starts to the new the season.'

Van der Gouw missed not only three opportunities to build fitness and improve match reactions, but also the chance for the squad to reconnect and bond. John Curtis, one of the youngest on tour, remembers the experience well. 'We went to see the Rolling Stones a few days before we played Brondby,' he recalls. 'The whole squad went in an executive box, it was great. I remember the night out, actually. We had a good night in Copenhagen. Pete [Schmeichel] took us into a restaurant and we all thought: "It's going to be boring, this." But within two hours, people were dancing on tables and stuff like that. It was fantastic for camaraderie.'

Denis Irwin, although not a Stones fan, adds: 'It wasn't my cup of tea, but I enjoyed the show. In Copenhagen, big Pete looked after us. In those days, we didn't go out that much during pre-season. The manager allowed you one night out, which I think is still the case now, and I think that was our night out. Although I can't remember that much of it, to be honest!'

Irwin scored a hat-trick in United's third and final game of the tour, a 4-0 defeat of SK Brann, to round off a satisfying stint away. 'Norway is the perfect pre-season as a player because you haven't got far to travel, the fans are fantastic over there and you're playing against teams who are in the middle of their seasons. It was a good test and a good place to go for pre-season,' says the Irishman.

Firing ten goals past Brondby and Brann without conceding had been one thing; silencing Arsenal's big guns was a different proposition entirely. Not only would United be facing buoyant Double-winners, but there was also the distraction of continued dissection of Beckham's every move – on and off the pitch.

Skipper Keane was sure his team-mate would handle whatever came his way, saying: 'As United players, the abuse we get already is unbelievable. I don't really see how it can get much worse. Becks will take it in his stride and, if anything, it should help to urge him on. I'll try to calm him down, but I don't think I'm one to talk! I know Becks can look after himself, but he's only human. I'm sure all the things that have been said have hurt him and his family. He just has to forget about the scumbags and get on with it.'

At Wembley, Beckham received the reception he'd been expecting – derision and chants of 'You let your country down' from the Arsenal supporters. Nothing new perhaps, and possibly nowhere near as bad as he'd envisaged, but still an irritation he'd have to handle in the coming months.

The somewhat half-hearted Beckham-baiting had made no impact on the player, but tougher to take had been the disappointing 3-0 Wembley defeat. Marc Overmars, Cristopher Wreh and Nicolas Anelka scored the goals to cap a miserable afternoon – one that Henning Berg, a second-half substitute, remembers well, but in perspective. 'The Charity Shield is the Charity Shield,' says the Norwegian. 'If you win it, then you say it is a fantastic trophy and if you lose it then you say it is good preparation for the league to start.'

Understandably, it was the latter stance that United adopted. Alex Ferguson found positives in the players gaining match fitness, especially for his improving skipper – although Keane admitted he had a long way still to go to reach peak performance. 'I expect to be really back into the same swing of things around the end of September – once I've been playing football for about six or seven weeks,' he said.

If the price for having been beaten to the title by Arsenal was that there was no automatic place in the Champions League, then the silver lining was a second chance to compete via a two-legged qualifier. Facing the Reds were Polish champions LKS Lodz, victors over FK Ganca of Azerbaijan in the first qualifying round. It was a favourable draw, at least on paper, and hopefully a backdoor route to another tilt at Europe's premier club competition.

Defeat to Monaco at the quarter-final stage had been one of the bitterest blows in the previous campaign, with United having looked as strong as any side in contention. Losing on away goals to the French side had been hard to take, but there were at least welcome words of encouragement from the strangest of sources. The great Zinedine Zidane, a member of the Juventus side beaten 1-0 in the final by Real Madrid, said of the Reds: 'All of us agree that Manchester United were the best team we faced in the Champions League this season. We are sure their time will come in the European Cup – sooner rather than later.'

In the first leg against the Poles, there were but glimpses of the free-flowing football that had caught Zizou's eye. But a 2-0 victory courtesy of goals from Ryan Giggs and Andy Cole put the Reds in control of the tie, while also further advanced fitness levels. With notoriously hard-working Leicester City to face in the opening Premiership fixture of the season four days later, those improved stamina reserves would be needed.

Even a month on from his supposed 'red card shame', David Beckham was still filling column inches. His contribution in every match since his return in Oslo had been monitored, his body language scrutinised. Questions continued to be asked. How would he react to provocations from fans and opponents? Would the off-field attention impact on his on-field displays? Would he ever be the same player again? Those on the outside believed the strain must surely be showing; those on the inside recall it quite differently.

'He wasn't really bothered, to be honest,' recalls Paul Scholes. 'It was a bit of a storm in a teacup and didn't affect his performances – he was brilliant. It was a little bit of something that comes sometimes when you've made a mistake. Footballers are pretty good at dealing with stuff like that. We had a manager who we knew could look after all that side of it, so we just concentrated on the football and that's what David was good at.'

Against Leicester he showed just how good. In a poor team

performance, he salvaged a point for United by inspiring a two-goal fight-back: cancelling out goals from Emile Heskey and Tony Cottee with an assist and an equaliser. His remarkable 95th-minute free-kick was the perfect riposte to visiting Foxes fans – famously fervent about the national side – who'd taunted him throughout. He was clearly taking Best's approach of 'the more you boo, the better I'll play'.

Beckham survived his next test of temperament, too – at West Ham United's notoriously partisan Boleyn Ground. Inside the compact East London stadium, the midfielder could hear every insult, was mercilessly reminded of his England misdemeanour and had his tolerance tested. That is until the blandness of the football took the fire out of the fixture and the game meandered to a goalless draw. It was a forgettable afternoon, but one in which Becks had again been his side's man of the match.

'Man United is great. Once you go through the doors of the training ground, it's almost like you're behind the Berlin Wall and nobody can touch you,' explains Phil Neville of the environment in which his famous former team-mate was allowed to recover and refocus. 'You've got this protective blanket around you and you're free from the outside world. Nobody else can touch you, you're given confidence, you're rebuilt, you're loved and that's what we had to do because every away ground we went to, Becks was getting stick bordering on criminal. But with Becks, it brought the best out of him. It actually made him improve his performances and, even though he was under immense pressure, I don't think his displays for United wavered one bit. I thought in terms of consistency, it was his best season by far, because he played in every game and he had a real determination to prove people wrong. You play for England and they're always looking for a scapegoat. Becks, he was that scapegoat. He got sent off. So what? He wasn't the reason England lost the game, so we move on.'

Van der Gouw agrees, and recalls that for Beckham there was

even an easing of the normally vicious dressing-room ribbing. 'We didn't take the p*** out of him, never,' says Raimond. 'He was one of us, an important player like everybody else and I had the feeling that everyone felt sorry for him, for the way he was being treated. Okay, people make mistakes on the pitch, but the consequences for him were massive and he went through it. But it's a big compliment to him when you look at how he handled everything and reacted over the course of the season.'

With camera lenses firmly fixed on the man with seven on his back, the debut of United's third summer signing – wearing No.19 – went largely unnoticed. Dwight Yorke's £12.6 million switch from Aston Villa had been protracted but finally completed, and he recalls his first impressions of the ranks he'd joined. 'It was a squad to be admired,' says Yorke. 'You are talking about the best goalkeeper in the world, Peter Schmeichel, and Jaap Stam had just joined the club prior to me. Of course, there were the ones who were already there, like Giggsy, Scholesy and Roy Keane, Becks … It was just full of star quality throughout the squad, and also unsung heroes like Denis Irwin – who was an unbelievable player. When you actually see him on a daily basis, practising, he was just first class. We had an unbelievable team and one that had star quality in every position that you can think of. Of course, Coley was there with Ole and Teddy, all international players. It was amazing.'

The Trinidadian was ineligible for United's next game, the return leg with Lodz in Poland, and another who missed out was Gary Neville. Champions League qualification had meant an early return after a shorter than usual break from football. While that clearly wasn't hindering a fired-up and firing David Beckham, Neville was visibly fatigued. He'd made the second-most appearances for the Reds the previous season (44 starts), second only to Beckham (45), but it was more the cumulative affect of non-stop football for three or four years that had taken a toll.

'I remember coming back at the start of the season and I was absolutely knackered. I hadn't had a break for three seasons, and this year we'd only had two or three weeks' break. We came back early because we had a Champions League pre-qualifying game against Lodz. You say football players shouldn't get tired, but you just do after so long continually playing. You can still play, but you know you are nowhere near where you should be,' recalls Gary.

'I remember coming off against West Ham and telling Kiddo, who was somebody I could speak to, I was absolutely f*****. They could see it, to be fair, and I remember the manager, who was brilliant like this, said: "Right, I don't want to see you for a week." I remember going away on my own and I sat on a sun bed – and I hate sun beds – for a week and I just lay there every day, occasionally pulling the umbrella over but just doing nothing. At night, I got something to eat with friends and then slept all night. I remember the week after, I felt completely different.

'I don't tend to rest that much, I'm not that type of person, but I just remember it had a massive impact on how I felt and the idea that the manager was willing to give you a week away was a big thing. He did it with Pete [Schmeichel] after Christmas, then later Giggsy during the international breaks, and Ronaldo and Nani. I had been to the World Cup – my first one – and it takes a lot out of you.'

In Lodz, United still cruised to a second consecutive goalless draw for a 2-0 aggregate win. There was no Yorke or Neville, but Ole Gunnar Solskjaer appeared as a second-half substitute having rejected the chance to move to Tottenham Hotspur.

'Spurs wanted to sign me,' confirms the Norwegian. 'The gaffer called me into his office and said Alan Sugar and Martin Edwards had agreed a transfer fee – five and a half million pounds, I think it was – so it was up to me to sign a contract. But the gaffer didn't want to let me go. "The clubs have agreed, but it's up to you. I don't want you to go. If you stay here, you'll get loads of games." So that was it for me, no chance I was leaving after that.

'I said: "I'll stay here if you want me, and then I'll do my best." I've never regretted it at all! I never contemplated it once the gaffer said I would play loads of games and be an important part of his squad. He had said that he was going to sign a striker because the year before it was me, Teddy and Coley, and he was going to sign Yorkie. It was no problem. I didn't mind. As long as I was being given a fair crack of the whip, I've never been afraid of that challenge.'

Solskjaer's potential move away was not the only transfer activity of the summer to come to nothing. Back in June a move for Marc-Vivien Foe to come into Manchester United had also fallen through. The midfielder had broken his leg in a pre-World Cup training camp with Cameroon, just as the Reds and his club Lens were negotiating a fee. Once recovered, Foe joined West Ham, moved to Lyon, before eventually making it to Manchester – playing for City on loan in 2002-03. A month after the Blues' season ended, he collapsed and died playing for Cameroon in the semi-final of the Confederations Cup in Lyon. He was just 28 and in his football prime.

The Reds' then chief scout Mick Brown recalls first seeing Foe and explains how he almost came to join United. He says: 'On my French scouting trips, I'd seen Mikael Silvestre play for Rennes and when I got back said to Alex: "I've got a player, and there's another one: [Marc-Vivien] Foe of Lens. He's a different player altogether, he's a holding midfielder. He is a big, strong lad. He's got a long throw as well, he hurls them in there, but he breaks things up, he's not easy on the eye but he doesn't make many mistakes. He's content to get it and give it. They're playing in a game next week in Rennes." Alex said: "I'll come with you."

'I thought: "Yeah, he's so busy, something will crop up." But he came with me, and by half time he'd have taken both of them off the park, stuck them on the plane and brought them back with us. "We'll have them." Suddenly I was going the other way: "Hang on a minute, you've only seen them for forty-five minutes." "No, fine. Buy them." So we went down the road of trying to get the lad, but things happened. The kid broke his leg and so the deal didn't go through. Things change and it was tragic what happened to him a few years later.'

Foe's injury meant that there were three not four reinforcements for what would be the club's greatest ever season – with one of their most lethal finishers also sticking around. Solskjaer's decision to stay would prove the defining decision of his career, and nine months later in the Nou Camp he'd have the season's final say.

Looking back, Solskjaer believes that the way the club rallied round Beckham played a huge part in the success that would follow – not just for the player himself, but also the collective. 'I was surprised. It was a shock. Going away and going to different places, seeing dolls of Becks being hung up and all that stuff . . . but that probably made him more determined,' says Ole. 'It made us more determined to look after him, I know that. That was the gaffer's point of view, too. Becks was one of us, one of that Class of '92 – I'll call them the Clan of '92 because they were together all the time – and he had the x-factor as well. I think the gaffer did really well looking after him – and Becks certainly paid him back.' And how.

Alex Ferguson had arguably his greatest-ever squad to choose from, two players for every position, and a team galvanised by their returning skipper and unified by their support of a victimised team-mate. Results in the first month of the new season were not particularly impressive, but the foundations for a successful assault on silverware had been laid.

Sunday 9 August 1998 | FA Charity Shield | Wembley |
Attendance: 67,342

MANCHESTER UNITED 0
ARSENAL 3 Overmars 33, Wreh 56, Anelka 71

This sweltering afternoon at Wembley was supposed to be the cur-
tain-raiser to the new campaign, but it felt more like a continuation
of the previous term. United supporters made the journey to the capital hoping for a result to lift the glum mood around Old Trafford
following the title capitulation in the latter half of the 1997-98
season. Instead, at the home of English football, the mood was sunk
further as the champions prevailed with a convincing 3-0 win.

It had all started so well for Alex Ferguson's men. There was the
welcome sight of shaven-headed Roy Keane back leading the Reds
into battle, main summer signing Jaap Stam was making a competitive debut, while David Beckham was cheered from tunnel to
halfway line by United's noisy 35,000 following.

The Reds even dominated the opening exchanges, enjoying
plenty of possession but they were unable to make it count. Slowly
that early impetus faded and Arsenal showed they were the fitter,
sharper and hungrier of the sides – just as they'd been in the 1997-
98 title run-in. From the moment Marc Overmars slammed in a
loose ball from ten yards the outcome appeared clear. Stam was
pulled out of position for Arsenal's second – prodded home by
Christopher Wreh – then was outpaced by Nicolas Anelka for the
demoralising third.

For United fans, the next day's press reports made far from enjoyable reading. 'The fitful nature of yesterday's performance suggested
last season's problems, far from going away, are already threatening
to multiply,' wrote the *Guardian*'s David Lacey. 'By the end, Keane
and his Old Trafford team-mates plus poor old boss Alex Ferguson

were tearing their hair out as Arsenal drowned them in an impressive tide of style, simplicity and laser-sharp finishing,' concluded John Dillon of the *Daily Mirror*.

An impressive win for the champions then, but not a decisive one in the view of the opposing bosses. 'I don't think this will help us beat United in the league but it will help us think we can win again,' was Arsène Wenger's assessment. 'It was a resounding win for Arsenal,' said Ferguson. 'But it was good for us to have a real match after the friendlies in Scandinavia.'

The message was loud and clear – just as had been the booing of Beckham's touches by Arsenal fans – there was no cause for concern. It was, however, a wholly inauspicious opening to a story with a wonderfully fairytale ending.

Arsenal: Seaman; Dixon, Adams (Bould 79), Keown, Winterburn; Parlour, Vieira (Grimandi 84), Petit (Boa Morte 72), Overmars (Hughes 67); Bergkamp (Wreh h-t), Anelka
Subs not used: Manninger, Vivas
Booked: Dixon, Keown

Manchester United: Schmeichel; G.Neville, Johnsen, Stam, Irwin; Beckham, Keane (Berg 76), Butt (Solskjaer 53), Giggs (Cruyff 69); Scholes (P.Neville 69), Cole (Sheringham 69)
Subs not used: Culkin, May
Booked: Irwin, P.Neville

Man of the Match: Roy Keane
On a forgettable afternoon for the men in red, the most notable display came from the returning skipper. Playing his first competitive game since damaging knee ligaments at Leeds 11 months earlier, Keane showed the leadership skills so missed during his absence.

Wednesday 12 August 1998 | UEFA Champions League 2nd Qualifying Round First Leg | Old Trafford | Attendance: 50,906

MANCHESTER UNITED 2 Giggs 16, Cole 81
LKS LODZ 0

'I'm happy with the performance and very pleased with the result,' said Alex Ferguson after watching his side rack up a 2-0 first-leg advantage over Polish champions LKS Lodz. The United boss would have preferred his side not to have had to play a Champions League qualifier so early in the season, but was still grateful of the opportunity to join the Continent's elite in the group stage. That prospect looked quite likely after Ryan Giggs stroked the Reds ahead in the first half and Andy Cole headed another late in the second for a healthy position in the tie. 'I thought it would end one-nil, which would have been frustrating,' admitted Ferguson. 'So the second goal was very important.'

United's pursuit of a fourth striker was continuing off the pitch, with a bid having been tabled to Aston Villa for Dwight Yorke. Meanwhile on it, Paul Scholes continued in an advanced role behind Cole. The only real change to the side that had started the Charity Shield was Giggs being given licence to roam, which he did throughout, regularly swapping positions with the front two.

It was that forward rotation that resulted in United's opener against Lodz, a team from 100 miles south of Warsaw. David Beckham drove a ball from the right-hand side deep into the visitors' penalty area, Scholes's cushioned header found Giggs and the Welshman sidestepped a defender then calmly scored with the outside of his wand of a left foot.

Observers inside Old Trafford and among the millions watching on television now expected the floodgates to open. However, they'd not accounted for the organised, unadventurous approach of a Polish side earning a £2,000 a man payout from a sponsor for shaving their heads. They were keen to enjoy their moment in the spotlight, and if that meant making life as difficult as possible for the famous Manchester United then so be it.

Despite the ten-man wall of white facing them, the Reds still produced 23 attempts at goal (10 on target, 13 off) only to find keeper Boguslaw Wyparlo in top form. Statistics don't always give a true reflection of dominance, and in truth the overall team display was only a marginal improvement on the showing at Wembley. Thankfully, Cole's goal ten minutes from time papered over some of the cracks – wasteful finishing chief among them. Denis Irwin advanced, exchanged passes with Giggs, then produced a cross from which Cole rose to head in at the far post. Cheers inside Old Trafford were tinged with relief.

'One-nil would have been better, but it is not all over,' insisted Marek Dziuba, LKS coach and former Polish international. 'We could score two goals [in the second leg], but really we need three and that is a monumental task. Manchester United is such a strong side, I would be happy to be able to call on their reserves for my team.'

Man of the match was undoubtedly the scorer of the first and contributor to the second, but Giggs preferred to focus on the collective contribution, saying: 'By the time we usually play our first game in Europe, we have five or six games under our belts, which has not been the case this season. A lot of the lads were also playing in the World Cup, which meant they came back a little bit later. But despite all that, I thought the lads looked sharp.'

A first win of the season, but the British press pack remained convinced that United required added firepower in order to challenge for honours, especially in Europe. 'His failure to sign a goalscorer of quality may well bring Ferguson nothing more than renewed frustration in his quest for European club football's most prestigious honour,' penned David Lacey in the *Guardian* newspaper. A week later that quality scorer arrived, and a serious assault for the European Cup was well and truly on.

Manchester United: Schmeichel; G.Neville, Johnsen, Stam, Irwin; Beckham, Keane, Butt, Giggs; Scholes (Solskjaer 82), Cole
Subs not used: Culkin, P.Neville, Berg, May, Cruyff, Sheringham
Booked: Butt

LKS Lodz: Wyparlo; Bendkowski, Pawlak, Krysiak; Omadiagbe (Jakubowski 85), Kos, Niznik (Carbone 57), Wyciskiewicz, Zuberek (Paszulewicz 72); Cebula, Wieszczycki
Subs not used: Slawuta, Pluciennik, Matys, Bugaj
Booked: Omadiagbe, Wyciskiewicz, Cebula

Man of the Match: Ryan Giggs
United's most impressive performer drew this praise from his manager. 'We've been trying to get Giggs to extend his role, and his work infield and out wide was excellent,' said Ferguson. 'He's getting better all the time.'

Saturday 15 August 1998 | Premiership | Old Trafford |
Attendance: 55,052

MANCHESTER UNITED 2 Sheringham 79, Beckham 90
LEICESTER CITY 2 Heskey 7, Cottee 76

The previous six weeks had been all about one man, and it felt inevitable that United's first Premier League game of the season would all be about him, too. David Beckham produced a stunning injury-time free-kick to save Manchester United from an embarrassing opening-day defeat, providing a resonant response to those hoping to drive him out of English football.

Tougher tests would come away from Old Trafford, of course, but lesser-willed players would surely have wilted under the intense media glare on him since England's World Cup disappointment. Instead, United's No.7 used the carping of his critics to fuel his desire to improve and against Leicester City he produced a man-of-the-match performance to claim a point for the Reds that was barely deserved.

Just as at Wembley six days earlier, Alex Ferguson's men produced a flat performance that did little to suggest a record trophy-winning season was underway. There were no changes from the team that had beaten LKS Lodz at Old Trafford in midweek, but the threat posed by Martin O'Neill's side was considerably greater.

Leicester went ahead after just seven minutes when Muzzy Izzet bundled his way to the United by-line and pulled the ball back for Emile Heskey. The big striker, having eluded league debutant Jaap Stam (who was taken off injured at half time), prodded in from five yards via the underside of the crossbar.

When that lead was doubled with 14 minutes remaining – Tony Cottee heading in a Robbie Savage cross – the game looked up for the Reds. Certainly visiting Foxes fans thought so, gleefully singing 'You're not very good' to an otherwise silent Old Trafford. Based on this performance, it was hard to deny. That gloating was soon proven premature, however, with the man they'd lambasted all game exacting his own personal revenge. 'Leicester is in the heart of England and they are fanatical about their country,' said Savage of his club's treatment of his former United youth team-mate. 'That goal should answer a few of his critics, though.'

That goal late in the game proved enough for a point after Teddy Sheringham had reduced the arrears with 11 minutes left. On as substitute, the striker had astutely redirected Beckham's speculative effort past Pegguy Arphexad to rally United and set up the charge for an equaliser. That came in the fifth minute of injury time when Beckham produced a wonderful 30-yard free-kick that soared over the wall then dipped low into the corner of Arphexad's goal. The midfielder's emotional celebration in front of the Leicester fans was understandable.

'We were pleased to get a point whether we deserved one or not,' said Alex Ferguson afterwards, before adding, defiantly: 'We're a little behind with our preparation. We will get better.'

Manchester United: Schmeichel; G.Neville (Sheringham 77), Johnsen, Stam (Berg h-t), Irwin; Beckham, Keane, Butt, Giggs; Scholes, Cole
Subs not used: Culkin, P.Neville, May
Booked: Sheringham

Leicester City: Keller (Arphexad 60); Sinclair, Elliott (Taggart 88), Walsh; Savage, Zagorakis, Lennon, Izzet, Guppy; Heskey, Cottee (Wilson 84)
Subs not used: Kaamark, Parker
Booked: Walsh, Guppy, Lennon

Man of the Match: David Beckham
It was thanks mainly to the Reds' No.7 that United claimed a point; he struck the shot that Sheringham flicked on with his head to halve the deficit, then produced a stunning free-kick for the late, late equaliser. A perfect riposte to the critics.

Saturday 22 August 1998 | Premiership | Boleyn Ground |
Attendance: 26,039

WEST HAM UNITED 0
MANCHESTER UNITED 0

The Boleyn crowd booed, David Beckham rose above it and Dwight
Yorke fired a blank on his debut. Unfortunately, not least for the
26,039 in attendance, that was the extent of the excitement on this
forgettable afternoon in the capital. It certainly wouldn't make the cut
for a season highlights package.

Despite being billed as the first test of fire for the sinner of
St Etienne, United's No.7 was subjected to little more than pantomime
catcalls from the not-so-baying Boleyn. The anticipated 'cauldron of
hate' failed to materialise, with Beckham's reception no worse than
he'd experienced on previous visits to the East London club. Still,
with a game that barely set pulses racing, the reaction to (and from)
the Leytonstone-born youngster at least provided a sub-plot to dis-
tract from the tedious main attraction.

'If this is the worst Beckham will have to face, then perhaps he
can start getting along with the rest of his life, baby and all,' wrote
the *Daily Mirror*'s Des Kelly, referencing the news that Becks and
fiancée Victoria Adams were expecting their first child.

Each time Beckham was jeered, United's 2,000 fans inside the
Upton Park ground cheered. 'You let your country down,' sang the
locals; 'Ar-gen-tina' and an invitation to 'stick England' where the sun
doesn't shine (or words similar) echoed from the away end. So muted
was the action that even the off-field soundtrack soon fell flat as the
Beckham-baiting turned into a slumber in the stands.

Yorke's first start, following his big-money move and just one
training session, was every bit as low-key as the match. He tried his
hardest to make an impact, but like the other 21 players on the pitch,

he could not find the spark of inspiration that had enticed United to pay so much for his services. For the new man it was a steady if unspectacular start.

As for the flow of the game, West Ham started brightly but lacked an attacking threat; United enjoyed plenty of second-half possession but also failed to find scoring opportunities. The closest Ferguson's men came to a goal was when Yorke's strike partner Andy Cole attempted to chip Shaka Hislop, only to be denied by the home keeper. For West Ham, Eyal Berkovic blazed over when well placed and John Hartson was tackled by Roy Keane with the goal at his mercy.

The stalemate was not what either side wanted and not something the United manager was inclined to talk about afterwards. He ignored post-match media duties, hurried his team onto the bus and back to Manchester. He knew this was not one to dwell on and that better days lay ahead.

West Ham United: Hislop; Pearce, Ferdinand, Ruddock; Impey, Lampard, Lomas, Berkovic (Abou 72), Lazaridis; Hartson, Sinclair
Subs not used: Forrest, Moncur, Keller, Margas
Booked: Lazaridis, Berkovic, Hartson

Manchester United: Schmeichel; G.Neville (P.Neville 52), Johnsen, Berg, Irwin; Beckham, Keane, Butt, Giggs; Cole (Sheringham 70), Yorke
Subs not used: Culkin, May, Scholes
Booked: Johnsen

Man of the Match: David Beckham
Booed, jeered and given the odd mouthful of abuse at corners, the adverse attention merely made him more motivated. It was nothing like as bad as expected, but the father-to-be took it all in his stride and showed all the usual traits to his game: pace, energy and determination.

Wednesday 26 August 1998 | UEFA Champions League 2nd Qualifying Round Second Leg | LKS Stadion | Attendance: 8,700

LKS LODZ 0
MANCHESTER UNITED 0

There had been little to excite four days earlier in the East End of London, and less still on this trip to Eastern Europe. Alex Ferguson's men had one mission: passage to the knockout phase of the Champions League, and were determined to achieve it with the minimum of fuss.

'Progress was the most important thing,' said Alex Ferguson, having watched his side control the game and cruise to a 2-0 aggregate win over the Polish champions. 'I would have liked to have won the game, but if you had been asked before if you would like to be in the Champions League, you would say "Yes".'

The combination of a 2-0 first-leg advantage and facing an injury-ravaged host suggested, correctly, that Manchester United's name would be in the Champions League draw the next day. The only real surprise was that the Reds were unable to add to their aggregate score against a side that had managed just one shot on target at Old Trafford.

With Dwight Yorke ineligible until the group stages and Andy Cole dropped to the bench, Paul Scholes played as the furthest forward of the five-man midfield behind lone striker Teddy Sheringham. The absence of a fatigued Gary Neville allowed his brother Phil a rare chance at right-back, while in central defence fit-again Jaap Stam replaced Henning Berg.

There was a solid look to this Reds line-up, which was more than you could say about sections of the LKS Stadion. The Polish side had wanted to fill the dilapidated ground to its 20,000 capacity, but UEFA soon quashed that idea and limited access to the two seated stands either side of the stadium. Among the 8,700 estimated crowd were 400 United fans from the UK, plus some 200 Polish Reds, among them Legia Warsaw fans who'd been smitten by United since their side had played them in the 1991 European Cup-Winners' Cup.

Injuries meant that the hosts chose not to fill their quota of seven substitutes, using only five of the available places. Yet their below-strength side showed more attacking intent in the first 20 seconds than they had in 90 minutes in Manchester. Rafal Nizik collected the ball in midfield, burst past Denis Irwin and fizzed a low shot a whisker wide of Peter Schmeichel's post.

That was a scare, albeit a small one, and suggested Lodz were intending to make it an uncomfortable night for United's millionaires. Ferguson's men were by now experienced European campaigners and, led by Roy Keane, immediately ensured they'd not become the first Reds side to lose a two-goal first-leg lead in Europe's leading competition. The skipper dominated possession, United passed and passed, and the hosts' early fire was easily doused.

David Beckham and Nicky Butt both had first-half chances, the former stinging the fingertips of Polish player of the year Boguslaw Wyparlo. And after the break it was his opposite number, Schmeichel, who was grateful to see a deflected Tomasz Kos free-kick drop over his crossbar. The better chances still fell to the white-shirted visitors: Beckham again tested Wyparlo, while Sheringham blazed the best chance of the night high and wide. No goals but a calm, assured performance from United to seal a place in the next day's draw.

'Now we are back in the Champions League and we proved last season that we can win our section,' continued Ferguson, moving from the victory to the challenge ahead. 'If we go into the group with the two seeds, then they have got to worry that we are in there, too.' They were to prove prophetic words from the United boss – both in terms of the draw and, four months later, the final group table.

LKS Lodz: Wyparlo; Pawlak, Bendkowski, Krysiak; Jakubowski (Bugaj 85), Wyciszkiewicz, Lenart (Pluciennik 82), Kos; Niznik; Zuberek (Matys 52), Wieszczycki
Subs not used: Slawuta, Paszulewicz
Booked: Kos

Manchester United: Schmeichel; P.Neville, Stam, Johnsen, Irwin; Beckham, Keane, Butt, Giggs (Solskjaer 64), Scholes; Sheringham
Subs not used: van der Gouw, Brown, May, Berg, Cruyff, Cole
Booked: Beckham

Man of the Match: Roy Keane
The United skipper marshalled the midfield throughout, ensuring that the Polish champions had no chance of getting back into the tie. He dropped deep to control the tempo of the game, put his foot in where necessary and clocked up another valuable 90 minutes in his drive for full match sharpness.

August in statistics

Pre-season friendlies:

Birmingham City 4 Manchester United 3
25.07.98, St Andrews, Attendance: 20,708
Scorer: Mulryne 3

Valerenga IF 2 Manchester United 2
27.07.98, Bislett Stadion, Attendance: 19,700
Scorers: Scholes, Solskjaer

Brondby IF 0 Manchester United 6
31.07.98, Parken, Attendance: 27,022
Scorers: Sheringham 2, Scholes, Cole 2, Cruyff

SK Brann 0 Manchester United 4
04.08.98, Brann Stadion, Attendance: 16,100
Scorers: Irwin 3, Cole

Premiership table (31 August 1998)

	P	W	D	L	F	A	GD	Pts
Liverpool	3	2	1	0	6	2	+4	7
Aston Villa	3	2	1	0	4	1	+3	7
Nottingham Forest	3	2	0	1	4	3	+1	6
Charlton Athletic	3	1	2	0	5	0	+5	5
Wimbledon	3	1	2	0	4	2	+2	5
Arsenal	3	1	2	0	2	1	+1	5
Leeds United	3	1	2	0	2	1	+1	5
West Ham United	3	1	2	0	1	0	+1	5
Leicester City	3	1	1	1	4	3	+1	4
Coventry City	3	1	1	1	2	2	0	4

Blackburn Rovers	3	1	1	1	1	1	0	4
Sheffield Wed	3	1	0	2	3	2	+1	3
Derby County	3	0	3	0	1	1	0	3
Tottenham Hotspur	3	1	0	2	2	6	-4	3
Manchester United	2	0	2	0	2	2	0	2
Middlesbrough	3	0	2	1	2	4	-2	2
Newcastle United	3	0	2	1	2	5	-3	2
Chelsea	2	0	1	1	2	3	-1	1
Everton	3	0	1	2	0	3	-3	1
Southampton	3	0	0	3	2	9	-7	0

August form (all competitions, excludes friendlies): LWDDD

Goals scored: 4   **Goals conceded:** 5

Most appearances: 5 each for Peter Schmeichel, Denis Irwin, Ronny Johnsen, David Beckham (450 mins each)

Players used: 17

Most goals: David Beckham, Andy Cole, Ryan Giggs, Ronny Johnsen 1 each

Most assists: Paul Scholes 2

Different goalscorers: 4

Quickest goal: Ryan Giggs, 16 mins [v LKS Lodz (h)]

Latest goal: David Beckham, 90+5 mins [v Leicester City (h)]

Watched by: 208,039

Average attendance: 41,608

Chapter 2

September – Slipping into Character

Five games, four goals and only one win. It was neither the scorching start to the season that Alex Ferguson had wanted from his stuttering side nor the early form in which to approach an unforgiving September schedule: Barcelona, Arsenal, Liverpool, Bayern Munich. United would be playing each of them within the space of a frantic fortnight that could potentially make or break the season, at least where Europe was concerned. The task ahead was clear: the new signings needed to settle in fast, skipper Roy Keane quickly reach his commanding best, while the collective had to shake off the lingering hangover of losing the 1997-98 title.

'We didn't start the season very well,' recalls Phil Neville, who played in five of the six September matches. 'We'd signed a few new players and it was taking a bit of time for everyone to gel. We were inconsistent. I was going through a disappointing spell personally, but I think the team were also going through a disappointing spell.'

While David Beckham had endured a very public World Cup

nightmare, Neville junior had suffered his own in private. Having played six times for England in the 12 months leading up to the tournament, exclusion from Glenn Hoddle's Three Lions squad for France '98 hit him hard. 'It was probably the lowest point for me. I was almost sure I was going, I got right down to the wire and when I wasn't selected it was a bitter blow,' reveals Phil.

'I think the disappointment of not going to the World Cup stayed with me for the first two or three months of the season. You look back and think: "Dear me, that was poor from me." But it was obviously a learning curve. It wasn't really until we got to probably November or December where we started to hit a bit of form.'

Manchester United's peak may have still been two or three months away, but the desired improvement was quickly forthcoming. The visit of Alan Curbishley's recently promoted Charlton Athletic provided the Reds with an opportunity not only to give home debuts to Dwight Yorke and Jesper Blomqvist, but to focus minds on events on the field of play. Broadcaster BSkyB had launched a proposed takeover of the club, a bid that had been accepted by the United board hours before the Addicks' visit. The Independent Manchester United Supporters Association fans' group immediately declared their disapproval. Hardly the backdrop against which to kick-start a season, although Alex Ferguson remained upbeat. 'I don't think the fans will take it out on the team,' he said. 'They recognise it's nothing to do with the players.'

Despite the distractions, the focus in Old Trafford's home dressing room remained firmly on landing a first league win of the season. 'I can't remember it being discussed and I would be very surprised if the takeover was a major conversation ahead of the game,' recalls Denis Irwin. 'We might have touched on it but, as a player, you ignore all that. You have to. We had a game to play.'

And play they did, putting in a vastly improved showing, led by grinning home debutant Yorke. The Trinidadian scored twice, likewise strike partner Ole Gunnar Solskjaer, to put a smile back on the faces of fans. Takeover issues could wait; at least the league campaign was up and running. Not only was the £12.6 million signing was making an impact on the field, but his bubbly personality was changing the dynamic off it.

Henning Berg, a second-half substitute in the 4-1 dismissal of Charlton, recalls clearly the introduction of the former Villa man: 'He could take the pressure off people just by smiling. Even when the manager had a go at him, he just sat there smiling – we couldn't believe it, even the gaffer started smiling. It was funny because everybody was quite down after losing the championship the year before and the dressing room was not happy; none of us. We needed personality and a guy like Dwight Yorke in the dressing room to liven things up, to not be too serious but have the right professionalism and work ethic at the same time. He was the missing link in the team. He made Andy [Cole] a better player. He made Roy Keane a better player. He made everyone smile a bit more. Everybody enjoyed themselves and we needed that at the time.'

Yorke was a scorer again a few days later when the Reds hosted Coventry City. Gordon Strachan's side never looked likely to cause an upset and were sent packing down the M6 with a 2-0 defeat that flattered them. Ronny Johnsen prodded in United's second, but it was again the Reds' new front man who caught the eye. 'What a waste of money!' had been the irony-coated chant from fans after his 20th-minute strike. All of a sudden smiles were back *en vogue* at the Theatre of Dreams, led by the man with the widest grin of all. 'The shining light was probably Dwight Yorke,' is how Phil Neville remembers the Reds' early September victories. 'He scored and he smiled and he lit the place up.'

While the striker's impact had been instant, and his introduction a lift for a dressing room struggling to offload the baggage of the previous campaign, Ferguson was keen to channel his new signing's

enthusiasm. He was the master of handling egos and closely monitored the behaviour of his newest arrival.

'I think maybe he did give the dressing room a lift, but he did
have some things to learn, I think, about Manchester United, and he
had to learn them quickly,' the then first team coach Jim Ryan
explains. 'I think the manager took him off [against Charlton] when
he had two goals and was on a hat-trick. I doubt that had ever happened to Dwight before. Maybe he saw that and it gave him a bit of
an education in how he should be at Manchester United. He maintained that . . . he was up, he wasn't sulking. He'll probably tell you
he learned a lot at Manchester United, and a lot of it was subliminal
learning.'

The next test for Yorke and his new team-mates was the UEFA
Champions League group stage, for which the draw had been
unkind. 'They don't come much tougher than Barcelona and Bayern
Munich, do they?' had been Alex Ferguson's reaction to being paired
with two fellow giants of European football, plus Peter Schmeichel's
former club Brondby. The press went further, instantly labelling
Group D the 'Group of Death' – a rather inappropriate term given
Manchester United's tragic experience in Munich in 1958. There was
no denying it was a tough group, however, potentially the toughest
in the competition.

The day after the draw, Barça's ranks were bolstered by the arrival
of Patrick Kluivert, for £8.6 million from AC Milan. United had
been keen to bring the Netherlands international to Old Trafford following his impressive showing at the '98 World Cup, and at first he'd
seemed keen to come. That interest soon cooled once the Spanish
league champions came calling.

'I remember it like it was yesterday,' says Andy Cole of an episode
that, had the transfer gone through, may have had ramifications for
his own career. 'The gaffer tried to buy Patrick Kluivert, but he said
no to Manchester United and moved to Barcelona. Now, I knew that

if he had come in then it could have been the end of me. I got to the stage where I thought, "Andrew, you can't afford to worry about that any more." If it was going to happen then it would happen. If it happens, then you give what you can up until that stage and if somebody else comes in and the manager says he is going to let you go, then you have to take it on the chin.'

Cole's positive outlook was to bring its rewards, just not right away. His September amounted to two substitute appearances: 22 minutes against Charlton and 20 against Liverpool. He had a fight ahead for a starting berth, yet put his personal frustrations aside to help out the latest man to threaten his place.

'When Yorkie came, I was the first one to try and help him out because I had no resentment to anyone,' he says. 'I knew my position, why would I have resented him? Yorkie came here from living in Birmingham at Aston Villa and he didn't know where to live. He came to my house and had dinner with my family; I showed him the best places to live and the things to do and not to do. I said to myself, why not? I was at that stage in my life.'

Back-to-back wins were the perfect preparation for the visit to the Theatre of Dreams of Spanish Double winners Barcelona. Even without Kluivert, ineligible for the group stage and watching from the directors' box, the visitors could boast an impressive cast list. Philip Cocu, a star of the Netherlands' World Cup run, was the lynchpin of the side. Brazilian Rivaldo and Portuguese Figo provided the flair. While Sergi, the left-back, was the only Catalan in a Barça team constructed by Louis van Gaal with a distinct Dutch flavour.

There was no goal from Dwight in this dramatic 3-3 draw but plenty more to delight. United raced into a two-goal lead – Ryan Giggs with a header and Paul Scholes a close-range shot – to provoke a salvo of Stretford End taunts aimed at Kluivert. A tactical switch soon swung the balance of the game back in favour of van Gaal's revitalised side, and silenced Mancunian barbs. Samba boys Anderson and Giovanni levelled inside 15 minutes of the second half, the latter a harshly awarded penalty against Jaap Stam. Man of the match Beckham then produced a fizzing, curling 25-yard free-kick to restore the Reds' lead, only for a second penalty from Luis Enrique (following a hand ball by Nicky Butt, punished by a red card) to make it a nervy end to the evening. A footnote to this bewildering game was the European debut of one Xavier Hernandez Creus, better known as Xavi, a man Reds would come to know only too well over the next decade. On this night he did not figure in the post-match patter, unlike team-mate Rivaldo.

Stam, the man adjudged to have felled the Brazilian for Barça's first penalty, was infuriated at its award: 'It was the wrong decision. People would have seen on TV that it wasn't a penalty. I didn't make any contact at all. Rivaldo tricked the referee. It was a clear dive. When I saw that the referee had given a penalty, I was stunned. It disappoints me as a professional footballer to see players diving like that. I saw it in the World Cup and now I've seen it again. It's an increasing trend, this cheating.'

No wonder United's most expensive defender was so incensed. He'd produced his finest display to date for his new club, yet the glare of media scrutiny monitored every aspect of his game. Four days later he'd be in the headlines again, as the Reds received a second 3-0 hammering from Arsenal inside six weeks.

Tony Adams out-jumped Stam for the Gunners' early opener. Nicolas Anelka eluded the Dutchman, as he'd done in the Charity Shield, to send Highbury wild with a second goal. Debutant Freddie Ljungberg rounded off a miserable afternoon for Ferguson's men with his first touch of the game – scoring with a delightfully impudent chip. Arsène Wenger's side climbed to fifth, becoming the first team in the Premier League era to inflict three defeats in a row on United, while the Reds dropped two places to tenth in the Premiership table.

Despite the humiliating loss, Henning Berg recalls no panic

among the squad, only a determination to improve. 'The league defeat was obviously not nice, but it was early in the season and everybody knows the season is not going to be decided at that time,' recalls the Norwegian. 'With the players and squad that we had, we knew that we could beat most teams anyway, and it was more about looking after ourselves and making sure we were the best we could be, then we would have a good chance. I don't think it mentally rocked us that much – the way we lost the championship the previous season was worse.'

Defeat at Highbury had clearly been a blow, but thankfully the Reds had recovered from worse. En route to retaining the 1996-97 title, Ferguson's side had been spanked 5-0 and 6-3 at Newcastle and Southampton. There was no great cause for concern yet; after all, trophies are handed out in May not September. Nevertheless, the Highbury horror show underlined the importance of a response against Liverpool four days later.

If the aim of the United manager was to keep attention off his inconsistent side, then he did so inadvertently. An ITV documentary on Ferguson filmed his team-talk ahead of Liverpool's previous visit in which he'd described Paul Ince as a 'big-time Charlie'. Broadcast two days before the latest meeting, it dominated the pre-match agenda.

'Incey was fantastic for this club and he spent the best of six or seven years here,' recalls Denis Irwin. 'He was part of the initial success and was a big, big player. He used to play in midfield and then with Keaney for a couple of years after Robbo left, and that was an immense midfield. Our fans didn't take too kindly to him after he went a roundabout way from Inter Milan to Liverpool. You always come up against former players. It's part and parcel of the game. Everybody gets a good reception when they come back here, but I don't think he did!'

Ince stuck two fingers up to the Stretford End as he left the pitch following United's 2-0 win, taunts of 'Charlie, Charlie, what's the score?' ringing in his ears. It had certainly been a frustrating night for the Liverpool captain. Irwin scored an early penalty, after a soft award for hand ball against Jason McAteer, and Scholes sealed the win with a faultless drive ten minutes from time. In between, the Merseysiders had a goal disallowed for offside and a hand-ball penalty shout of their own turned down.

The pace and verve of United's play, especially in the first half, gave renewed hope that Sunday's slump to the champions had been little more than an off-day. Keane won his battle with pantomime villain Ince; Scholes was a constant menace to the Liverpool defence; Stam and Gary Neville forged a firm alliance in United's back line.

It was that new partnership in defence that was the real feature of the victory. Midfield and attack had been functioning well, but the pairing of Stam and Neville senior was the fourth tried in just ten matches. Injuries had played a part in the changes, but Ferguson really needed to find a steadying influence to support Stam through his acclimatisation to Premiership football.

United's chief scout at the time was Mick Brown, assistant manager during Ron Atkinson's Old Trafford tenure, and he'd been to watch Stam ahead of the club's approach to PSV Eindhoven. He had no doubt whatsoever that the big Dutchman would prove a success in England.

'I'd seen Jaap play a bit when I was working with Roy Hodgson at Blackburn, prior to coming back to United. He was a wonderful player – one of my all-time favourite players, in fact. He was a defender and I think they're viewed as second-class citizens in football. Yet nobody ever wins anything unless they've got good defenders – look at how important Nemanja Vidic has been to United. But Jaap had that x-factor about him, this iconic figure "big Jaap Stam" who had such great pace.

'He was a bit unlucky at the start in that he came to the club at a time when we had no stability at centre-half through injury and different things. You've got a lad here coming in from Dutch football, where they're used to playing one-on-one at the back: "He's mine, I'll stop him." He's gone from that to playing in an English back four and learning how the two balance off each other. It's different.

'Everybody takes six months to a year to adjust, but Jaap came in and everybody who looked at him saw this fella who got stuck in, won tackles, got the ball and you're thinking "bloody hell". I thought he was magnificent. It's like Blackpool rock. If you wanted a player with a stamp on him which said "Manchester United player", he was my man.'

Stam's display against Liverpool promised much, but the Reds' stand-out performance came from his vocal adjutant at the back. 'Gary Neville was marvellous,' said Ferguson. 'His reading of situations and organisational ability were excellent, and his determination to win the match was superb.'

Next up for Manchester United and its new defensive axis was an emotional trip to Munich. In his pre-match press conference Ferguson was understandably reluctant to talk about the historical resonance of the tie, United's first in the city since the 1958 Air Disaster, saying only: 'It's a very emotional part of the club, but we're just here for the game.'

'It's just another big match,' concurred captain Keane, by now looking more like his old self with every game.

The Reds' second Group D fixture – ahead of which was held a minute's silence to mark 40 years since the air crash – is one that Gary Neville remembers well. 'Then came the game away in Munich, we drew two-two, and me and Jaap were centre-halves again. I was playing against Carsten Jancker, who was six foot four, and again, it was absolutely brilliant,' says the now club ambassador.

'I was having a brilliant period, because I was playing at centre-half against the best teams in Europe in the best stadiums. But we were conceding all of the time and we conceded in the last minute there when Peter came out and tried to punch one. We drew and it was like, s***, how has that happened?'

It was a tough night for both Nevilles, with Phil playing at left-back against Bayern's not-so-jolly German giants. 'That was one of the toughest games I've ever played,' he admits. 'They got a last-minute equaliser from a long throw and we drew two-two. Physically, they were massive: Effenberg, Jancker, Salihamidzic, Jeremies, Matthaus, Kuffour, Basler, Babbel, Elber ... they were strong and powerful and experienced. This was the first of two tough group games against them.'

All had being going well until Schmeichel's injury-time aberration. Ferguson's side had overcome Giovane Elber's 11th-minute strike to level through a Yorke diving header, then lead through Scholes's dash into the box for a tap-in. A historic away result looked likely, only for the goalkeeper's error to result in a combination of Elber and Teddy Sheringham bundling home an equaliser.

Three wins, two draws and one defeat was a reasonable return for a month's work, especially given the calibre of opposition, but it could have been better. At least in the recollection of Gary Neville: 'In the early parts of the season, you are just working it out and finding the right things. Defensively we were poor, all over the place, as if we weren't taking it seriously. The attacking bit was going well between Yorke, Sheringham, Cole and Solskjaer. We had the best midfield in Europe. The defensive bit was the problem.'

Nevertheless, it was a team effort, says Andy Cole, but with one real difference in the dressing room, lightening the mood and bringing invaluable *joie de vivre* to the squad. 'Yorkie was a breath of fresh air,' says Cole of the man who became his good friend. 'He lived his life saying: "I don't give a monkey's, I'm living my life to the full." And when you get somebody like that in your dressing room, it is totally different to anyone else. He came in with a spring in his step saying:

"I'm here and I'm Dwight Yorke and I'm here to enjoy my football, I'm going to liven up the dressing room being the personality that I am." And Jesus, did he liven up that dressing room straight away.'

With Yorke immediately assimilated, Stam steadily finding his feet and Blomqvist featuring in four of September's six games as he found match fitness, Alex Ferguson's summer business looked increasingly shrewd. Slowly but surely, United were on the up, and that trajectory would spike markedly in October.

Wednesday 9 September 1998 | Premiership | Old Trafford | Attendance: 55,147

MANCHESTER UNITED 4 Solskjaer 39, 63, Yorke 45, 48
CHARLTON ATHLETIC 1 Kinsella 32

Against the backdrop of takeover talk, Dwight Yorke staked his Old Trafford claim with a two-goal home debut as the Reds got their Premiership campaign up and running. After days on the front pages following BSkyB's approach to take control of the club, subsequently approved by the board, the £12.6 million signing dovetailed with Ole Gunnar Solskjaer to ensure Manchester United a place on the back pages, too. Both strikers found the net twice, cancelling out Mark Kinsella's shock opener for Charlton, to claim a first league victory of the season and move the Reds out of the top division's bottom five.

'I was very proud because, yes, when we went behind, it could have become very difficult after all that has gone on,' said Alex Ferguson referencing the off-field distractions for his improving side. 'My players were focused and concentrated, and they did really well under the circumstances.'

This was the first hint that the United of old was re-emerging. The swagger was back. Even before Kinsella's 30-yard hit had been diverted past Peter Schmeichel in the 32nd minute, the hosts had regularly carved open the visitors' defence. Yorke played like he'd been a key component of the Red machine for years rather than weeks, and his link-up with Solskjaer and David Beckham eventually enabled United to power past Alan Curbishley's newly promoted side.

Seven minutes after Kinsella's opener, the Norwegian exchanged passes with the Trinidadian to fire a right-foot shot beyond Charlton goalkeeper Sasa Ilic. Then, on the stroke of half time, it was the new man's turn: the unmarked forward heading home an inch-perfect free-kick. Beckham cross, Yorke goal – it was to become a familiar refrain. The pair combined again for the third goal, the striker finishing the winger's low cross with a right-foot strike. And it was four when Solskjaer, who snubbed a transfer to Tottenham weeks earlier, headed in his second goal from a Henning Berg cross.

Jesper Blomqvist had made his own impressive debut, but there was no mistaking the main man on this particular evening. 'There was no mention of the takeover in the dressing room and I think you can tell that by the way we played,' said a beaming Yorke. 'It was business as usual – that's what Manchester United is all about. I am looking forward to having more nights like this.' And there were to be plenty in the coming months.

Manchester United: Schmeichel; P.Neville, Stam, Johnsen, Irwin (Berg 57); Beckham, Keane, Scholes, Blomqvist; Yorke (Cole 68), Solskjaer (Sheringham 68)
Subs not used: van der Gouw, Wilson

Charlton Athletic: Ilic; Mills, Brown, Youds, Powell; Newton (Mortimer 56), Kinsella (K.Jones 76), Redfearn, Robinson; Mendonca (S.Jones 71), Hunt
Subs not used: Petterson, Balmer

Man of the Match: Dwight Yorke

Opened his account with the Reds, converting David Beckham crosses either side of half time and looking every inch a £12.6 million striker. Appeared comfortable holding the ball up, passed well throughout and was a real threat when running at defenders.

Saturday 12 September 1998 | Premiership | Old Trafford | Attendance: 55,193

MANCHESTER UNITED 2 Yorke 20, Johnsen 48
COVENTRY CITY 0

Normal service resumed. Four days after the exertions of seeing off Charlton Athletic, the Reds slipped back into the old routine of playing within themselves to dispatch Gordon Strachan's Coventry City. The Sky Blues had beaten Alex Ferguson's side 3-2 at Highfield Road the previous campaign, the first of five damaging league defeats in the second half of the season, but there was never a hint of a reprisal from the West Midlands club.

'You could sense something was wrong from the beginning,' said Strachan after watching his side muster just one strike on goal in the 90 minutes – a Paul Telfer free-kick. 'We were like somebody going to the dentist knowing there's pain coming some time soon. We weren't brave enough to play against them.'

That was a one-sided assessment of the game; United were determined that the Sky Blues would not extract even a hint of joy from their afternoon's work. Jaap Stam shrugged off premature criticism with a commanding display in the heart of defence, combining well with second-half scorer Ronny Johnsen, and all across the midfield the visitors were harassed and harried out of possession. In attack, Dwight Yorke and Ole Gunnar Solskjaer picked up where they'd left off in midweek, linking up with the midfield and menacing the Coventry defence. The Reds were intent on building momentum, not losing it.

It took 20 minutes for the breakthrough, Yorke shinning the ball past Magnus Hedman from a Paul Scholes pull-back, and once the lead was secured the outcome was never in question. 'One-nil to the Sky TV,' chanted the pocket of visiting Coventry supporters, reminding the home hordes of the continuing takeover distractions. They'd have little other reason to raise their voices.

Three minutes into the second half, the game was won when Johnsen, still upfield for a corner, diverted a Scholes long-ranger past Hedman. Those expecting an ensuing Reds onslaught were left disappointed, though: at 2-0 it was all over. Preservation of energy became the order of the day, with thoughts clearly on the visit of La Liga champions Barcelona in midweek. Watched on by their assistant manager Gerard van der Lem, the game petered out.

'The second goal came too early for us in the second half and the game dipped very badly after that,' said an unsatisfied Ferguson. It was a clear message to his players, who moved to fifth in the Premiership table, that nothing but full tilt for the whole 90 minutes would be good enough against Rivaldo, Cocu and Figo.

Manchester United: Schmeichel; G.Neville, Stam, Johnsen, P.Neville; Beckham (Butt 78), Keane, Scholes, Giggs (Blomqvist 78); Yorke, Solskjaer
Subs not used: van der Gouw, Berg, Cole
Booked: Yorke, Beckham

Coventry City: Hedman; Shaw, Wallemme, Breen, Burrows; Edworthy, Quinn, Boateng, Telfer; Huckerby (Hall 73), Dublin
Subs not used: Ogrizovic, Williams, Soltvedt, Shilton
Booked: Burrows

Man of the Match: Dwight Yorke

Following his midweek double-scoring debut, United's No.19 was on a roll with a third goal in four days. The Stam-inspired defence looked untroubled, but it was the Yorke-led attack that truly impressed.

Wednesday 16 September 1998 | Champions League Group D | Old Trafford | Attendance: 53,601

MANCHESTER UNITED 3 Giggs 17, Scholes 25, Beckham 64
FC BARCELONA 3 Anderson 47, Giovanni 60 (pen),
Luis Enrique 71 (pen)

Old Trafford has hosted some classic European nights since Matt Busby's Babes first rallied against the continentals, but few encounters have had the thrills and spills of this stunning six-goal set-to. The rampant Reds raced to a two-goal advantage thanks to Ryan Giggs and Paul Scholes, and looked almost certain to avenge their 4-0 hammering in the Nou Camp five years earlier. Instead, Barcelona twice fought back, first through Sonny Anderson and a Giovanni penalty, then via a second spot-kick from Luis Enrique to cancel out David Beckham's wondrous free-kick. This was Champions League football at its finest, and fans left the ground disappointed and yet also relieved.

If Alex Ferguson's men were to reach the knockout stage of the Champions League, then it would it would be done the hard way. Opponents in Group D – surely 'B' would have been more fitting? – were Barça, Bayern Munich and Danish champions Brondby. There was no margin for error, one slip and it'd be six group matches and out of the European Cup for another season.

It was a prospect the Reds boss was unwilling to entertain in his pre-match press conference. 'It's a key game. I'm aware of that,' said

Ferguson to the assembled journalists, many wanting to talk takeovers rather than tactics. 'A defeat would put Barcelona on the back foot, which is important because they are the biggest danger to our progress.'

It was a message he'd clearly shared with his team, which, dressed in all white, made a blinding start. Captain Roy Keane set the tempo; Champions League debutant Dwight Yorke caused mayhem between the Barça lines; while their full-backs had no answer to the winged threats of Beckham and Giggs. Louis van Gaal's side, not enjoying the best of times domestically, were totally overrun.

Shortly after Ole Gunnar Solskjaer had rattled Ruud Hesp's crossbar from a Beckham centre, Giggs headed the hosts ahead from another inch-perfect Becks cross. Eight minutes later, the England man centred again with equally devastating effect: Yorke's overhead kick was parried out by Hesp and Scholes gleefully gobbled up the rebound. 'Kluivert, Kluivert, what's the score?' sang the Stretford End in the direction of the cup-tied Dutchman, watching from the directors' box.

Van Gaal realised his side had been too open in the first half, but recognised it was a trait shared by United that they too could exploit. Full-backs Luis Enrique and Sergi pushed further forward, while Luis Figo moved into a more central role. It had the desired effect. Two minutes after the break, Anderson capitalised on confusion in the Reds' rearguard and crashed the ball home to halve the deficit. Further pressure from the visitors ensued and the scores were level when Rivaldo won his side a penalty, collapsing under minimal attention from Jaap Stam. Giovanni despatched the contentiously awarded spot-kick. Two all. Game on.

Now it was United's turn to regroup and the man in the No.7 shirt appeared particularly affronted by the Catalans' fightback. Four minutes after Barça's equaliser, he produced one of the finest free-kicks of his career, generating both power and precision to send the ball swerving high into Hesp's top-right corner. Two goals in four minutes soon became three in 11. Barça exerted frenetic pressure and amid the melee Nicky Butt deliberately blocked a shot with his hand. Figo prodded the ball in, but the penalty was given, Butt dismissed, and Luis Enrique stepped up to make it 3-3.

Ten-man Reds battled to ensure a point, which afterwards Ferguson was delighted to take. 'It wasn't too bad a result in the end, considering that we conceded two penalties and had a man sent off,' said the boss, before switching attentions to the challenge ahead. 'Brondby's win against Bayern [2-1] has thrown the group wide open. It's still all to play for.'

Manchester United: Schmeichel; G.Neville, Stam, Berg, Irwin (P.Neville 79); Beckham, Keane, Scholes, Giggs (Blomqvist 84); Yorke, Solskjaer (Butt 55)
Subs not used: van der Gouw, May, Cole, Sheringham
Booked: Yorke, Beckham
Sent-off: Butt

FC Barcelona: Hesp; Luis Enrique, Reiziger, Abelardo, Sergi; Giovanni (Xavi 68), Cocu, Rivaldo; Luis Figo, Anderson, Zenden
Subs not used: Vitor Baia, Oscar, Ciric, Okunowo, Roger

Man of the Match: David Beckham
The midfielder looked totally at home on the Champions League stage and gave one of his most compelling performances. His deep cross picked out Giggs for the opener, he caused pandemonium in the Barça box for Scholes's second before producing a stunning, curling 25-yard free-kick, possibly his best for the club, in the second half.

Sunday 20 September 1998 | Premiership | Highbury |
Attendance: 38,142

ARSENAL 3 Adams 14, Anelka 44, Ljungberg 80
MANCHESTER UNITED 0

'We were second best,' said Alex Ferguson after seeing his side unseated in the first real test of the 1998-99 title race. Losing to the reigning champions for the second time in six weeks was hard to take. The Charity Shield defeat at Wembley had been dismissed as a mere stretching of legs ahead of the season proper, but the margin of victory here was harder to dismiss. 'There are some days when I can't find any excuses,' added the boss.

Despite starting the day eighth and tenth respectively, this meeting was still billed an early-season 'title decider' – and little wonder. United and Arsenal had amassed a total of 15 trophies between them over the previous decade – the Reds nine, Gunners six – and the bookies had them down as the two most likely to mount a genuine challenge again. Sadly, the evidence of this game suggested more a procession to trophy retention for Arsenal than a ten-month fight to the finish. The hosts raced into an early lead and Ferguson's men spent the afternoon attempting to play catch-up.

Arsenal started brightly and, once in front, simply trampled all over the side they'd deposed as champions four months earlier. On 14 minutes, home skipper Tony Adams rose above Jaap Stam to head in a Stephen Hughes free-kick. On the stroke of half time, Nicolas Anelka fired in at the second attempt after Peter Schmeichel had parried his first effort. Nicky Butt was sent off for the second time in a week, halting Patrick Vieira's gallop through on goal. Then debutant and new signing Freddie Ljungberg rounded off the humiliation with his first touch of the game – a delicious chip – with ten minutes remaining.

It was a champion effort from the hosts, with Vieira the outstanding player on the pitch, winning his battle with Roy Keane hands down. For United, it was just a bad day at the office with only David Beckham, who struck the woodwork, finding anything like top form. 'You're only one-season wonders,' had sung 2,000-plus visiting Reds in response to the incessant cries of 'champions' that echoed around Highbury. By the end even that ditty had been turned against them. 'We're only one-season wonders,' sang the giddy Gunners, as disappointed United fans made an early exit with their side 3-0 down and outplayed.

'It's one I want to forget,' concluded Ferguson. 'Hopefully, this will not be repeated. When did you last see my team play as badly as this?'

Manchester United: Schmeichel; G.Neville, Stam, Berg, Irwin;
Beckham, Keane, Butt, Blomqvist; Yorke, Giggs
Subs not used: van der Gouw, P.Neville, Scholes, Cruyff, Solskjaer
Booked: Keane
Sent-off: Butt

Arsenal: Seaman; Dixon, Adams, Keown, Winterburn; Hughes, Parlour,
Vieira, Overmars; Bergkamp, Anelka (Ljungberg 80)
Subs not used: Manninger, Bould, Garde, Wreh
Booked: Hughes, Ljungberg

Man of the Match: David Beckham
Had the bit between his teeth against Barcelona and produced another workhorse display at Highbury. The only United player to truly hit his straps, Becks was the visitors' main threat and responsible for six of the Reds' seven goal attempts.

Thursday 24 September 1998 | Premiership | Old Trafford |
Attendance: 55,181

MANCHESTER UNITED 2 Irwin 19 (pen), Scholes 80
LIVERPOOL 0

Manchester United versus Liverpool doesn't need sub-plots. The mere presence on the same rectangular patch of grass is generally more than ample to spark the imagination. But while added spice wasn't required for this Thursday evening fixture, it was there in abundance. Paul Ince, one-time lynchpin of United's midfield, was coming back to Old Trafford just days after being labelled a 'big-time Charlie' by his former boss. It was more a quirk of TV scheduling than a well-timed barb from Ferguson – a throw-away line in a team talk shown in a documentary – but the press loved it.

'I'm not even bothered about what he might have said about me,' was Paul Ince's pre-match reaction. 'Keane against Ince will be good to watch,' stated an equally dismissive Ferguson.

This was a totally different United performance to the limp surrender at Highbury. The Giggs/Yorke partnership trialled against the champions was abandoned and in came Ole Gunnar Solskjaer, Henning Berg and Paul Scholes. 'I hope my players realise how badly they let themselves down,' had warned the boss. He got an emphatic early response.

There was an intensity to the Reds' first-half play that overwhelmed the Merseysiders. Ryan Giggs, Roy Keane and Solskjaer all went close before Denis Irwin struck the breakthrough from the penalty spot on 19 minutes. Brad Friedel flapped at a David Beckham corner, Jason McAteer was adjudged to have handled the loose ball, and Irwin ignored Liverpool protestations to slam home. United had further chances, but Liverpool's only threatening moment came via a deflected Ince shot saved by Peter Schmeichel in the final minute of the half.

Joint bosses Gerard Houllier and Roy Evans demanded more from their side after the break and got it. Suddenly it was Liverpool monopolising possession, with United content to contain and counter. Patrick Berger spurned a hat-trick of half-chances and Karl-Heinze Riedle had an effort correctly disallowed for offside. Gary Neville, who'd switched to centre-half alongside the equally impressive Jaap Stam, ensured the Reds' lead remained intact.

A feisty game of eight bookings – Ince inevitably among them – was finally settled with ten minutes remaining. Substitute Andy Cole pulled a cross towards Dwight Yorke, he helped the ball on, and Scholes fired a rising left-foot shot high into the Stretford End net.

'Charlie, Charlie, what's the score?' chanted the ecstatic home fans as pantomime villain Ince left the stage. His two-fingered response did little to help reduce the simmering enmity, nor did it alter the fact Manchester's Reds had reigned supreme and leapfrogged Liverpool into third.

Manchester United: Schmeichel; P.Neville, Stam, G.Neville, Irwin; Beckham, Keane, Scholes (Butt 88), Giggs; Yorke, Solskjaer (Cole 70)
Subs not used: van der Gouw, Berg, Blomqvist
Booked: P.Neville, Stam, Scholes, Giggs

Liverpool: Friedel; McAteer, Carragher, Babb, Bjornebye; McManaman, Redknapp, Ince, Berger; Riedle (Fowler 75), Owen
Subs not used: James, Matteo, Heggem, Leonhardsen
Booked: Carragher, Ince, Berger, Redknapp

Man of the Match: Gary Neville
Effortlessly switched to centre-half, earning this praise from Ferguson: 'His reading of situations and organisational ability were excellent, and his determination to win the match was superb.'

Wednesday 30 September 1998 | Champions League Group D |
Olympiastadion | Attendance: 53,000

BAYERN MUNICH 2 Elber 11, Sheringham 90 (og)
MANCHESTER UNITED 2 Yorke 30, Scholes 49

This maiden competitive match in Munich was not only Manchester
United's first visit to the city since the Air Disaster of 1958, but it was
very nearly one of the Reds' greatest European results. Giovane
Elber's early opener had been seen and raised by goals from Dwight
Yorke and Paul Scholes, only for Bayern to capitalise on a Peter
Schmeichel blunder deep in the final minute of normal time to claim
a point. And while Alex Ferguson's men would have taken a draw at
the start of the evening, there was an inevitable feeling of deflation
at having come so close to claiming a famous win.

'They are a big team and taller than us, which could be a
problem at set plays. In open play, however, I think we have the ability to impose ourselves on parts of the game,' Ferguson had noted
ahead of the contest, with what turned out to be typically accurate
foresight.

After an impeccably observed minute's silence for the Busby
Babes, 40 years on from an ill-fated refuelling stop-off that claimed
the lives of 23 people, including eight players, the Germans went
ahead through diminutive Brazilian Elber. He started and finished an
11th-minute move, albeit from an offside position, to bring the game
alive.

Following a brief period of consolidation came United's time for
imposing their presence in the match. Encouraged by 3,000 travelling fans, the majority having enjoyed the offerings of the
Oktoberfest, Yorke equalised on the half-hour. David Beckham,
enjoying a fascinating duel with World Cup winner Bixente Lizarazu,
shrugged off his marker to send a superlative cross onto the head of

the diving Trinidadian. It was a goal worthy of being the Reds' 150th in the European Cup.

United's ascendancy continued after the break and within four minutes of the restart Scholes struck. Having run onto a Yorke pass, his heavy touch looped up off Matthaus, enticing Oliver Kahn to the loose ball. Both players went for it, both missed it, but Scholes's momentum allowed him to nudge the ball over the goal-line unopposed. Ferguson's men were ahead and on course for a memorable, and potentially decisive, Group D victory.

Further chances fell United's way – Teddy Sheringham, Roy Keane and Beckham all going close – but Ottmar Hitzfeld's side then upped their tempo. It was only thanks to a string of saves from Schmeichel that the Bavarians were kept at bay, but then came the last-minute twist. The Dane rushed through a crowded penalty area to punch clear a long throw, only to miss the ball and allow it to drop into the goal as Elber challenged Sheringham.

'It was an error of judgement,' said Ferguson of the late concession. 'Unfortunately, Peter decided to come for the ball and that's what happens in football. It was a kick in the teeth and Peter didn't deserve that. He was magnificent tonight.'

Schmeichel's skipper Keane supported his manager's stance. 'Just before that goal Peter had made two tremendous saves to keep us in the game. So there's no player in the dressing room blaming him for what happened,' insisted the Irishman, who'd barely put a foot wrong in his battle with Stefan Effenberg.

So no victory for United but there was at least an admirer picked up in the course of the evening. Bayern president Franz Beckenbauer, who'd caught up with his fellow doyen of the game, Sir Bobby Charlton, said: 'United are a great team, and I still think they are good enough to win the Champions League. I am saying that ahead of my own team Bayern. This United side is strong enough to win the title. But I haven't told my good friend Bobby Charlton that yet.'

Neither Beckenbauer nor Charlton knew at the time, but they'd meet twice more before the season was over, with even greater injury-time drama to come.

Bayern Munich: Kahn; Babbel, Matthaus, Linke; Strunz, Jeremies (Fink 82), Effenberg, Lizarazu; Elber, Jancker (Daei 63), Salihamidzic (Goktan 63)
Subs not used: Scheuer, Kuffour, Tarnat
Booked: Matthaus

Manchester United: Schmeichel; P.Neville, Stam, G.Neville, Irwin; Beckham, Keane, Scholes, Blomqvist (Cruyff 69); Sheringham, Yorke
Subs not used: van der Gouw, May, Brown, Berg, Cole, Solskjaer
Booked: Beckham, Cruyff

Man of the Match: Paul Scholes
Scored for his third consecutive game, persistence and opportunism resulting in this latest strike, and deserved for it to be the evening's decisive strike. Scholes was the centre point of all United's finest moments.

September in statistics

Premiership table (30 September 1998)

	P	W	D	L	F	A	GD	Pts
Aston Villa	7	5	2	0	8	1	+7	17
Derby County	7	3	3	1	6	3	+3	12
Wimbledon	7	3	3	1	11	9	+2	12
West Ham United	7	3	3	1	7	5	+2	12
Newcastle United	7	3	2	2	13	7	+6	11
Manchester United	**6**	**3**	**2**	**1**	**10**	**6**	**+4**	**11**
Leeds United	7	2	5	0	8	4	+4	11
Liverpool	7	3	2	2	12	9	+3	11
Chelsea	6	3	2	1	10	7	+3	11
Arsenal	7	2	4	1	6	3	+3	10
Sheffield Wednesday	7	3	0	4	8	5	+3	9
Middlesbrough	7	2	3	2	8	8	0	9
Tottenham Hotspur	7	2	2	3	8	14	-6	8
Charlton Athletic	7	1	4	2	11	10	+1	7
Everton	7	1	4	2	4	5	-1	7
Nottingham Forest	7	2	1	4	5	9	-4	7
Leicester City	7	1	3	3	6	8	-2	6
Blackburn Rovers	7	1	2	4	5	10	-5	5
Coventry City	7	1	2	4	4	12	-8	5
Southampton	7	0	1	6	3	18	-15	1

Champions League, Group D table (30 September 1998)

	P	W	D	L	F	A	GD	Pts
Barcelona	2	1	1	0	5	3	+2	4
Brondby	2	1	0	1	2	3	-1	3
Manchester United	**2**	**0**	**2**	**0**	**5**	**5**	**0**	**2**
Bayern Munich	2	0	1	1	3	4	-1	1

September form (all comps): WWDLWD

Goals scored: 13   **Goals conceded:** 9

Most appearances: 6 each for Peter Schmeichel, Jaap Stam, Roy Keane, Dwight Yorke [540 mins each]

Players used: 18

Most goals: Dwight Yorke 4

Most assists: Dwight Yorke, David Beckham 4 each

Different goalscorers: 7

Quickest goal: Ryan Giggs, 17 mins [v Barcelona (h)]

Latest goal: Paul Scholes, 80 mins [v Liverpool (h)]

Watched by: 310,264

Average attendance: 51,711

Chapter 3

October – Starting to Click

In September Dwight Yorke had lifted the Manchester United dressing room with his cheerful disposition; in October it was his partnership with Andy Cole putting smiles on faces. The exciting new pairing produced nine goals in five of the Reds' six matches, missing only the Worthington Cup tie with Bury. Yorke scored four times and Cole five, as the seemingly telepathic duo set about making headlines. But they weren't the only two making an impact. Teenager Wes Brown emerged from the Reserves to impress as replacement right-back for Gary Neville. Jaap Stam appeared ever more at ease in English football. The worth of bringing in Jesper Blomqvist to challenge and support Ryan Giggs was increasingly seen. It was clear that the shortcomings of the previous season were fast being resolved and that things were falling into place.

Having matched up to some of Europe's pre-eminent clubs the previous month, October was more about grafting for victories against sides better known for fortitude than free-flowing football. Away visits to the Dell, Pride Park and Goodison were winnable but a worry. At Old Trafford, Wimbledon loved nothing more than upsetting the big boys in their own back yard, much like Division One side Bury, who had climbed the leagues thanks to a pragmatic approach. In among those matches was a trip to Parken to face Brondby, a side thumped by Keane and co in pre-season, but that had since beaten Bayern. It was neither a daunting schedule nor one to be taken lightly.

Fortunately for Alex Ferguson, his new signings were beginning to settle, although the manager identified another overriding reason for recent progress. 'We've hit a rich vein of form after losing at Arsenal. That gave us a rude awakening – and sometimes you need that,' insisted the boss. 'The players have responded in the right way.'

That assertion came after the Reds had followed up victory at bogey side Southampton with a wonderful attacking display against Wimbledon. Goals were flowing and the source was a front two first tried at the Boleyn Ground but not in the six weeks since. Yorke had injected energy and enthusiasm into United's forward line, effortlessly linking midfield and attack in a way not sustained since Eric Cantona's retirement two years earlier. All he needed now was an established strike partner. Against the Saints he got one.

'Southampton at the Dell,' responds Cole without hesitation when asked to pinpoint the moment his partnership with United's new man first clicked. 'Yorkie had played with Giggsy, Scholesy, Teddy and then Ole. For some reason, we went down to the Dell and the manager just decided to give me a go and if it worked out then it worked out. I said to myself: "You are going to get a game today, so just enjoy it."

'Before the game or even during the game, nothing was worked on. We trained but nothing was specifically trained on. Everything we did just worked a dream, peeling off wide, coming short and spinning in behind. The movement was just . . . Wow! Afterwards, the manager said he had stumbled on something. And it *was* stumbled on, because it wasn't like he was buying Yorkie for me. It wasn't like when I was at Newcastle and Kevin Keegan bought Peter Beardsley to play with me. This was just stumbled on and that's just what happens sometimes.'

It was an instant rapport that appeared to stem from their off-field friendship, which had blossomed after Cole helped Yorke to settle into his new surroundings. Yet United's No.9 was every bit as surprised by the recent arrival's sunny disposition as most of the Reds' dressing room had been.

'I don't think anybody at Man United had seen that type of personality. You get cocky people, but this guy's attitude towards football was totally different. It was sunshine football. He thought he was going to have a laugh and a joke: "If you like me then you like me and if you don't then you don't."

'People used to wonder how we got on so well together because we are total opposites. Yorkie was the life and soul and a "have a look at me" type, while I was the other way and wanted to keep things quiet. But opposites attract. I loved his personality and he loved mine for what I was. We got on so well and to this day we still get on so well, because we are two totally different people who approach life in two totally different ways.'

Whatever the secret, the on-pitch chemistry was eye-catching and at Southampton, despite big talk beforehand from their fiery full-back Francis Benali, both strikers scored in a convincing 3-0 victory. 'We're looking forward to playing them,' Benali had said, only to spend much of the afternoon being tormented by Beckham and watching the Reds' new strike duo run rings around his fellow defenders.

Having hit upon a winning combination, the United boss wasn't about to tinker and the pair were among the goals again a fortnight later. International football's untimely interruption could have slowed their momentum, but there was little sign of that as Wimbledon were walloped 5-1. Post-match, Ferguson revealed that the break – at least for those not called up by their country – had been put to good use.

'It's hard to single out players after an excellent team performance like this, but Andy Cole and Dwight Yorke have done really well together,' said the Reds boss. 'They've been training on their own as a pair – perhaps they were getting to know each other!'

On the receiving end of United's latest scoring spree had been Scotland's new number one goalkeeper, Neil Sullivan. Despite his disappointment at fetching the ball from his net five times – thanks to Cole twice, Yorke once – the Dons stopper was fulsome in his praise. 'There was great movement from Yorke and Cole. They were fantastic,' said Sullivan. 'They look like they have been playing together for years. And there are times when you just have to hold your hands up and say you have been beaten by a very good side. Our back four have been together now for a few seasons and we don't often concede many goals, so that says it all, really. I think the Cole–Yorke combination is definitely the best we have played against this season.'

Yorke had been one of dozens of names linked with the Reds through the summer, with established world stars Gabriel Batistuta, Alessandro Del Piero, Andrei Shevchenko and the rising Marcelo Salas among them. 'We looked at all of those players,' recalls United's then chief scout Mick Brown. 'There were plenty more we supposedly were watching but weren't. We counted up once over a year how many players we were supposed to be interested in, in the close-season, and it got to some fantastic, ridiculous number.'

Having scouted Stam, Brown also recalls how Yorke's name first came to be mentioned at the Cliff training ground. 'I walked into the office one day and there was the manager and some members of the coaching staff, and we had a little bit of a meeting and that's when the question was asked: "If you could sign any player for Manchester United, who would it be?" That's when I came out with the name Dwight Yorke.

I got one or two funny looks as I remember it – I won't say from whom – but I later found out that somebody had said: "What the hell do we want him for?" To be fair, the question was asked, I gave the answer and then I was asked, "Why do you say that?" I replied, "Because he can play in three positions, for a start, but he will love it at Old Trafford. He's got a mentality where his a*** isn't going to fall out and he is one of those who will step up." Of that I was convinced. I know you can't guarantee anything in football, but I was really, really positive about that.'

As one of those expecting the Trinidadian to be a success, Brown was obviously delighted when the man he'd recommended combined so well with Cole. 'As chief scout, you don't very often get to see your own team, so when I did get the opportunity to see us, I thought his partnership with Andy Cole was probably the last we've seen of two out-and-out strikers,' he recalls.

'Nobody plays pure four-four-two like we did then, with Beckham and Giggs on the wings and those two up front. Some of their combination play, step-overs, joining in getting second and third balls . . . I thought that was top-class stuff. You can see Dwight's smile from ten miles away, you never knew where Andy was at, but you could see the enjoyment in the two of them playing together. That was some partnership, those two.'

For the man himself, who would come to be seen as the last piece in the jigsaw of the all-conquering Treble team, arriving at United took his game up a level. Yorkie was loving life as a Red and benefiting from playing with an intensity in training that mirrored that of the matches.

'That was a big difference,' recalls Yorke of sessions at the Cliff. 'Villa was very good and competitive, but when I went to Manchester United I realised that, even though we were good at Villa, we were nowhere near as good as these guys. Training was competition every time you turned up. Because there was so much star quality within the squad, that lifted everyone and when you were not at it there were people ready to pull you up and say "What are you playing at?" Roy in particular! That improved you as a player.

'At Villa, where I was for ten years, you could go through the motions and people wouldn't have a go at you, because their standard was maybe not quite as high. Even though your average day in training at Villa would still have probably been better than at most clubs, you couldn't be average at United because you looked really out of place and it showed up a lot more. That was a huge difference.'

Next to face United, and their ever-improving strike force, was Brondby, Peter Schmeichel's first club. Their coach Ebbe Skovdahl had been at Old Trafford for the five-goal demolition of the Dons and clearly feared a possible repeat against his own Danish champions. 'It seems I can't put my head on the pillow at night without seeing United scoring goals in my sleep,' he joked. 'I was very impressed. The only surprise for me was that United didn't get four or five more.'

His worst fears were confirmed when Giggs scored twice, Roy Keane and Ole Gunnar Solskjaer chipped in, with Cole and Yorke making their now-customary contribution. Schmeichel had returned from injury in time for his sort-of-homecoming, but made two uncharacteristic blunders for Brondby's goals. Even so, the 6-2 away win set a new Champions League record.

Third of United's five games in a fortnight was a visit to Derby County, another club that had enjoyed success against the Reds in recent campaigns, but few could foresee anything but a first Pride Park win for Ferguson's men. Even Rams skipper Spencer Prior was apprehensive. 'I deliberately refused to switch on the television to watch United's six-two midweek win over Brondby because I realised it would ruin my sleep,' said the County captain. 'Wimbledon boss Joe Kinnear called United "frightening" after taking a five-one hammering at Old Trafford last weekend, and I know exactly what he means. Unless we work like dogs, and cut out the clever-clever stuff, which has plagued our recent performances, we are going to get slaughtered.'

Prior and his Pride Park pack claimed a point and possibly deserved to take more from a wholly forgettable 1-1 draw – Jordi Cruyff's bobbling shot late on cancelling out Deon Burton's tap-in opener. The goal for the Catalonian-bred Dutchman was his second of the month, following a volley at Southampton, and drew praise from his manager. 'He's had so many ups and downs with injuries and settling in here. And of course he has always had to live with his father's name,' explained a sympathetic-sounding Ferguson. 'All these things present certain challenges and he's had to come through them. He has outstanding ability. You can't question that. The main problem for him is that he's not had enough football because of his injuries.'

Having scored 14 goals in three October fixtures, the dropped points at Derby were a surprise – as was the seeming lack of urgency until falling a goal behind. Was it simply an off day? Or was it a result of weariness from midweek's European sojourn? Ferguson insisted it wasn't the latter. 'We are in Europe all the time,' he dismissively told journalists. 'We gave the ball away too easily, that was the problem. There was a lot of carelessness from us.'

If there *were* heavy legs in his dressing room then the boss was given the perfect opportunity to rest them. Bury made the ten-mile journey across Manchester, with 10,000 fans in tow, hoping to pull off a shock against their illustrious neighbours. For their chairman, Terry Robinson, the outcome – a 2-0 Reds win after extra time – was secondary to the financial boost for his club.

'When I heard all the other so-called smaller clubs getting good matches, I kept thinking we'd miss out, then we got the best draw of the lot,' said the Shakers supremo. 'No one will ever know how much this match will mean to Bury.'

The game was also much anticipated by the Neville brothers, coming against their home-town club, for whom their father worked as commercial manager. Phil recalls: 'The Bury tie was good. I was captain, I think. It was great because I was playing even though I shouldn't have been. I'd played a few games before that but I really wanted to play against Bury and the manager let me.'

While the younger Neville brother got to enjoy a memorable occasion, his elder sibling watched from the stands after adopting a different approach. 'I didn't play but I wanted to,' remembers Gary. 'I've never asked to play in a game, it's not a question you ask, but I remember being really disappointed at not playing because I knew the chance of playing them again was small. I was disappointed, it was a big thing for Bury and I enjoyed the night, but I wish I had played.'

Of the tie itself, Phil adds: 'They played really well on the night, Bury, and we couldn't score, until we eventually got a couple late in extra time. What was great was that there were so many fans there. Bury only get two or three thousand for a home game and they got ten thousand in the K-Stand that night. It was a proud moment for a Bury lad, really.'

The tie was eventually settled by Norwegians Solskjaer and Erik Nevland at either end of the second segment of extra time. For the latter, scoring the clinching goal represented a huge personal milestone. 'A dream,' he recalls. 'I had posters of United's players on my bedroom wall when I was at home in Norway – even up to when I joined the club – so to score at the Stretford End within a couple of years was just an incredible feeling.'

Phil Neville was the only player from the trip to Derby to play in the League Cup match, and he was in the next starting line-up, too, as the Reds made a third Premiership away trip of the month to play Walter Smith's Everton.

Dwight Yorke had proven the star addition to the swelled Reds ranks and he scored again in this (eventually) comfortable 4-1 victory – but Jesper Blomqvist and Jaap Stam were making their mark, too. Conceding five goals in six October games was steady rather than outstanding, but a huge improvement on the nine shipped a month earlier. Stam played in five of those matches, partnering Gary Neville in the heart of defence and was showing the kind of form that prompted United's record outlay for a defender.

For the likes of Henning Berg, who had been a regular at the back throughout the previous campaign, it meant just one appearance all month and that in the League Cup with fringe players and youngsters. Some players would have sulked; the Norwegian took a patient, philosophical approach.

'Well, it was just competition,' Berg explains. 'Pallister left that summer and, although he was not always number one on the teamsheet, he was always a regular. When he was going, you expected the manager to sign another player and then Jaap came in. It was like an exchange, so my competition for the team was more or less the same. It was obvious Jaap would be playing and it was just a case of who would be playing with him – Ronny [Johnsen], me or David May? Ronny had a lot of injuries and Gary Neville could play there as well, but we didn't have that many right-backs either.

'There was competition for places, but I know that Jaap coming in didn't change anything for me. I thought it was good. He was a great talent, had a lot of potential and was a very good player – you could see that straight away. You want the club to sign good players because you want the team to have the best chance. Obviously, he had a great season, there is no doubt about that. I liked playing with him, we had different qualities but I enjoyed playing with him.'

Stam was clearly settling in to life in England, but it was the new Swedish wide man who produced the man-of-the-match performance on Merseyside. Blomqvist headed United's fourth goal to cap a display that left Everton midfielder John Collins impressed. 'With

Yorke up front they have terrific movement, and Keane's return from injury has given them far more bite in midfield. He looks as though he never had an injury,' assessed Collins. 'But I think Blomqvist is important to them because he has added further quality to a high-quality squad, which is always very difficult. I think they did miss Giggs last year, but they won't so much this time around.'

Blomqvist's contribution was also being appreciated by his new team-mates, not least those playing with him on the left-hand side. One of those, Denis Irwin, recalls the impression the Swedish international made on him.

'The manager is always out there and looking to improve the team. He made three great signings. Jaap was built for the Premier League. We knew about Yorkie, because we had played against him; I had marked him a few times at Villa and we knew he was a really good player, a good scorer as well as someone who could hold the ball up. Of course, his link-up play with Coley was fantastic that year as well. But Jesper was really underrated,' says Irwin. 'When Giggsy didn't play Jesper played in front of me a few times. He would work his socks off, he was more skilful than people thought and had a bit of pace. He was a good character as well and he was very much underrated. Of course, we needed him in the European Cup final.'

Cruelly, that Nou Camp appearance seven months later was to be the winger's last for the club. He sat on the sidelines for the next two years with a serious knee injury, moved on to Everton in 2001, was briefly at Charlton, before returning to Scandinavia. He never recovered from his injury and played 40 competitive games in a decade. Every reason, then, to remember his part in the incredible Treble triumph.

'Jesper Blomqvist? Fantastic professional,' recalls Phil Neville, who, like Irwin, played behind the Swede. 'Brilliant understudy for Giggsy. Giggsy could be rested or played in the middle, Jesper would come in. Brilliant trainer, trained hard. He was fantastic for us.'

Alex Ferguson had promised that United would be back stronger after losing the league to Arsenal and three months in the signs were promising. Yorke was the spark up front, Stam was finding his feet at the back and Blomqvist was now providing a viable alternative to a perceived over-reliance on Giggs.

'Those three were fantastic for us,' continues Phil. 'Fantastic characters. I was friends with all three of them. At the time, it was quite easy to come into the dressing room because there was a great spirit. They probably found it hard because the levels of expectation and intensity in training were obviously more than what they'd been used to, but I think they settled in really well.

'It was the season when the manager's rotation policy really began to bear fruit and everyone got the games, so everybody felt welcome and a part of it. Even though there were only eleven players on the field, you knew that the week after you would be playing. The manager kept eighteen players unbelievably happy and feeling part of things. That was the key to the whole season.'

Saturday 3 October 1998 | Premiership | The Dell | Attendance: 15,251

SOUTHAMPTON 0
MANCHESTER UNITED 3 Yorke 12, Cole 60, Cruyff 75

Missing a flight back from Munich was not ideal preparation for a visit to your bogey ground. Even against a Southampton side bottom of the table with just one point from seven matches, there remained real concern that the disruptions could hinder hopes of avoiding a fourth successive away defeat to the Saints.

'We know Manchester United don't much enjoy coming to the Dell,' had boasted Francis Benali ahead of the game, but clearly someone had forgotten to tell Manchester United, who eventually made their way back from Germany and quickly trained their sights on ending their barren run on the south coast.

Dwight Yorke and Andy Cole were paired for only the second time and, unlike at West Ham, struck up an obvious on-pitch rapport – each finding the net in a comfortable victory rounded off by a Jordi Cruyff volley. 'It was a determined performance by us,' was the verdict of the United boss, pleased but ever the perfectionist.

Benali and Matt Le Tissier were the only two starters for Southampton to have featured in their hat-trick of Dell victories against the Reds: 3-1 and 6-3 in April and October 1996, then 1-0 in January 1998. For United, the build-up may have been far from perfect, but this was a squad chock full of options. In came Raimond van der Gouw and Nicky Butt for the injured Peter Schmeichel and Paul Scholes, while Teddy Sheringham dropped to the bench for Cole.

After an early escape when David Howells headed over unmarked in the second minute, the visitors slipped into an increasingly familiar and fluent rhythm. On 12 minutes it brought reward in the form of a first goal of the season for the soon-to-be-prolific Cole and Yorke partnership.

Cole broke down the left-hand side, crossed to Yorke, and the former Villa man stretched out his right leg to prod in his fifth goal in eight games. It was United's first away strike of the campaign, to which more would have been added by the break had David Beckham and Jesper Blomqvist not missed the target.

Saints boss David Jones afterwards claimed his side had matched the Reds for the first hour, but in truth three points had looked secure long before Cole marked his first start in seven matches by etching his name on the scoresheet. Released into the inside-left channel by Blomqvist, the Reds No.9 advanced on goal and fired past Paul Jones with aplomb. Fifteen minutes later it was 3-0 and game over when substitute Cruyff followed up a Jones save of a Cole shot to acrobatically volley in.

Dell hoodoo halted, away goals account opened and United up to second in the table. It was a thoroughly satisfactory way to end a challenging few weeks and a solid way to begin another busy month.

Southampton: Jones; Warner, Monkou, Lundekvam (Gibbens 56), Benali; Ripley (Beattie 64), Howells, Palmer, Bridge; Ostenstad, Le Tissier
Subs not used: Moss, Basham, Hiley
Booked: Palmer

Manchester United: van der Gouw; P.Neville, Stam, G.Neville, Irwin (Brown 79); Beckham, Keane, Butt, Blomqvist (Cruyff 73); Yorke (Sheringham 73), Cole
Subs not used: Berg, Solskjaer
Booked: Keane

Man of the Match: Roy Keane
The driving force in midfield was at his expansive best. Against Bayern he'd provided a foundation for others to foray forward; here he was back near his marauding former self. 'He's been getting better and better all the time,' said a delighted Ferguson.

Saturday 17 October 1998 | Premiership | Old Trafford |
Attendance: 55,265

MANCHESTER UNITED 5 Cole 19, 88, Giggs 45, Beckham 47, Yorke 52
WIMBLEDON 1 Euell 39

So much for the theory that top sides always struggle after an international break. Following a fortnight without a game, Manchester United produced a five-star display to rout eighth-placed Wimbledon, making it the perfect preparation to the midweek must-win Champions League trip to Copenhagen.

Peter Schmeichel, Denis Irwin, Teddy Sheringham, David May and Ronny Johnsen were all out injured, with Nicky Butt still suspended after his red card at Arsenal. But even that couldn't stop United from moving through the gears. Roy Keane continued where he'd left off at the Dell. Ryan Giggs looked more comfortable in central midfield than he had at centre forward. David Beckham was at his effervescent best down the right, playing ahead of debutant right-back Wes Brown, aged 19, who was only pipped to the man-of-the-match award by the brilliant Andy Cole.

The Dons, so often Premiership party poopers, were seldom given a sniff of an opportunity to pull off a shock. Cole scored twice and Dwight Yorke once to continue the link-up that had blossomed on the south coast, while Giggs and Beckham were also on target. Wimbledon boss Joe Kinnear, for whom the only highlight was Jason Euell's 39th-minute equaliser, offered an honest assessment. 'There's no shame getting beaten by a side like United, who were better than us in every department,' said the Dons chief.

It was specifically the United front two that Kinnear's visitors could simply not contain. Cole claimed his and United's first from 18 yards after being played in by Beckham. Giggs then headed in a Jesper Blomqvist cross to reinstate United's lead six minutes after Euell had levelled, and the scoring continued after the break. Beckham rifled a low drive in from 30 yards, and Yorke made it four by harassing a mistake out of the Wimbledon defence to roll the ball beyond Scotland's new first-choice goalkeeper Neil Sullivan. It was five when the Reds' finest performer Cole took another Beckham pass, nutmegged Dean Blackwell and finished precisely.

Alex Ferguson was glowing after his team's display, commenting: 'An excellent performance. We've responded the right way to losing at Arsenal, and that's the measure of good players.'

Next to try to stop United's dynamic duo were Brondby, whose coach Ebbe Skovdahl was at the game. Having seen his side hit for six by the Reds in pre-season, and after witnessing this equally destructive display at first hand, he'd been left with plenty to ponder.

Manchester United: van der Gouw; Brown, Stam, G.Neville, P.Neville (Curtis 74); Beckham (Cruyff 57), Keane, Giggs (Scholes 66), Blomqvist; Yorke, Cole
Subs not used: Berg, Solskjaer
Booked: Stam

Wimbledon: Sullivan; Cunningham, Perry, Blackwell, Kimble (Ardley h-t); Thatcher, Earle, Roberts, Hughes; Leaburn (Gayle h-t), Euell
Subs not used: Heald, Kennedy, Cort
Booked: Roberts

Man of the Match: Andy Cole
Played with a smile on his face and continued his seemingly natural partnership with Yorke. The Reds' top scorer the previous season was back at the top of his game, leading Ferguson to reveal: 'Cole has picked himself for the game in Denmark.'

Wednesday 21 October 1998 | Champions League Group D | Parken | Attendance: 40,315

BRONDBY IF 2 Daugaard 35, Sand 90
MANCHESTER UNITED 6 Giggs 2, 21, Cole 28, Keane 55, Yorke 60, Solskjaer 62

We often score six, but we seldom score ten. The words of the Reds' fan anthem have rarely seemed so apt. Alex Ferguson's men netted half a dozen times but squandered enough clear-cut chances to have comfortably made it to double figures against the Danish champions. Manchester United truly were the pride of all Europe on this wet Scandinavian evening, scoring more goals away from home than any side since the inception of the Champions League in 1992. 'It was a bit like a tennis match,' said Brondby coach Ebbe Skovdahl, 'We have lost six-nil [in pre-season] and now six-two, and I don't know what will happen in the third game.'

The Reds made two changes from the side that had thumped Wimbledon so emphatically four days earlier. Peter Schmeichel replaced Raimond van der Gouw after proving his fitness in a double training session the day before departure, and also into the starting XI came Paul Scholes for the suspended David Beckham, with Ryan Giggs moved from central to right midfield.

It took just two minutes for the wiry Welshman to make an impact. European debutant Wes Brown progressed unimpeded into the final third, then claimed an assist when his cross was fumbled by Brondby goalkeeper Mogens Krogh for Giggs to tuck away the rebound. By half time United had scored twice more. Giggs was at it again on 21 minutes, heading in a Jesper Blomqvist centre (for the second time in five days), then seven minutes later the Dwight Yorke and Andy Cole partnership conjured yet another goal, with the latter providing the finish. The Reds' No.9 collected a Yorke pass, wrong-footed Kenneth Rasmussen and then sent a right-foot shot curling beyond Krogh.

The next Dane to make a mistake in this game was Schmeichel, who allowed an accurate but tame free-kick from Kim Daugaard to squirm past him and into the net. It wasn't exactly the return to his former club the great Danish hero had been hoping for, although the 1-3 scoreline was probably a fair reflection of the first 45 minutes – the visitors excellent in attack, if slightly wasteful, but rather sloppy at the back.

More of the same followed after the break, with the Reds striking three times in seven minutes only to concede again in injury time. The imperious Roy Keane, taking yet another step towards his finest form, was next to score. He played a one-two with Yorke to break open the Brondby defence and make it 1-4 with a shot in off the post. Provider then turned finisher, with Yorke heading a deserved fifth for United from Phil Neville's high cross to the far post. Number six came from (don't call him 'super') sub Ole Gunnar Solskjaer, who rounded off the rout on 62 minutes by firing in a Yorke lay-off with his first touch of the game.

More United goals seemed a certainty, only for profligate finishing and a drop in tempo to allow the hosts to pull one back in injury time. Ebbe Sand capitalised on another Schmeichel handling error – spilling a shot into the path of his international team-mate – to make it 2-6.

It was a comprehensive and record-breaking away win for United, and while Ferguson was understandably delighted with the half-dozen goals, he was less pleased his side's overall display. Afterwards he said: 'It was not a great performance. The conditions were difficult for both teams and that created a carelessness and sloppiness in our play, and we gave the ball away too much. Still, you can't dismiss the goals we scored and that was the main feature of the game for me.'

The result, allied with Bayern Munich's 1-0 home win against Barcelona, moved the Reds to the top of Group D. 'It's been a great night for us and we got the result we wanted in Munich,' said Ferguson. He may not have been entirely happy, but there was a growing feeling among United supporters that – in the words of the supporters' song – this was developing into 'one of those teams that you (only) see now and then'.

Brondby IF: M.Krogh; Colding, Rasmussen, Nielsen (M.Jensen 31), B.Jensen (Vragel 27); Bjur, Daugaard, Ravn, Lindrup; Sand, Hansen (Bagger 67)
Subs not used: Anderson, Thygesen, S.Krogh, Olsen

Manchester United: Schmeichel; Brown, Stam, G.Neville, P.Neville; Beckham, Keane, Giggs (Cruyff 61), Blomqvist; Yorke (Wilson 66), Cole (Solskjaer 61)
Subs not used: van der Gouw, Berg, Clegg, Curtis
Booked: Cruyff

Man of the Match: Ryan Giggs
This was the Welshman at his unplayable best. He scored after two minutes and netted again after 21 to give the Reds the perfect start in a rain-drenched Parken. In his hour on the pitch, Giggs exposed the Danes' lack of pace and cut them open with countless trademark slalom runs.

Saturday 24 October 1998 | Premiership | Pride Park | Attendance: 30,867

DERBY COUNTY 1 Burton 75
MANCHESTER UNITED 1 Cruyff 86

Three consecutive defeats for the hosts and 14 goals in three games for the visitors suggested only one outcome to this late October fixture. Sadly, at least for travelling Reds, United were held at Derby for the third season running as the goals dried up and the Rams went on the raid.

In truth, and Alex Ferguson admitted as much, Jim Smith's side had done their homework and probably deserved to win the game through Deon Burton's 75th-minute goal. Yet a late triple substitution from the United boss claimed the impetus for his side with one of the new arrivals, Jordi Cruyff, salvaging a point with four minutes of normal time remaining.

'Derby tried to block out the width of our game. At times they were successful. It made it quite a dour game,' summarised Ferguson afterwards. There was certainly not the anticipated level of enter-tainment, at least not for those expecting United to pick up where they'd left off in Copenhagen.

Here, as in Denmark, a saturated pitch did little to help the Reds' high-tempo passing game. Nor were the home side going to allow Roy Keane, Ryan Giggs, Dwight Yorke and Andy Cole the space to counter-attack as they'd done at Parken. 'We had talked about it with the manager before the game and reached the conclusion that we couldn't outplay them, but we could outfight them,' said Darryl Powell of the Rams' collective commitment. 'That was the case. They didn't like the way we played and we felt they were disheartened.'

Derby's bold approach of playing three up front – Burton, Dean Sturridge and Paolo Wanchope – kept United's backline busy and the hosts made a weary-looking United contest every ball. Ferguson refused to blame European exertions for the low-key performance, but recognised the difference fresh legs could make by introducing his own trio (of substitutes) with eight minutes left.

Trailing to Burton's right-foot connection to a Powell cross, the Reds replaced Gary Neville, Nicky Butt and Giggs with Paul Scholes, Jesper Blomqvist and Cruyff and the latter ensured a point with time running out – hitting a bobbling low shot beyond Russell Hoult.

'It was a sensible throw of the dice. When you're one-nil down you have to do something like that. I would have brought on four if I could have done,' joked a relieved Ferguson. 'We were pretty poor, to be honest, and didn't deserve even to draw the game.' A fair assess-ment, but what is it they say about picking up points when not playing well?

Derby County: Hoult; Delap, Prior, Stimac, Laursen (Dorigo h-t), Schnoor; Carsley, Powell; Sturridge, Wanchope, Burton
Subs not used: Poom, Carbonari, Elliott, Baiano
Booked: Schnoor, Powell, Delap

Manchester United: Schmeichel; Brown, Stam, G.Neville (Scholes 82), P.Neville; Beckham, Keane, Butt (Cruyff 82), Giggs (Blomqvist 82); Yorke, Cole

Subs not used: van der Gouw, Berg

Booked: G.Neville, Beckham, Cole

Man of the Match: Wes Brown

The youngest player in red was also the most sprightly, keeping Sturridge quiet and tearing up and down the right flank all afternoon. He was even rewarded with a new song, a proud moment for any player, with regular renditions of 'We've got Wesley Brown' from the away section.

Wednesday 28 October 1998 | Worthington Cup 3rd Round | Old Trafford | Attendance: 52,495

MANCHESTER UNITED 2 Solskjaer 106, Nevland 115
BURY 0

United set off on the third of four routes to silverware – with the FA Cup to follow in January – by registering a 2-0 victory against Greater Manchester neighbours Bury. Two Norwegians did the damage for the Reds, with Ole Gunnar Solskjaer and substitute Erik Nevland netting in the second half of extra time for a battling third round League Cup win.

Alex Ferguson made ten changes to the side that had been held at Derby, handing a debut to Jonathan Greening and places to fellow youngsters Michael Clegg, John Curtis, Mark Wilson and Phil Mulryne. while guiding them through this wet and windy night were experienced heads David May, Phil Neville, Henning Berg, Solskjaer and Jordi Cruyff.

Bury adopted the same obdurate approach that had served them so well in their climb to the second tier of English football, and for 105 minutes it worked to perfection. Neil Warnock's team, cheered on by almost 10,000 fans, set out to make the game as difficult as possible for United's overhauled side. During normal time United enjoyed possession, passed well and poured forward, only to be repelled by two banks of white-shirted Shakers.

Wilson and Greening went close for the hosts in the opening half, while for the visitors Chris Lucketti headed wide from a Mark Patterson free-kick. Sadly, at least for the home fans, chances remained at a premium after the interval, too. Inductee Nevland went close for the Reds, while Andy Woodward almost snatched a shock victory for the Division One side with just minutes remaining. When there were no goals in the first half of extra time, thoughts began to turn to the prospect of penalties.

That nail-biting prospect was eventually avoided thanks to the contribution of replacements Paul Scholes and Wes Brown. A minute into the second period of overtime, Solskjaer struck, squeezing the ball in via a post after being teed up by Scholes and Greening. The clinching second goal, coming from a Brown cross, was gleefully turned in at the far post by Nevland.

'Shame they changed the rules, we could have done with a replay,' said Warnock after the game. Still, Bury had landed an esti-mated £400,000 from the almost sell-out tie, a season's takings at Gigg Lane, and Alex Ferguson had given valuable experience to his youngsters. 'It certainly turned into a long night, but there were some good points, especially being able to expose some of the young play-ers to the pressures and expectancy of this club,' said the boss, who, upon hearing his side had been handed a home draw against Nottingham Forest in the fourth round, added: 'There could well be a chance for the youngsters again.'

Manchester United: van der Gouw; Curtis, May, Berg, Clegg (Brown 70); Cruyff, Wilson (Scholes 70), Mulryne (Nevland h-t), P.Neville; Greening, Solskjaer
Subs not used: G.Neville, Cooke

Bury: Kiely; Woodward, Lucketti, Redmond, Swailes, Barrick; Daws, Patterson (Matthews 100), Johnrose; D'Jaffo (Preece 57), Ellis (James 63)
Subs not used: Kenny, Foster

Man of the Match: Jonathan Greening
The signing from York City enjoyed an impressive debut, linked up well with Solskjaer and, eventually, played a part in his strike partner's breakthrough goal. Went close in the first half of normal time and remained a handful for the Shakers all evening.

Saturday 31 October 1998 | Premiership | Goodison Park | Attendance: 40,079

EVERTON 1 Ferguson 31
MANCHESTER UNITED 4 Yorke 14, Short 23 (og), Cole 59, Blomqvist 64

'Jesper is a very talented player with a lot of grit,' said Alex Ferguson after watching his summer signing put in a match-winning performance against Everton, his best since arriving from Parma for £4.4 million. The Swede had enjoyed plenty of game time in his fledgling Reds career, having been bought to provide cover and competition for Ryan Giggs, and in this Goodison Park engagement he ably filled the injured Welshman's boots.

That's not to say that the former Gothenburg man was the only

United player to excel on this particular afternoon; Roy Keane was up for the scrap in midfield, Andy Cole and Dwight Yorke dovetailed again, both scoring, and the defence held together (just) under intense Everton pressure either side of half time. A week on from the subdued showing at Pride Park, the Reds were back on track, producing a devastating display of finishing.

Duncan Ferguson almost scored after just 12 seconds, but it was the Reds who eventually went ahead – on 14 minutes – courtesy of an eye-catching move. Blomqvist passed to Cole, he picked out Paul Scholes with a delightful chip, and the midfielder squared the ball to the advancing Yorke – who crashed in the rebound of his first saved attempt.

David Beckham swung in one of his customary crosses for a panicked Craig Short to head beyond his own goalkeeper for 0-2. Then Ferguson, the Toffees' bruising centre-forward rather than the United boss, reduced the arrears with (almost inevitably) a towering header from six yards. That goal on the half-hour lifted the hopes of the home side, not to mention the volume levels inside Goodison. Roared on, Walter Smith's side twice hit the woodwork only to then fall further behind. In the 59th minute, Blomqvist raced onto a Scholes pass, played in Cole and his angled shot beat Thomas Myhre via the far post. The score became 1-4 when United's man of the match ended a lightning counter-attack by firing at Myhre then heading in the rebound.

The scoreline didn't necessarily reflect Everton's part in this entertaining game, and a reflective Alex Ferguson was keen to pay the Toffees their dues: 'Goals change games and after Duncan Ferguson had scored they were genuinely back in the match. The third goal for us killed it and we were comfortable after that.'

Fittingly, the final word was left to the man of the hour. 'I love it,' said a beaming Blomqvist of life as a Red. 'I am really enjoying my football. For my goal I was really pleased to see the ball go in, but I was equally pleased that we won.'

Everton: Myhre; Short (Dunne 67), Watson, Materazzi, Unsworth; Cadamarteri, Dacourt, Collins, Ball; Bakayoko, Ferguson
Subs not used: Gerrard, Cleland, Grant, Milligan
Booked: Ball, Short, Unsworth, Bakayoko

Manchester United: Schmeichel; Brown, Stam, G.Neville, P.Neville (Irwin 67); Beckham, Keane, Scholes, Blomqvist; Yorke, Cole
Subs not used: van der Gouw, Berg, Cruyff, Solskjaer
Booked: G.Neville, Keane, Scholes

Man of the Match: Jesper Blomqvist
The Swedish winger was bought to ease the over-reliance on Giggs and he more than proved himself in the Welshman's absence. United's No.15 set up Cole for the third goal then scored the fourth himself, his first for the Reds, to cap off an impressive afternoon's work.

October in statistics

Premiership table (31 October 1998)

	P	W	D	L	F	A	GD	Pts
Aston Villa	10	6	4	0	11	3	+8	22
Manchester United	**10**	**6**	**3**	**1**	**23**	**9**	**+14**	**21**
Arsenal	11	5	5	1	13	5	+8	20
Liverpool	11	4	4	3	18	12	+6	16
Middlesbrough	10	4	4	2	16	11	+5	16
Chelsea	9	4	4	1	13	9	+4	16
Leicester City	11	4	4	3	11	10	+1	16
West Ham United	11	4	4	3	12	12	0	16
Leeds United	11	2	8	1	11	8	+3	14
Derby County	11	3	5	3	10	9	+1	14
Newcastle United	11	4	2	5	15	16	−1	14
Wimbledon	11	3	5	3	16	19	−3	14
Tottenham Hotspur	10	4	2	4	12	16	−4	14
Charlton Athletic	10	3	4	3	17	14	+3	13
Everton	11	2	6	3	7	10	−3	12
Sheffield Wed	11	3	2	6	8	10	−2	11
Blackburn Rovers	11	2	3	6	11	15	−4	9
Nottingham Forest	10	2	2	6	7	16	−9	8
Coventry City	11	2	2	7	7	17	−10	8
Southampton	11	1	3	7	6	23	−17	6

Champions League, Group D table (22 October 1998)

	P	W	D	L	F	A	GD	Pts
Manchester United	**3**	**1**	**2**	**0**	**11**	**7**	**+4**	**5**
Barcelona	3	1	1	1	5	4	+1	4
Bayern Munich	3	1	1	1	4	4	0	4
Brondby	3	1	0	2	4	9	−5	3

October form (all competitions): WWWDWW

Goals scored: 21   **Goals conceded:** 5

Most appearances: Phil Neville 6 (531 mins)

Players used: 25

Most goals: Andy Cole 5

Most assists: Jesper Blomqvist, Dwight Yorke 4 each

Different goalscorers: 10

Quickest goal: Ryan Giggs, 2 mins [v Brondby (a)]

Latest goal: Erik Nevland, 114 mins [(aet) v Bury (h)]

Watched by: 234,487

Average attendance: 39,081

Chapter 4

November – The Long Goodbye

Peter Schmeichel had been pelted with plastic bottles during United's win at Everton as October drew to a close, but as November began the giant Dane was more concerned with the barrage of criticism hurtling his way.

Widely acknowledged as the world's finest goalkeeper for much of the 1990s, Schmeichel's patchy start to 1998-99 had not gone unnoticed, and widespread probing from the media prompted Alex Ferguson to insist: 'He's a fine goalkeeper, the best I have ever had and the best that Manchester United have ever had. Great players are always going to be examined more closely than others and their mistakes will be highlighted to a greater degree. That is what has happened here.

'Sometimes people are hoping you make mistakes, because otherwise they think you are flawless. But people wouldn't be human if they didn't make mistakes. There have been very few from Peter during his time here and they have certainly been outweighed by the number of marvellous performances he has contributed.'

But while the goalkeeper's previous excellence still had him firmly in credit with his manager, there was no mistaking the change in United's No.1. 'He was not in the best form,' recalls Schmeichel's understudy, Raimond van der Gouw. 'I'd played for two seasons with him and I thought he would never make mistakes at all, but that season he made some crucial ones, and I was really surprised to see what had happened to him.'

Of course, van der Gouw, like the rest of the club – save Schmeichel, Ferguson and Martin Edwards – was blissfully unaware that the Dane had long since taken the decision to leave United at the end of the campaign. Though increasingly dogged by his enormous secret, Schmeichel's mood was at least temporarily lifted by the Champions League visit to Old Trafford of his former club, Brondby.

Denmark's finest had taken poundings in October's 6-2 stroll and August's pre-season 6-0 whitewash, both at Parken, and coach Ebbe Skovdahl displayed remarkable candour in his pre-match press conference ahead of the sides' Group D encounter. 'So far it has been like a tennis match,' he grimaced, before shrugging: 'I really don't know what we're going to do for the third match.'

That perplexing pep talk unsurprisingly did little to help his side's cause at Old Trafford, with United four goals ahead inside half an hour and eventually sated by a 5-0 victory. Back-to-back wins over the Danes put the Reds in control of Group D, but Bayern Munich's six-point haul in their own double-header with Barcelona threatened to eliminate one of the pre-tournament favourites, unless they could overturn United in Catalonia later in the month. For Brondby, however, the ignominy of their pastings would last far beyond their early exit, according to Schmeichel, who shared his former side's pain as United ran riot.

'A couple of years later, the Brondby chairman told me it was those results against United that tipped everything the wrong way for the club,' says the giant Dane, now a club ambassador for United.

'They've gone further and further down ever since. In all fairness, the six-two win was good because it gave us three points and it gave us a cushion on goal difference, but even that hurt me. It did. It was just a tiny bit too much.

'Brondby beat Bayern Munich before we played them, so in many ways at least they'd shown they were competitive. It was great to beat them, but it was probably one of those games where you think four-two would have looked better for everyone. The five-nil at Old Trafford could have been fifteen, but we held back. I'm glad we held back. I was really, really pleased we held back. It hurt the club. It hurt Brondby for sure and they basically haven't had a good run in Europe since. They've had sniffs here and there, but that was really tough for them and it obviously gave us the edge over the other two, Bayern Munich and Barcelona. In the greater picture, I suppose it was very important that we did that.'

The second victory over the Danish champions was achieved without Ryan Giggs, sufferer of a fractured foot against Derby County, and the Welshman was joined on the sidelines by Phil Neville, who scored against Brondby but was withdrawn with a hamstring injury after half an hour. When Ronny Johnsen sustained a twisted ankle in the Reds' next outing, a goalless draw with Newcastle, it seemed Lady Luck was working against United. In fact, the spate of setbacks – which reached a zenith later in the month when three players suffered injuries against Blackburn – was attributed to a far more troubling variable: the Old Trafford pitch.

Relaid ahead of the season with a revolutionary, Australian-conceived turf interwoven with nylon mesh, the grass was already suffering as a dreary summer trudged into a sodden autumn. The situation had worsened notably after the Reds' Worthington Cup victory over Bury at the end of October, a 120-minute epic conducted amid a near-biblical downpour.

Faced with the prospect of four successive home games in 11

days, head groundsman Keith Kent came up with a drastic means of saving the pitch: introducing blue-nosed lob worms in their thousands in order to aid drainage, but it proved to no avail. After the Reds' draw with Newcastle, the clumps of deadened turf strewn about the field laid bare the direness of the situation, and Kent joined Alex Ferguson and Bill Casimaty – managing director of Strathayr, suppliers of the pitch – for an emergency meeting.

Casimaty quickly identified the problems: an unavoidably Mancunian climate and a maddening Old Trafford schedule. In five months since the pitch had been laid, it had enjoyed five days of sunshine and hosted 23 events, providing woefully insufficient conditions for the grass to root. The interim solution would be to see out the quartet of home games, rip up the troublesome turf and lay a thick, temporary replacement to carry through until the end of the season, before regrowing it in May.

Schmeichel would not be there to see Old Trafford's newest stage, and he felt compelled to admit as much amid the incessant speculation around his future. Having called a press conference at Old Trafford, the Dane told the assembled media: 'Manchester United is the ultimate place to play football, but it has been getting too much for me.'

The announcement gave the green light for a transfer speculation overdrive, with goalkeepers from all over the world tipped as potential replacements. Mark Schwarzer, Richard Wright, Carlos Roa and Gianluigi Buffon were all quickly proffered, but the recurring names belonged to Mark Bosnich and Edwin van der Sar. Both would ultimately represent United, but it would be the former who would arrive first, on a free transfer from Aston Villa, a week after the Reds overcame Bayern Munich in Barcelona.

Looking back on his decision to announce his intentions, Schmeichel admits: 'There were so many rumours around that I just wanted to clear things up. I was playing really poorly and with so much speculation, we decided it was best to announce it then. I wasn't sure how the decision would go down with the fans, but they were great with me.'

United's No.1 made the announcement the day after watching from the stands as a heavily rejigged Reds side navigated a route past Nottingham Forest and into the quarter-finals of the Worthington Cup. Once again, the competition had been used as a proving ground for the younger members of the squad and a run-out for their senior peers.

'It was very enjoyable – all the young lads liked the Worthington Cup,' says midfielder Mark Wilson. 'I'd come on over in Brøndby in October for my Champions League debut, and starting a game at Old Trafford so soon after that just puts you on such a high. The pitch was awful, but you just didn't care because you were out there in that United shirt, playing against seasoned pros for proper prizes.'

Though no injuries were sustained during the relatively routine tie, settled by two clinical Ole Gunnar Solskjaer finishes, the turf would claim three more victims in United's 3-2 Premier League victory against Blackburn Rovers, with Solskjaer, Jordi Cruyff and Paul Scholes all injured during the course of play. A Scholes brace and another goal from Dwight Yorke was almost overturned by a second-half fightback from the ten-man visitors, but Rovers manager Roy Hodgson was nevertheless irate with his side, venting his spleen during post-match drinks in Alex Ferguson's office.

First-team coach Jim Ryan, among the backroom staff members invited into all such gatherings with his manager, recalls: 'That's one of the things I remember most about all the post-match drinks we had. Probably ninety-seven per cent of the time, the game that has just happened is never mentioned, but that day Roy was very unhappy about two or three of his players. He started criticising them, saying: "Can you believe them? How can they do that to us?" He wasn't saying anything about us or the way we played, he was just disappointed at his own players.'

With Rovers struggling towards the foot of the table, the defeat would prove to be Hodgson's penultimate game in charge at Ewood Park. Blackburn owner Jack Walker's search for a new man to helm his club would soon bring him back to Old Trafford, but at the time it was another manager, Glenn Hoddle, who briefly concerned Alex Ferguson.

Unlike several clubs – including Rovers, who fielded Damien Duff and Jeff Kenna at Old Trafford – the United boss had rested Denis Irwin and Roy Keane in order to help the Republic of Ireland ahead of their Euro 2000 qualifier against Yugoslavia. Relations between Ferguson and England's manager, however, were less amiable.

The United manager took exception to Hoddle's public vilification of David Beckham after England's exit from France '98, and the winger came under widespread media scrutiny after United's win over Blackburn for a perceived over-reaction which contributed to Tim Sherwood's dismissal at Old Trafford. Beckham then prepared to join up with Hoddle for England's midweek friendly against Czech Republic, but the Three Lions manager again went public with his views, insisting: 'I will be speaking to David about what happened. There is still an element that can be improved on and he has got to deal with it.' The following day, after an impassioned phone conversation with his United counterpart, Hoddle told the press: 'I've spoken to Alex and it is no longer an issue, but this is something I really could have done without on the eve of a big game.'

Amid the international break fell United's Annual General Meeting, which was a far from mundane affair in light of the mooted BSkyB takeover, which continued to rumble on under the consideration of the Monopolies and Mergers Commission. With almost a thousand shareholders crammed into Old Trafford's Manchester Suite, the atmosphere began at sweltering and didn't cool until its climax over two and a half hours later.

Martin Edwards spent much of the afternoon fielding abuse from disgruntled supporters, with repeated demands for the United chairman to leave his post – to his total lack of surprise. 'I felt that a lot of supporters who were against the bid would turn up and voice their opinions, and that's what happened,' he admitted. 'I'm used to being abused at this club; I have had it for twenty years, probably more as a family. It's something you have to accept. You know you are going to have to make decisions which aren't popular with everyone, but you have to do what you feel is in the best long-term interests of the football club.'

In the short term, it was undoubtedly in the Reds' interests to exploit a fortnight-long window without a home tie, and the Old Trafford turf was duly resurfaced. Away from home discomforts – and once the players had returned from international duty – the Reds would travel to two contrasting opponents: Sheffield Wednesday and Barcelona.

Firstly, to the less salubrious Hillsborough, where the Reds missed the chance to go top of the Premier League table as they matched defeats for Aston Villa and Arsenal with a shock reverse against Danny Wilson's struggling Owls. Peter Schmeichel found himself quickly back in the headlines after fumbling a routine Niklas Alexandersson shot into the net and, though Andy Cole neatly levelled, United's performance levels dropped off after the break and Wim Jonk's finish and a clinching second from Alexandersson sealed the Reds' demise. For Schmeichel, enough was enough.

'It really wasn't working out for me,' he recalls. 'I was playing really poorly and after the game at Sheffield Wednesday I found myself thinking: "Christ, how bad can it be? How bad can it become?" I went in to the manager's office a day or two after that game and said: "I'm really sorry for my performance, but it's not happening for me. I really need to go away. I need some time." He actually looked, right there and then, in his calendar and said: "Well, we've got a period in January where we've only got one game . . . you can go away for ten days." Just knowing that was on the horizon was enough to put me at ease for the next few weeks.'

The Dane would actually be jetting away to sunnier climes just two days later, although the prospect of facing a Barcelona team frantic for victory was hardly an ideal way to unwind and combat stress. For Alex Ferguson, the return to Camp Nou was a return to the scene of what he termed: 'My worst European experience with United.'

Trounced 4-0 by the Catalan giants in the 1994-95 group stage, United had learned from that chastening evening, but still bore the scars. 'The players who played last time in Barcelona can't forget that kind of a night in a hurry,' added the manager. 'They've learned from that and they know if we make mistakes we will get punished by a team like Barcelona. Now we are relishing this challenge.'

In a mouth-watering epilogue to his pre-match press conference, the boss set the scene for a night to remember. 'We'll have a right go at them,' he promised. 'We've got to make sure we give their defence a thorough examination. They haven't been doing well defensively, while we have been scoring a lot of goals in Europe. It's a hell of a match and all the players are ready.'

Few were prepared for the spectacle which unfolded into one of the all-time great Champions League thrillers. Tactics counted for little as two teams married to the notion of attack simply duked it out. Forget football, even forget basketball, it was more like air hockey in end-to-end terms. The final score, a 3-3 draw, eliminated the hosts and left United still needing a positive result against Bayern Munich at Old Trafford to progress to the final eight, either as group winners or as one of two best-placed runners-up, but although work remained to be done, the encounter still invokes positive memories among those involved.

'Both games against Barcelona were absolutely brilliant,' grins Gary Neville. 'I remember coming off in the Nou Camp at full time and thinking it was one of the best games I had ever played. I gave two goals away, but I thought I was brilliant! Sonny Anderson did me for the first goal and then Rivaldo pulled one down with his chest over Jaap's head and overhead-kicked it into the net when I was running in. After the game in the dressing room, at three-three, I couldn't believe how end-to-end it had been.'

That United had gone toe-to-toe with such a dangerous attacking force as Louis van Gaal's Barcelona – and held their own – owed much to a forward pairing of Yorke and Cole which was at its deadliest. The former bagged a brace, but it was the latter's solitary strike which became the partnership's signature goal.

'It was natural; we just played what we saw,' smiles Cole. 'Roy got the ball in midfield, turned and fizzed it in to Yorkie . . . Yorkie went over it and then he pulled off at an angle, I gave it him back with one touch and made a run, opened myself up on the angle where the centre-half was trying to push in, he gave it to me back with one touch and I took two touches to finish it. That is just what it was. When you play one-touch football at pace, like we did, you can't get near it anyway. Everything was so precise, from Roy's pass onwards.'

'Our attacking play from Yorke and Cole was the best I've ever seen,' concurs Neville. 'Sometimes in a match, you don't recognise how well some people are playing. It sounds odd to say, but you are just playing the game so that's what you're concentrating on. But we were watching them from the back and we were thinking: "They are unbelievable." They were unstoppable that night and it was a brilliant match.'

In keeping with a theme which would underscore United's season, there would be no let-up after such a sapping, starry encounter. In just four days, United went from the free-spirited magnificence of Barcelona in Camp Nou to the nitty-gritty of Leeds at Old Trafford; akin to an expressive dance show followed by a round of bare-knuckle boxing.

For all David O'Leary's pre-match insistence that he was endeavouring to emulate his United counterpart – saying: 'That's what I want to do: build a team for the future in the Alex Ferguson way' – the first whistle at Old Trafford dissolved any admiration or imitation in favour of two sides ready for a scrap. It was hardly a surprise with Roy Keane and Alfie Inge Haaland appearing on the same pitch for the first time since the 1997 spat which had culminated in the latter berating the former, as Keane nursed ruptured cruciate knee ligaments. Keane hadn't forgotten the Norwegian's taunts but, on this occasion, the enmity merely simmered throughout.

United trailed to Jimmy Floyd Hasselbaink's cracker, led after goals either side of half time from Solskjaer and Keane, were pegged back by Harry Kewell's neat strike and then finally nabbed the points with a sharply taken late winner from Nicky Butt which capped a man-of-the-match display from the Gorton midfielder.

But while Butt and his colleagues could celebrate their position of power in two domestic competitions and the Champions League as November drew to a close, one of their closest members of staff was drifting away from Old Trafford. Blackburn Rovers had approached Martin Edwards to request a meeting with Brian Kidd about the Ewood Park vacancy, and the Reds' long-serving number two felt compelled to hear Jack Walker's offer. For several parties, a season-defining twist lay in wait.

Wednesday 4 November 1998 | UEFA Champions League Group D | Old Trafford | Attendance: 53,250

MANCHESTER UNITED 5 Beckham 7, Cole 13, P.Neville 15, Yorke 27, Scholes 63
BRONDBY IF 0

Ryan Giggs prods home the opening goal of United's season, teeing up progress to the Champions League proper at the expense of Poland's LKS Lodz.

After a summer of torment, David Beckham airs his delight after a late, late free-kick to salvage a Premier League point against Leicester City.

The smile says it all. Procured from Aston Villa for a then-club record fee after a summer-long wrangle, Dwight Yorke is paraded to the nation's press.

Yorke immediately takes to life at Old Trafford, producing a stunning overhead kick in the build-up to Paul Scholes's goal against Barcelona in a 3-3 thriller.

Scholes scores again, this time at Bayern Munich, but once again the Reds are unable to finish the job and are held to a 2-2 draw.

A partnership is born. Andy Cole and Dwight Yorke both score as Southampton are comfortably brushed aside at The Dell.

Ole Gunnar Solskjaer thunders home goal number six as United romp to a first win in Group D, running amok against poor Brondby at Parken stadium.

Peter Schmeichel offers advice to his defenders against Blackburn, in his first appearance since announcing his intention to leave United at the end of the season.

A trademark forward surge from the world's most expensive defender, Jaap Stam, cannot prevent the Reds' shock 3-1 defeat to Sheffield Wednesday.

Paul Scholes chances his arm in another six-goal thriller with Barcelona, a result which eliminates the Catalans and leaves United on the brink of the Champions League knockouts.

Having capped a man of the match display with a superb winner, Nicky Butt wheels away in delight during a 3-2 thriller with Leeds United at the Old Trafford.

All smiles as Paul Scholes celebrates putting the Reds ahead at Aston Villa, only for the league leaders to bounce back and secure a 1-1 draw.

King for a day. Jim Ryan leads the warm-up ahead of his unexpected debut as caretaker manager. In Alex Ferguson's absence, the Reds suffer their final defeat of the season, against Middlesbrough.

Ryan Giggs takes the initiative as United close out 1998 with a hard-fought goalless draw against title-chasing Chelsea at Stamford Bridge.

New year, new start. Giggs is congratulated by Phil Neville after sealing a comeback win over Middlesbrough in the FA Cup third round.

Dwight Yorke thunders an effort on goal as the Reds overcome a pre-match power failure to register a comfortable 4-1 win over West Ham United.

Lighting the fuse. Ole Gunnar Solskjaer sparks pandemonium at Old Trafford with an injury-time winner to dump rivals Liverpool out of the FA Cup.

Solskjaer celebrates one of four goals in eleven minutes as United register a Premier League record 8-1 away win at Forest.

Roy Keane battles with Coventry City's George Boateng during an attritional trip to Coventry, decided by Ryan Giggs's late winner.

Dwight Yorke leaps to head home the first of two invaluable goals against Internazionale in the Champions League quarter-final, first leg.

Chelsea are dumped out of
the FA Cup in a quarter-final
replay, with brace-scorer
Yorke leading the celebrations
in tribute to new arrival
Brooklyn Beckham.

Semi-finals, here we come. A
nerve-shredding night in the San
Siro has a happy ending as Paul
Scholes's late strike seals a 3-1
aggregate win over Inter.

Gary Neville is congratulated after
a rare appearance on the scoresheet
in a routine 3-1 win over Everton.

The greatest. One of English football's very best games is settled by one of its greatest goals: Ryan Giggs's solo winner to overcome Arsenal in the FA Cup semi-final replay.

Giggs's goal is the cue for an overspill of joy as travelling Reds mob their heroes on the Villa Park pitch; a mini-invasion repeated more emphatically at full time.

'They are several levels above us,' Brondby coach Ebbe Skovdahl gravely told his post-match press conference. For shock factor, the declaration was found wanting. A nine-goal difference over 180 minutes had provided a detailed spoiler. Following on from the Reds' 6-2 stroll in Copenhagen a fortnight earlier, another Danish pasting was dished out as a rejigged United side put five past Brondby without reply. After the Reds' 6-0 pre-season triumph at Parken, they were only a goal shy of a tennis scoreline over the three games.

David Beckham, Andy Cole, Phil Neville, Dwight Yorke and Paul Scholes all struck in a victory that was assured by a breakneck start at Old Trafford. 'I don't think the players will be complacent,' Alex Ferguson had warned his pre-match press conference, and his players bore out that message with a devastating first-half display.

Just over five minutes had passed when Kenneth Rasmussen fouled Cole, 30 yards out and wide left of the area. Though the position was far from inviting, Beckham chanced his arm and whipped in a fine free-kick which undulated rapidly enough to clear the wall, yet bounce on the line as it sped into the back of Emeka Andersen's net. After Per Nielsen had headed against his own post, Cole scored the goal of the evening. Following a mesmerising run from Jesper Blomqvist down the left flank, the striker dummied the Swede's ball infield, took Yorke's return pass in his stride and clipped a sumptuous finish over the onrushing Andersen.

A minute later, Cole was involved again, this time playing a supporting role in a one-two with Phil Neville which culminated in the swashbuckling full-back ramming home his first Old Trafford goal for the Reds. While Neville's celebrations aped close friend Blomqvist, United were soon again indebted to the Swede, who revelled in the absence of the injured Ryan Giggs. This time Blomqvist surged forward from inside his own penalty area, beating three opponents on a 60-yard run which culminated in the ball being switched to

Beckham. His delivery for Yorke was exemplary, while Andersen's attempts to keep out the striker's header were not.

'The first-half performance was one of the best I've seen at United,' Ferguson said afterwards. 'The speed of the passing was superb, as was the imagination of the play. Some of the goals were stunning.'

Another would follow on the hour mark, as Scholes struck after a rare solo run, bursting into the right side of the penalty area, slaloming between two challenges and slipping a left-footed finish inside Andersen's near post to bag the game's final goal.

While Brondby's shock opening-night win over Bayern had enabled United to build an advantage in Group D, the Danes had stuck to their fancied role of whipping boys as the Reds ran riot. 'Frankly, I hope they win the trophy now,' sighed Skovdahl, 'because it will put our two results against them in perspective and make these defeats easier to cope with.'

Manchester United: Schmeichel; P.Neville (Brown 31), G.Neville, Stam, Irwin; Beckham, Keane, Scholes, Blomqvist (Cruyff h-t); Cole (Solskjaer 53), Yorke
Subs not used: van der Gouw, Butt, Johnsen, Curtis

Brondby IF: Andersen; Colding, Rasmussen, Nielsen, Skarbalius; Daugaard, Ravn, J.Jensen, Bagger (Thygesen 67); Bjur (S.Krogh 72), Sand (Hansen 74)
Subs not used: Drejs, Bjerregaard, Vragel, M.Jensen

Man of the Match: Jesper Blomqvist
Though involved for only 45 minutes, the Swede tore Brondby apart, laying on two goals with thrilling individual surges and generally revelling in the absence of Ryan Giggs.

Sunday 8 November 1998 | Premier League | Old Trafford |
Attendance: 55,174

MANCHESTER UNITED 0
NEWCASTLE UNITED 0

Funny business, football. After his sacking by Chelsea in February 1998, Ruud Gullit returned to the Netherlands to gain further coaching qualifications and, while studying, the Dutchman received an unexpected offer. 'Alex [Ferguson] invited me a couple of times to go to Old Trafford and watch his training sessions,' revealed Gullit. 'It was a very nice gesture. I was tempted to go, but I had a course to do in Holland for my coaching badge and there wasn't enough time for me to go to Manchester.'

Gullit didn't have to wait long. Less than six months passed before he was installed as manager at St James' Park, and he was still guiding the Tynesiders through choppy waters when the Magpies' trip to Old Trafford beckoned. Treating the encounter as a blank canvas, Gullit seemingly used a tombola to select his side, throwing in debutants Andy Griffin and George Georgiadis, as well as 19-year-old birthday boy Aaron Hughes.

Gullit's approach played on the hope that United's cakewalk against Brondby had proven taxing on some hidden level. With a record of just 11 wins from the previous 23 Premier League games immediately following Champions League action, the Reds were, seemingly, prone to sluggishness after continental exertions, and so it proved again.

There were flashes in which United slipped into character, most notably in the opening exchanges when backheeled flicks from both Andy Cole and Dwight Yorke teed up Paul Scholes to drive wide of Shay Given's goal, but for the most part United were a shadow of the side which had plundered 26 goals in its previous seven games.

A disjointed opening half was perfectly captured when Peter Schmeichel's shanked clearance thudded against the back of Roy Keane's head, to the skipper's inevitable and animated ire.

The visitors even appealed long and loud for a penalty when Paul Dalglish was bundled over by Denis Irwin, but referee Steve Dunn saw nothing more than a juddering yet fair shoulder charge. An errant backpass from Wes Brown early in the second half provided the Magpies with their one glaring chance of the afternoon, only for Schmeichel to hurtle from his line and block Dalglish's shot. 'I don't know how he makes some of his saves; he seems to have elastic legs,' the striker later lamented.

Clear openings were at a similar premium for United, but the hosts' golden chance was passed up by David Beckham midway through the second period. Released by Gary Neville's incisive pass, the winger drew Given from his line but dragged a left-footed finish past the far post.

A frustrating afternoon was compounded when substitute Ronny Johnsen's return from ankle injury was curtailed by Alan Shearer's robust challenge within 25 minutes of coming on, and Alex Ferguson was left with much to contemplate after watching his side fail to score at Old Trafford for the first – and last – time in 1998-99. 'I don't think the pitch helped as I thought it was really poor,' he stressed. 'But Newcastle's tactics were terrific. Ruud Gullit made a brave selection. I hadn't heard of a couple of their players when I was told their side, but they deserved their point.'

Manchester United: Schmeichel; G.Neville, Brown (Johnsen 58 (Butt 83)), Stam, Irwin; Beckham, Keane, Scholes, Blomqvist (Solskjaer 88); Cole, Yorke
Subs not used: van der Gouw, Cruyff
Booked: Stam, Beckham, Blomqvist

Newcastle United: Given; Hughes, Charvet, Dabizas, Griffin; Georgiadis, Hamann (Speed 66), Batty, Glass; Shearer, Dalglish
Subs not used: Harper, Barton, Pearce, Solano
Booked: Shearer, Dabizas, Charvet

Man of the Match: Gary Neville
A rock-solid defensive display alongside Stam in the heart of defence, and Neville would have had a superb assist had Beckham not spurned United's clearest chance.

Wednesday 11 November 1998 | Worthington Cup 4th round | Old Trafford | Attendance: 37,237

MANCHESTER UNITED 2 Solskjaer 57, 60
NOTTINGHAM FOREST 1 Stone 68

The deterioration of the Old Trafford pitch during United's goalless draw with Newcastle had prompted a hastily arranged meeting between Alex Ferguson, head groundsman Keith Kent and turf consultant John Souter ahead of Nottingham Forest's Worthington Cup visit.

'They are perplexed; they couldn't believe it,' revealed Ferguson. 'We think we know the reason, but until they have had a full investigation we won't be certain. It's fingers crossed that's for sure.' The turf was relaid in patches, rendering a green and brown patchwork effect, which also symbolised the manager's team selection: a mishmash of youngsters and senior players in need of minutes.

That news was of little consolation to Forest manager Dave Bassett, however. 'United have already proved this season that they are the strongest in the Premiership and are getting even stronger,' he said. 'They have seven players in their reserves who would get into most Premiership teams – I would love to be in that situation.'

Despite the strength on show in both sides' ranks, they served up a dreadful first period bereft of any meaningful action. David May's calf injury prompted the introduction of Ronnie Wallwork at half time, providing almost the only talking point of the game to that point.

After the break, however, two moments of shared vision and incision from Jordi Cruyff and Ole Gunnar Solskjaer decided the tie. On 57 and 60 minutes, the Dutchman released the Norwegian with sublimely weighted passes to bear down on goalkeeper Dave Beasant, and the outcome was never in doubt.

'The Worthington Cup may be no more than an exercise yard for Manchester United's second string, but Ole Gunnar Solskjaer is grateful for any opportunity to demonstrate his finishing skills,' noted the *Independent*'s Derick Allsop.

Despite the Norwegian's goals, and the eye-catching bluster and industry of Jonathan Greening, Mark Wilson and Phil Mulryne, it was Cruyff who stole the show with his role as Solskjaer's attacking benefactor. 'Jordi was absolutely superb, and his imagination and vision of his passing is tremendous,' enthused Ferguson.

After Steve Stone's thunderous effort had reduced the arrears, Solskjaer might twice have clinched a hat-trick, lobbing wide of an open goal from long range and then having his effort impressively tipped onto the woodwork by Beasant, but instead the hodgepodge Reds were content to settle for a narrow margin of victory and a quarter-final trip to Tottenham.

With the majority of the established contenders already ousted from the competition – including under-strength Arsenal's 5-0 home exit at the hands of Chelsea – the White Hart Lane meeting would pit the bookies' favourites against one another. Spurs were priced at 5-1, United at 6-1, even though Ferguson insisted that he would again blood youth in the last eight. 'They will play against Tottenham,' said the manager of his youngsters. 'We have said what our policy is and we want to do well. We will pick a team which we think will win, but also using my pool to its utmost advantage.'

Manchester United: van der Gouw; Clegg, Berg, May (Wallwork 46), Curtis; Greening, Wilson, Butt, Mulryne; Solskjaer, Cruyff
Subs not used: Notman, Nevland, Teather, Ford
Booked: Curtis, Mulryne

Nottingham Forest: Beasant; Louis-Jean, Chettle, Armstrong, Rogers; Stone, Bart-Williams, Gemmill, Gray; Freedman, Harewood (van Hooijdonk 63)
Subs not used: Quashie, Crossley, Darcheville, Lyttle
Booked: Rogers

Man of the Match: Jordi Cruyff
'Our groundstaff worked round the clock, and so did Jordi,' marvelled Alex Ferguson, who watched on in delight as his playmaker embossed a typically poised display with two superb assists.

Saturday 14 November 1998 | Premiership | Old Trafford | Attendance: 55,198

MANCHESTER UNITED 3 Scholes 32, 58, Yorke 44
BLACKBURN ROVERS 2 Marcolin 65, Blake 74

What had, for an hour, all the makings of a convincing victory over struggling Rovers descended into a worrying study in sloppiness and complacency as the ten-man visitors almost recovered from three goals down at a jittery Old Trafford. The Reds were already two goals clear when Tim Sherwood was dismissed for lashing out at David

Beckham. Having furthered their lead, United switched off and were left clinging on to the victory as Roy Hodgson's side commendably struck twice.

Fittingly, the tone for a baffling afternoon was set by preceding confusion over the involvement of both sides' members of the Republic of Ireland squad, with a vital European Championship qualifier against Yugoslavia looming four days later. Alex Ferguson and Hodgson had agreed to rest a pair of players apiece – Roy Keane and Denis Irwin, Damien Duff and Jeff Kenna respectively – only for FIFA to rule that the Republic could not invoke a ruling to prevent all four players partaking.

Nevertheless, there was some solace for Republic manager Mick McCarthy when Ferguson stuck to a gentleman's agreement and left Keane and Irwin on the United bench. The ramifications for the Reds were most evident in defence, with highly rated rookie John Curtis making just his fourth league start.

Behind the greenhorn, Peter Schmeichel strode out for his first appearance since announcing his impending departure from the club, and the Dane received a rapturous reception from the thronging home support. Blackburn's tribute was to abstain from involving Schmeichel for much of the opening hour.

Shorn of injured first-choice goalkeeper Tim Flowers, Rovers looked shot of confidence from the off, and it was no surprise when Dwight Yorke dispossessed Christian Dailly and fed Paul Scholes to slide a left-footed finish across John Filan. Yorke's display oozed confidence and class throughout, and when Nicky Butt clipped Beckham's pass into the striker's path, his emphatic finish was a foregone conclusion. So too, apparently, was the game's outcome when Sherwood needlessly swung an arm at Beckham shortly after the interval. The amount of contact made was questionable – Hodgson later remarked: 'The lad played on for the rest of the game; the last time someone elbowed me in the face, my nose was broken' – but the intent was not, and Sherwood could have few arguments.

Ten minutes later, Scholes and Yorke combined again, with the former buying time while the latter skipped out of the way to goal, and Scholes duly drilled an angled finish across Filan to seemingly put the game to bed. United took that as their cue to ease up, but Rovers dragged themselves back into contention when substitute Dario Marcolin drilled home Darren Peacock's knockdown, and then Nathan Blake powered in a header.

Though 15 minutes remained, United were able to arrest the shift in momentum, despite the loss of Scholes, Ole Gunnar Solskjaer and Jordi Cruyff to injuries all later attributed to the patchwork pitch. Nevertheless, Ferguson could only bemoan what he termed 'a careless performance', after an alarming final half-hour.

Manchester United: Schmeichel; P.Neville, Stam, G.Neville, Curtis; Beckham, Scholes (Cruyff 61 (Keane 80)), Butt, Blomqvist (Solskjaer 66); Yorke, Cole
Subs not used: Irwin, Berg
Booked: Stam, Scholes

Blackburn Rovers: Filan; Kenna, Peacock, Henchoz, Davidson (Croft 55); Johnson, Sherwood, Dailly, Duff (Marcolin 51); Blake, Davies (Gallagher 77)
Subs not used: Fettis, Dunn
Booked: Davies, Henchoz, Johnson
Sent off: Sherwood

Man of the Match: Dwight Yorke
Another eye-catching shift from the new boy, scoring one, creating two and waving the Reds' attacking baton all afternoon.

Saturday 21 November 1998 | Premiership | Hillsborough |
Attendance: 39,475

SHEFFIELD WEDNESDAY 3 Alexandersson 14, 73, Jonk 55
MANCHESTER UNITED 1 Cole 29

United stuttered to only their second defeat of the season proper, but
a miserable afternoon in Yorkshire heralded the start of a run of only
one win in nine games. From the off, so error-strewn was United's
performance that it was inevitable that Danny Wilson's Owls would
be given the chance to spring an upset. Sure enough, Peter
Schmeichel encapsulated the afternoon by fumbling Niclas
Alexandersson's routine shot over his own line after just 14 minutes;
a new nadir in his struggling form and ideal ammunition for a press
pack struggling to hide itchy trigger fingers.

'If Schmeichel had not already told United that they will need a
new goalkeeper, they might have come to that conclusion unaided,'
speculated the *Independent*'s Dave Hadfield. 'He will certainly have
conceded few worse goals in his long, distinguished career.'

United responded positively, however, with enough cohesion in
attack to constantly trouble the home defence. Pavel Srnicek was well
protected throughout, but the Czech was left exposed when Andy
Cole and Dwight Yorke combined in simple yet incisive fashion to
leave the England striker with a simple finish.

The sudden upsurge in United's play looked certain to overrun the
hosts, especially with Wednesday on the ropes for the remainder of the
half. Cole, Jesper Blomqvist and Denis Irwin came close, while Paul
Scholes was booked for palming the ball past Srnicek, but the interval
acted as a leveller. After returning to the field, the Reds were possessed
by the same lax play that had proved so detrimental in the early stages,
and Wednesday again moved ahead in sloppy circumstances.

A pedestrian move from the hosts carved apart a sluggish United defence and, though Schmeichel saved Andy Booth's close-range effort from an Alexandersson cross, nobody reacted quicker to the loose ball than Wim Jonk, who tapped home a simple rebound. Having operated at such sub-standards for much of the afternoon, and with Wednesday galvanised by retaking the lead, United rarely looked like recovering for a second time, and defeat was assured when David Beckham and Jaap Stam contrived to lose possession inside their own area, giving Alexandersson the opportunity to round Schmeichel and slide in the clincher.

With a trip to Barcelona looming large, Alex Ferguson saw fit to question whether or not his side already had one eye on the Camp Nou, at the cost of focus on matters closer to home. 'There were mistakes all over the pitch today,' lamented the United manager. 'You can't put it down to one individual. You wonder whether you're turning into a big-match team. They let themselves down today, but you know that, come Wednesday, they will probably excel.'

Sheffield Wednesday: Srnicek; Atherton, Walker, Emerson, Hinchcliffe; Alexandersson, Jonk, Rudi, Sonner; Carbone, Booth
Subs not used: Clarke, Stefanovic, Humphreys, Magilton, Sanetti
Booked: Jonk

Manchester United: Schmeichel; P.Neville, G.Neville, Stam, Irwin (Brown 66); Beckham, Keane (Solskjaer 83), Scholes, Blomqvist (Butt 58); Cole, Yorke
Subs not used: van der Gouw, Berg
Booked: Scholes

Man of the Match: Andy Cole
Amid a spate of off-colour displays from those in red, Cole again put forward his case for an England recall with a sharp, pacey display headlined by a neatly taken finish.

**Wednesday 25 November 1998 | Champions League Group D |
Camp Nou | Attendance: 67,650**

FC BARCELONA 3 Anderson 1, Rivaldo 57, 73
MANCHESTER UNITED 3 Yorke 25, 68, Cole 53

Rarely do sequels outstrip the original. But, though September's slugfest between United and Barcelona had oscillated with dizzying verve and pace, the rematch at Camp Nou was an even more consuming spectacle.

Successive defeats to Bayern Munich rendered the game a must-win for the Catalans, while United's looming group finale against the Germans meant that, whatever happened in Spain, a last-day win at Old Trafford would secure qualification. Nevertheless, Alex Ferguson had his sights set on victory over Louis van Gaal's injury-hit side, who didn't even have enough fit personnel to fill their substitutes' bench.

'We don't have that Italian type of mentality,' said the United manager, of the notion that United would try only to stifle the spectre of defeat. 'We know we will be virtually guaranteed to go through by winning, and we plan to have a right go at them. We've got to give their defence a thorough examination. I'm not saying I expect a hatful in Barcelona, I'll be happy with just a couple.'

The early signs suggested that United's attackers would need to be on their game. Under a minute had elapsed when Sonny Anderson pounced on shoddy defending to fire Barcelona ahead, and the hosts completely dominated the early stages, with Rivaldo quickly coming to the fore, where he would remain all evening.

It took heroic efforts from Peter Schmeichel to fend away a stinging shot from the Brazilian, while the Dane also heroically flung himself to flick the loose ball away from Anderson after Luis Figo's rasping effort had been parried back into the danger zone. But, as

United swayed against the ropes, they suddenly sprung forth and landed a heavy sucker punch with their first swing of the evening.

Jesper Blomqvist, shining in place of the injured Ryan Giggs once again, motored down the left flank and astutely switched play infield for Dwight Yorke, who had dropped into space. Finding that gap still unoccupied, the striker made a beeline for Ruud Hesp's goal and drilled a low effort inside the Dutchman's post to haul United back on terms.

The remainder of the first period bore the closest resemblance to caution that the game would see, with both sides stepping back to assess the situation. Half time brought a shared realisation that neither had much to lose from going for the win, prompting a breathtaking second period illuminated by four fabulous goals.

The first of them would become the signature goal of the Cole–Yorke partnership. Cole dummied Roy Keane's infield ball, allowing it to run to Yorke, whose first-time return pass flummoxed Samuel Okunowo to the border of collapse and gave Cole the simple task of tucking away a finish.

Cue Rivaldo, who quickly curled a free-kick inside Schmeichel's right-hand post when the Dane had moved the other way. United had led for just four minutes, but were far from disheartened, especially with David Beckham growing in influence after a low-key first half. With 22 minutes left, the England winger curled an unstoppable cross to Hesp's near post, where Yorke dived and twisted to direct his header into the net.

Yet again it would not be enough. Five minutes on, Rivaldo somehow found time and space between Jaap Stam and Gary Neville to control Sergi's cross on his chest and thread an overhead kick inside Schmeichel's post. And this time United were rocked. Rivaldo thundered a 30-yard shot against the bar, then released Giovanni to bring a brilliant one-on-one save from Schmeichel.

Only a last-gasp save from Hesp denied Cole a winner, but a

share of the spoils was only fair reward for two sides who had thrown everything into a 90-minute showcase of attacking expression. The *Daily Record*'s David McCarthy could only marvel: 'Every now and again a game of football grabs you by the throat and grips you so tight you can hardly breathe. This was one.'

Though tinged by a whiff of disappointment to have twice sur-rendered a lead, Alex Ferguson could only concur: 'When you score three goals at Nou Camp, you've got to be happy. Matches like this stretch the nerve ends to the limit.' Past breaking point, in fact, for Barça. The Catalans were out, leaving United and Bayern to duke it out for top spot in Group D.

FC Barcelona: Hesp; Celades, Okunowo, Reiziger, Sergi; Giovanni, Xavi, Rivaldo; Figo, Anderson, Zenden
Subs not used: Arnau, Cuadrado, Roger, Ciric, Mario

Manchester United: Schmeichel; Brown, Stam, G.Neville, Irwin; Beckham (Butt 82), Keane, Scholes, Blomqvist; Cole, Yorke
Subs not used: van der Gouw, P.Neville, Solskjaer, Berg, Curtis, Wilson
Booked: Irwin, Blomqvist, Keane, Scholes

Man of the Match: Dwight Yorke
A livewire display from the striker, whose superb brace was outshone by his combined work with Andy Cole for the Reds' mesmerising second goal.

Sunday 29 November 1998 | Premiership | Old Trafford |
Attendance: 55,172

MANCHESTER UNITED 3 Solskjaer 45, Keane 46, Butt 77
LEEDS UNITED 2 Hasselbaink 29, Kewell 52

A cross-Pennines derby with Leeds appeared a million miles from the glitz and glamour of fronting up Barcelona in Camp Nou, yet both sides served up a spectacle to warm the chilliest northern cockles on a wintry Sunday afternoon at Old Trafford.

While both teams limped into the afternoon beset by injuries, neither manager saw fit to do anything other than pursue victory from the off. David O'Leary, in his first visit to Old Trafford as a manager, had already won at Anfield with his exciting young team, and unabashedly admitted: 'They go to the Nou Camp and give as good as they get against Barcelona. Fantastic. Anyone would applaud that.'

The Reds' exertions in Catalonia meant an enforced rest for David Beckham, Jesper Blomqvist and Denis Irwin, while the afternoon came too soon for Ronny Johnsen and Teddy Sheringham to recover from their own longstanding injuries, and Ryan Giggs was only fit enough for the bench.

Leeds, for their part, went into the game without Lucas Radebe and Lee Bowyer, and they were soon rocked when both Martin Hiden and Nigel Martyn suffered injuries in the opening half-hour. The latter swigged down painkillers after crashing, back-first, into the post in brilliantly tipping Nicky Butt's header over the bar. The Leeds goalkeeper was given the perfect pick-me-up when Jimmy Floyd Hasselbaink thundered a low shot in off the inside of Peter Schmeichel's post just before the half-hour, sending the travelling supporters wild. Chided pre-match by their manager for 'unacceptable' domestic lapses in the early part of the season, United's response was positive.

Though Harry Kewell spurned a presentable chance to double the Whites' lead, it required a string of fine saves from Martyn to preserve the visitors' lead, with Ole Gunnar Solskjaer and Andy Cole denied, before the Norwegian striker took a Dwight Yorke pass on the stroke of half time and arrowed a low finish into the far corner of Martyn's net.

Leeds made an unavoidable interval change, with Martyn making way for Paul Robinson, and the 19-year-old was beaten within 20 seconds as Paul Scholes circumnavigated Ian Harte and pulled a ball across the box for the onrushing Roy Keane to steer home. It was a moment of huge satisfaction for the United skipper, in his first appearance against Leeds – and Alf Inge Haaland – since rupturing cruciate knee ligaments in a tangle with the Norwegian at Elland Road 14 months earlier.

Yet Leeds struck back almost immediately, as Wes Brown missed David Hopkin's header and Kewell strode through on goal before lifting a calm finish over Schmeichel. The game continued to swing from end to end before the outstanding Butt had the decisive say, cushioning Phil Neville's pass into his own path and stabbing a wonderful finish high into Robinson's goal to move United within a point of league leaders Aston Villa.

Manchester United: Schmeichel; Brown, Stam (Berg 76), G.Neville, P.Neville; Scholes (Sheringham 71), Keane, Butt; Yorke, Cole (Giggs 64), Solskjaer
Subs not used: van der Gouw, Curtis
Booked: P.Neville

Leeds United: Martyn (Robinson h-t); Halle, Hiden (Wetherall 25), Woodgate, Harte; Haaland, Hopkin, McPhail, Ribeiro (Smith 84); Hasselbaink, Kewell
Subs not used: Wijnhard, Granville
Booked: Ribeiro, Haaland

Man of the Match: Nicky Butt
The Gorton midfielder's season sprang into life with a superb all-round display, embossed by a huge role in Keane's goal before his own clinically taken winner.

November in statistics

Premiership table (29 November 1998)

	P	W	D	L	F	A	GD	Pts
Aston Villa	14	8	5	1	22	12	+10	29
Manchester United	**14**	**8**	**4**	**2**	**30**	**16**	**+14**	**28**
West Ham United	15	7	5	3	20	16	+4	26
Arsenal	15	6	7	2	15	7	+8	25
Chelsea	13	6	6	1	22	13	+9	24
Leeds United	15	5	8	2	22	14	+8	23
Middlesbrough	15	5	8	2	24	17	+7	23
Liverpool	15	6	4	5	26	19	+7	22
Derby County	15	5	6	4	15	14	+1	21
Wimbledon	15	5	5	5	19	25	-6	20
Newcastle United	15	5	4	6	19	19	0	19
Tottenham Hotspur	15	5	4	6	19	23	-4	19
Leicester City	15	4	6	5	16	18	-2	18
Everton	15	4	6	5	10	15	-5	18
Charlton Athletic	15	3	7	5	22	23	-1	16
Sheffield Wednesday	15	4	4	7	14	15	-1	16
Coventry City	15	4	3	8	13	21	-8	15
Nottingham Forest	15	2	5	8	12	24	-12	11
Southampton	15	2	4	9	12	31	-19	10
Blackburn Rovers	15	2	3	10	14	24	-10	9

THE IMPOSSIBLE TREBLE

Champions League, Group D table (25 November 1998)

	P	W	D	L	F	A	GD	Pts
Bayern Munich	5	3	1	1	8	5	+3	10
Manchester United	5	2	3	0	19	10	+9	9
Barcelona	5	1	2	2	9	9	0	5
Brondby	5	1	0	4	4	15	-1	3

November form (all competitions): WDWWLDW

Goals scored: 17   **Goals conceded:** 11

Most appearances: Andy Cole, Gary Neville, Jaap Stam, Peter Schmeichel, Paul Scholes, Dwight Yorke 6 each

Players used: 26

Most goals: Dwight Yorke 4

Most assists: Dwight Yorke 7

Different goalscorers: 8

Quickest goal: David Beckham, 7 mins [v Brondby (h)]

Latest goal: Nicky Butt, 77 mins [v Leeds United (h)]

Watched by: 363,156

Average attendance: 51,879

Chapter 5

December – Real Gone Kidd

Time and again during his seven years at Manchester United, media conjecture had hustled Brian Kidd towards the Old Trafford exit, with the country's leading assistant manager universally acknowledged as a number one in-waiting. The overtures of Everton and Manchester City had been rejected in the previous 18 months, but it was the interest of Blackburn Rovers which finally proved too alluring to resist.

On the night that United and Blackburn both exited the Worthington Cup quarter-finals, to Tottenham Hotspur and Leicester City respectively, Rovers' bid to take Kidd to Ewood Park was initially rejected by Reds chairman Martin Edwards, only for Alex Ferguson's assistant to ultimately agree to discuss the move.

While conflicting claims were never cleared up – Edwards insisted that Kidd was offered a new, extended contract, which Kidd denied – it was clear that, after seven years as a number two, taking on a managerial hot-seat had become irresistible. Kidd missed

United's trip to White Hart Lane, giving the United players their first hint that major changes were afoot. Looking back, the squad remains split on whether or not the warning signs had been there.

'Yes, we did see it coming, because I think you always had the sense that he wanted something more than being the first team coach,' says Ole Gunnar Solskjaer. 'He wanted to decide himself. He thought he had a manager in him.' Andy Cole, conversely, insists: 'Did we see it coming? No, did we hell. I couldn't believe it. This was Kiddo, not some run-of-the-mill coach, so we couldn't believe the club would let him go. We were talking about Brian Kidd, a fantastic coach. We used to call him Capello because he always used to go over to AC Milan when Fabio Capello was there, so we used to call him Kiddo Capello. So when he left, a lot of us were devastated. How do you replace Kiddo?'

Understandably, the news was most keenly felt among the squad's home-grown members. 'At the time it was a big loss for the players because he was a friend of ours,' says Gary Neville. 'He had brought some of us up from the age of twelve or thirteen. He was like a father figure in some ways to a lot of us, particularly the ones who had been there all the way through. He had known us from the youth team to the first team. He had been through everything with us. He believed in us massively – obviously the manager did as well – but he promoted the young local lads more than anybody, as well as Nobby [Stiles]. They were huge for us.'

'I thought it was the end of my world,' continues Phil Neville, 'because you thought nobody would ever come in who was as good as Kiddo. Kiddo was the best number two and he'd had us since we were ten years old. He was almost like family. He'd pick you up if you were out of the team and he'd keep you on your toes and make sure you didn't get carried away if you were in the side. He was the essence of the ethic about Manchester United, particularly with the young players. We'd put so much trust in him and he put so much faith in us; there was an unbelievable bond there and even now when I see him, he is still the same Kiddo. He's a football man and he still speaks about our time in the youth team, A-team, B-team, reserve team. You just couldn't imagine someone else coming in to be number two.'

In the interim, Alex Ferguson enlisted reserve team coach Jim Ryan to fill the vacancy, and the first test of their collective mettle would come in a high-stakes trip to Premier League leaders Aston Villa. John Gregory's side had survived and thrived in the wake of Dwight Yorke's high-profile transfer to United, which perhaps aided the Villa manager's mood ahead of the striker's return to the Midlands. Upon learning from Yorke that he wanted to leave Villa, Gregory famously admitted: 'If I'd had a gun at the time, I think I would have shot him.' Almost four months later, the sentiment had softened, slightly.

'My feelings towards Dwight were back to normal after I had got my initial disappointment off my chest,' he claimed. 'It didn't hurt that he wanted to play for Manchester United, it just annoyed me when he said he didn't want to play for my club. But that's water under the bridge now.

'I believe it would be totally out of order for anyone to give Dwight a hard time when he comes back to Villa Park. I hope he gets the warm reception he deserves from our fans. This is the first opportunity to thank him for what he did for Aston Villa over nine good years. Let's give him a standing ovation before the game and after 3pm he can become the enemy in the right manner.'

Yorke, for his part, was happy to accept the enmity, stressing pre-match: 'I'm going there to make sure we get three points which will take us top.' In actuality, the Trinidadian exerted little influence on a 1-1 draw in which Paul Scholes's opener was quickly cancelled out by a deflected Julian Joachim strike.

'It was probably one of my worst games for United, I think,' laughs the striker. 'Villa were top of the table and doing well and for a moment I wondered if I'd made the right move because they were constantly getting better and getting results, while we were sitting second or third. I was thinking: "F*****g hell, why does it have to happen when I leave?" But I have a great affiliation with the fans and the people who were at the club at the time. Villa is part of my home and it had to be something like United to drag me away.

'When somebody like United comes in for you, you have to make the right move. And although it proved that later on, of course, they didn't see that. But going back to Villa, there were mixed emotions and I was desperate to do well, but maybe the emotion got the better of me. I was crap and it was the worst game I had played for any team. My friends like Ugo [Ehiogu] and [Mark] Bosnich were desperate for me not to score, and I talked to them the night before and told them I was definitely going to score. I got it wrong on the day in terms of my play – there were too many emotions. Even though you've been at the club and you did great for them, when you go back after leaving you get the boos and I thought that was harsh because of what I had done and the number of years I had spent at the club. I can understand it because I was arguably one of their best players, but I hope in the long run that they recognise I made the right move in the end.'

A major motive behind Yorke's move was the prospect of Champions League football and, with five goals in as many Group D games, the striker was ready for a mouth-watering group finale against Bayern Munich. Victory would assure the Reds of qualification as group winners, while a draw would be enough to sidle through in one of two slots allocated to the group runners-up with the highest points total, depending on favourable results elsewhere.

For Alex Ferguson, the tie would pit him against a familiar foe, Ottmar Hitzfeld. The German had ousted United at the semi-final stage two years earlier with Borussia Dortmund, and whereas popular wisdom suggested that the difference between the two sides in 1997 had been the Reds' profligate finishing, ahead of his return to Old Trafford Hitzfeld suggested that obsession had proved United's undoing.

'I felt in that game that United were too nervous, that somehow they were too keen to win the trophy,' he proffered, at his pre-match press conference. 'That was why we won. They were the favourites and everybody expected them to beat us and win the final, so I can understand the real disappointment for Ferguson.

'I know it is something that burns away inside him still. In any game like that, it's a question of the nerve of the players. For whatever reason – maybe because Ferguson wanted it too much and expressed that feeling – his side were too inhibited. That allowed us to impose our game on them in a way which we could not have done if they had been more natural.'

In the opening five group games of 1998-99, United's play had been entirely uninhibited, with caution permanently thrown to the wind. It had yielded only two wins over Brondby, while leads had been squandered against Barcelona twice, plus Bayern in Bavaria, but the Reds' attacking instincts had captured the imagination of many onlookers and peers around European football. Prophetically, Bayern poster boy Stefan Effenberg opined ahead of the game: 'The best thing would be if both of us went through, then we could meet in the final.'

And so it transpired, ending up as a curious 1-1 draw in which the final stages were played at a pedestrian pace when it became clear that both sides were in line to qualify; Bayern as group winners, United as the competition's second-best runners-up behind Real Madrid. Hasan Salihamidžić cancelled out Roy Keane's opener and prompted a jittery air inside Old Trafford, but the news that Lens and Galatasaray were losing midway through the second period was quickly passed from the away dugout to those in the home equivalent, and both United and Bayern recognised that there was little to gain but much to lose from attempting to force the issue at Old Trafford.

'The Munich players were coming up to my team and telling them just to keep the ball in the final few minutes,' revealed Ferguson. 'In fact, I was aware ten minutes before the end that as things stood we were through. It was the Germans who were telling us. They always have very good lines of communication. They never get things like that wrong.'

Though United had squeaked in as the eighth qualifiers for the quarter-finals, skipper Roy Keane was in no doubt about how far his side could go, insisting: 'There's a belief now in the whole camp that we can get through. It's our third season of qualification for the later stages and that's a great achievement for the club. But quarter- and semi-finals are no good. You want to be winning trophies, especially the European Cup. We're now capable of going on to win it.

'We hope we have come through a period of learning. We know we conceded too many goals looking at the group. We know we have to cut that out, but that's probably being over-critical of the team. We really wanted to go for a win against Bayern, but the experience of the last few years has told us that a goal was enough. Now everyone keeps asking us if we are a better squad than the one from two years ago which won the Double. I think honestly yes we are. We do have a stronger squad. Maybe going back to the Double-winning side it was a better eleven. But to do well in Europe and the Premiership you need a better squad, which we have. We have a European mentality now. We're better equipped than previous teams. There are a lot of quality teams left, but hopefully a few of them will want to avoid us. We struggled a few years ago to get to the final stages. Now we're through and any of the eight teams left are capable of winning it. And we're one of them.'

Alongside United and Bayern, the remaining six qualifiers all posed pitfalls. Holders Real Madrid, serial finalists Juventus, tournament favourites Internazionale, plus dark horses Dynamo Kiev, Kaiserslautern and Olympiakos all awaited. 'This last eight is as formidable as it gets,' quivered the *Daily Mail*'s preview piece, before adding: 'The draw is not so much a knockout as a death trap.' Imagine the doom-mongering on Fleet Street, then, when the Reds were paired with Inter, replete with the talents of Ronaldo, Roberto Baggio and Diego Simeone, the latter still a hot topic in English football for his histrionic role in David Beckham's World Cup dismissal.

The Argentine midfielder was quick to align himself with Beckham, who had been subjected to icy receptions at away grounds all over England ever since the events of St Etienne. 'It makes me mad to hear all of these things happening to David,' sniffed Simeone. 'This is the sort of lynch-mob mentality which is not only highly dangerous but totally unfair. I find it incredible. If it would help, I would be prepared to meet him any time anywhere. The past is gone, and the present is here. I am going to Manchester to play my football and I think the fans will be fair with me.

'In reality, David didn't do anything in our last game. I went for the ball, didn't get it and obviously fouled him. I fell on him and when he was getting up he reacted. These are reactions that referees think done with the intention of doing harm. Possibly the kick was not so strong. He gave me a slight blow which made me lose my balance and fall. I thought he would have had a yellow card and that would have been enough.'

While the reunion between Simeone and Beckham would provide an absorbing sub-plot to the tie, United had more consuming short-term goals; firstly picking their way through a tricky festive fixture list. Ten days after exiting the Worthington Cup, the Reds were back at White Hart Lane to face George Graham's Spurs. Once again, David Ginola would be heavily involved, but this time the Frenchman's role in proceedings was drastically different to his match-winning contribution in the cup.

Ole Gunnar Solskjaer's close-range double had the Reds in full control, only for the hosts to ultimately pilfer a point through Sol Campbell's late pair of headers. The game's turning point came with the visitors two goals ahead, as Gary Neville picked up two bookings for fouls on Ginola. Even now, the United defender feels the Frenchman could have avoided giving referee Uriah Rennie the platform to brandish a red card. 'He wasn't a good referee,' recalls Neville. 'That's the first thing to say. For the first booking, I went for a tackle in midfield, slid in and mistimed it and got a yellow card. The second one, Ginola knocked it down the line, skipped over me and went down. He could have kept me on the pitch, but he didn't.'

Neville's suspension wouldn't kick in until the Boxing Day visit of Nottingham Forest, but Alex Ferguson still had concerns over the availability of several others for the intervening home games with Chelsea and Middlesbrough – two of the Premier League's form teams. Solskjaer had left the fray at White Hart Lane with an ankle injury, Dwight Yorke had been hampered by a thigh strain sustained against Bayern Munich and Ryan Giggs was still searching for full fitness after returning from a broken foot. Denis Irwin and Paul Scholes were shaking off the after-effects of flu, while Jaap Stam was playing through the discomfort of a shin injury.

Chelsea sat fourth in the table ahead of their trip north, but had announced their arrival in the title race with an injury-time win over leaders Aston Villa on the same night United had edged into the Champions League knockout stages. Though Arsène Wenger had insisted his Arsenal side 'are not title contenders and have a lot of worries', a four-way fight for the title appeared to be forming, and Ferguson could see new-found steel in a Chelsea side unbeaten since the opening day of the season.

'It's going to be a terrific match against Chelsea,' he predicted. 'They have been in very good form this year and they have got a consistency about them which maybe Chelsea teams have lacked in the past.' Even factoring in the shortcomings of their forebears, the Blues arrived at Old Trafford keen to add to an intimidating record at the home of the Reds, having lost just twice in 23 visits, and they narrowly avoided defeat again as Gianfranco Zola nabbed a late equaliser to cancel out Andy Cole's sharply taken opener.

After five games without a victory, the manager's plans to lead his side back to winning ways were scuppered in tragic circumstances ahead of Middlesbrough's visit. The Ferguson family was rocked by a bereavement and – with the club's full blessing – Alex joined them rather than welcome Bryan Robson's side to Old Trafford. Instead, for one day only, that role went to Jim Ryan.

'I got the call on the morning of the game as I was going out of the door for pre-match,' recalls the Scot. 'The gaffer explained what had happened and that there was no other choice. I had to change some of the things I was doing before the game. I had to change all that in the car on the way over, and you forget about all that and just concentrate on the new plan. But you just go and do the best you can. In the team talk I just said to them: "Look, you know the situation: the manager's not here. I'm here and I'm going to try and do the best I can, cover all the bases and see. I want you to do the same. Be as if he's here and try and play as if he is." Then I went through the team. Of course, we had no tactical talk either. The manager used to do a tactical report, so I just started with the team, then the bench and who we'd use if such and such happened. I'd had a conversation with the manager, but it was only two or three minutes long, so I went through a couple of tactical things, just normal things, not a lot, and tried to use the fact that the manager was away as a motivational thing. Without success!'

United slipped to a shock 3-2 defeat, a result most noteworthy for the sloppy nature of the goals conceded. Gary Neville still cringes on recalling the afternoon: 'Defensively, we were all over the place, it was as if we weren't taking it seriously,' he grimaces. 'I'll always remember that game because it was a turning point, ultimately, but it was embarrassing at the time. Jim Ryan was manager and Eric Harrison was his assistant, and I remember Eric at half time saying: "The midfield need to protect the defenders because by f*** do they need protecting!" It was quite embarrassing at the time, because I was a defender and we were all over the place.'

'I was really disappointed, really distraught in a way,' adds Ryan, 'and that's mainly because I'm a Manchester United supporter, and it was me in charge as a supporter and I'd lost the game for us. Although I never thought of it as me having managed Manchester United for a day, everyone always says to me that I did, which is nice to think of, so I guess I reached the peak of management, albeit briefly. Unfortunately my best wasn't good enough that day!'

The festive fixture list generously presented the Reds with the visit of table-propping Nottingham Forest on Boxing Day, providing an inviting opportunity to register a first victory in almost a month. First, however, would come an event which still invokes misty-eyed grins at its mere mention: the players' Christmas party.

'It was great, that's all I can say,' beams Dwight Yorke. 'It was the most memorable thing of the first six months of the season,' adds Gary Neville, who continues: 'Me and Yorkie organised it. Yorkie organised the guests and I organised the logistics, shall we say. There's no point having guests if you didn't have the right drink, food or security. We had an unbelievable party. I just remember Keano's speech at the end of the night, closing it up. It was an absolutely brilliant day. That Christmas do still gets talked about to this day.'

'I was the architect of certain things, I take full responsibility for certain things and I'm not ashamed of that,' adds Yorke. 'What I can tell you is that everyone involved in the team went, and whoever didn't drink, drank. I was a single guy and the onus was on me to deliver certain people in the club. I was the main culprit; the lads can blame me for having such a great night. In the history of the club nights out, that must rank as one of the best, that's all I can say. People do still shake their heads about it so it was a top night.'

On the field, Yorke remained sidelined by a thigh injury for the visit of Forest, who were brushed off in a one-sided contest made remarkable by a rare brace for central defender Ronny Johnsen. The Norwegian, whose pair of goals was complemented by a superb finish from Ryan Giggs, recalls: 'I was good at coming to chances, but finishing them off? Not so good. That's why I became a defender! I played as a striker until I was twenty-four, even a few games for the Norwegian national team, but I understood my place in the end and became more concerned about not conceding goals. We had so many good finishers in that United team so it wasn't a problem. My job was to keep the balance!'

Three goals, a clean sheet and a routine victory represented the kind of balance United had only occasionally struck in the first half of the season. Having secured only a sixth clean sheet of the Premier League season to date, the Reds' defenders would need to be on their mettle again for the final challenge of 1998: the daunting trip to face Chelsea at Stamford Bridge.

The Blues' impressive performance at Old Trafford was still fresh in the memories of both camps, but Alex Ferguson was in bullish mood when assessing the fixture's curious habit of favouring the away team whenever United and Chelsea met. 'Our record at Chelsea has been brilliant,' he said. 'We have been excellent down there just like they have been up at Old Trafford.'

In the event, United were once again fortunate to avoid defeat, especially when Peter Schmeichel performed a trademark one-on-one save to thwart Gianfranco Zola in the late stages of the game. There was, however, a noticeable solidity in the Reds' performance which had been missing for much of the month; a resolve to fend off genuine title rivals and take anything tangible home to Manchester. A point apiece left Chelsea and United trailing leaders Aston Villa by two and four points respectively, with Arsenal level on points with the Reds but lagging on goal difference. The latter pair of protagonists would remain neck-and-neck for much of the remainder of the season.

Crucially, however, a new mindset had gripped the squad in the wake of defeat to Middlesbrough; a setback which would ultimately prove a watershed as 1999 began. 'It was a big moment,' recalls Peter Schmeichel. 'It was one of those games where in the dressing room afterwards we were all like: "How the hell did we do that? Why the hell did we do that? This is bad, let's make sure we win the rest of the games," and we started just for the fun of it, saying that if we won the rest of the games, we'd have had an unbelievable season. It sort of carried on and carried on from there!'

Wednesday 2 December 1998 | Worthington Cup quarter-final | White Hart Lane | Attendance: 35,702

TOTTENHAM HOTSPUR 3 Armstrong 48, 55, Ginola 86
MANCHESTER UNITED 1 Sheringham 71

United's bid for a clean sweep of major honours came unstuck as George Graham's Tottenham gradually overpowered a rejigged Reds side to book a berth in the Worthington Cup semi-finals. While Spurs viewed the tie as a glaring opportunity to march back towards European football, Alex Ferguson – as promised – used the trip to blood youngsters and afford invaluable playing time to players on the first-team fringes.

That included Ryan Giggs, returning from a broken foot, Ole Gunnar Solskjaer, Teddy Sheringham, Nicky Butt, Ronny Johnsen and

Henning Berg, while David Beckham and Jesper Blomqvist were on the bench. Despite prioritising the Premier League and Champions League, with Aston Villa and Bayern Munich waiting in the following week, Ferguson was intent on prolonging a four-lane charge for glory.

For much of the first period, the two teams were evenly matched. Butt's low shot was saved by Ian Walker, while fellow central midfielder Phil Neville drove off-target from an awkward position after Giggs's superb through-ball. For all Spurs' bluster and the encouragement of a baying home crowd, it was United who shaded the first 45 minutes.

After the break, however, the hosts landed a quick one-two which sent the Reds reeling. Three minutes into the second half, Allan Nielsen's centre was flicked on by the diminutive Ruel Fox, and Chris Armstrong's precise header arced over Raimond van der Gouw, sending White Hart Lane wild. Spurs were virtually out of sight seven minutes later as Armstrong headed in his second of the game, racing to the near post to power home David Ginola's cross.

Regardless of the sharpness and experience of the personnel on show, Ferguson's players remained unfamiliar with the concept of a lost cause. Solskjaer and Butt both came close to finding a route back into the game, before a beautifully worked move culminated in Neville crossing for Sheringham to deftly head home against his former club.

United applied plenty more pressure, but few chances arose. The game was settled when Ginola, scattering his brilliance sporadically about the evening, fashioned space and thundered a 25-yard cracker past van der Gouw with five minutes remaining. Spurs were immediately installed as competition favourites, a status validated when they overcame Leicester City at Wembley to win the trophy.

Contemplating his side's exit, Ferguson was rueful. 'I'm very disappointed,' he said. 'I don't think the scoreline reflected the balance of play. We played some good football and once we'd scored we should have done better with the chances we had.'

Yet, as the *Independent*'s Glenn Moore noted, presciently: 'While Spurs dream of Wembley, United can concentrate on every other competition.'

Tottenham Hotspur: Walker; Carr, Calderwood (Fox h-t), Campbell, Young; Anderton, Nielsen, Sinton, Ginola; Iversen, Armstrong (Ferdinand 86)
Subs not used: Baardsen, Wilson, Clemence

Manchester United: van der Gouw; Clegg, Berg, Johnsen, Curtis (Blomqvist 86); Greening (Beckham 86), Butt (Notman 72), P.Neville, Giggs; Sheringham, Solskjaer
Subs not used: Culkin, Wallwork

Man of the Match: Henning Berg
A typically classy, ice-cool display alongside compatriot Ronny Johnsen, as the veteran defender made the most of a rare outing, catching the eye particularly with a fabulous last-ditch challenge to deny Allan Nielsen a certain goal.

Saturday 5 December 1998 | Premiership | Villa Park |
Attendance: 39,241

ASTON VILLA 1 Joachim 55
MANCHESTER UNITED 1 Scholes 47

United missed the chance to take pole position in the Premiership, but Alex Ferguson was left satisfied with a point after his side survived a rousing second-half display from John Gregory's league leaders at Villa Park. Paul Scholes opened the scoring within two minutes of the second half commencing, only for Julian Joachim's deflected effort to loop over Peter Schmeichel and level matters within eight minutes.

The looming visit of Bayern Munich and the potentially detrimental effects of expending too much energy and emotion at Villa Park undoubtedly affected a Reds display which was largely self-contained. Villa, even without a suspended Stan Collymore and injured Paul Merson, looked hungrier going into the first of three successive games against the remaining top four teams.

Dwight Yorke's Villa Park return added spice to the occasion, and he was afforded a mixed welcome. Yorke was unquestionably lacking sharpness and his search in vain for form embodied a game which never truly ignited.

'The reality was that as summits go this match was about as intoxicating as high tea with buttered scones,' wrote the *Guardian*'s David Lacey. 'Satisfying up to a point but hardly a feast.'

Schmeichel and his opposite number, Michael Oakes, might well have joined Lacey in the press box for much of the first half, such was the dearth of goalmouth action, but 90 seconds into the second period there was a short-lived flurry of activity. Andy Cole's industry down the right flank culminated in Oakes palming his drilled cross out into a dangerous area, and the onrushing Scholes thumped a left-footed shot between the goalkeeper's legs.

Yet, rather than attack, United sought to contain and conserve. Though Jaap Stam brilliantly negated the threat of free-scoring Dion Dublin all afternoon, there was little the Dutchman could do to prevent Joachim's quick-fire leveller, a 20-yard shot which struck Denis Irwin and looped over Schmeichel.

The equaliser owed much to good fortune, but Villa were spurred by parity while United were rocked. Alan Thompson's rocket of a free-kick thudded fiercely against a post just after the hour, prompting Ferguson to replace Cole with Nicky Butt. The move stymied Villa's rhythm and allowed the game to drift towards a stalemate; a result deemed acceptable by both sides.

'We didn't deserve anything more,' admitted Ferguson. 'Villa are an excellent side, and I expect them to stay to the forefront in the title fight. They were the better team in the second half, so we won't complain about going home with a valuable point, and we came out of it with no injuries.'

Aston Villa: Oakes; Watson, Southgate, Ehiogu, Wright; Hendrie, Taylor, Barry, Thompson; Joachim, Dublin
Subs not used: Rachel, Lescott, Grayson, Ferraresi, Vassell
Booked: Ehiogu

Manchester United: Schmeichel; Brown, G.Neville, Stam, Irwin; Beckham, Keane, Scholes, Blomqvist (Giggs h-t); Cole (Butt 70), Yorke
Subs not used: van der Gouw, Johnsen, Sheringham
Booked: Yorke, Irwin, G.Neville

Man of the Match: Paul Scholes
All afternoon Villa made trouble for a United team clearly distracted by Bayern Munich's impending Old Trafford visit. However, Scholes's point-salvaging goal brought the sort of marginal gains champions survive on in winter.

Wednesday 9 December 1998 | Champions League Group D | Old Trafford | Attendance: 54,434

MANCHESTER UNITED 1 Keane 43
BAYERN MUNICH 1 Salihamidžić 56

Amid an undulating, confused atmosphere at Old Trafford, United crept into the quarter-finals of the Champions League by virtue of a curious draw with Bayern Munich. Alex Ferguson's side failed to register the win required to usurp the Germans at the top of Group D, yet still qualified alongside Real Madrid as the two best-placed runners-up in the group stages. Roy Keane's thumping opener was cancelled out by Hasan Salihamidžić early in the second period, and both sides squandered chances to win the game before realising that a share of the spoils would suit everybody.

That dwindling climax was at odds with a game which pulsated for long periods, both sides oozing class and technical ability. Roared on by a vocal home support, Dwight Yorke blazed narrowly over early on, then midway through the half Andy Cole rolled an effort fractionally wide of Oliver Kahn's post.

Bayern, however, gave as good as they got. Alexander Zickler's header was hacked to safety by Keane and Wes Brown twice had to be alert to clear before Giovane Elber could pounce, while the Brazilian glanced a header wide of Peter Schmeichel's goal. Crucially, as nerves began to affect the home support's mood, Keane struck before the interval. Ryan Giggs mis-controlled and then recovered David Beckham's crossfield ball, faked Thomas Strunz into touch and rolled the ball into the path of Keane to crash home a 20-yard cracker.

That lead might have been doubled early in the second period, but Ronny Johnsen – on for the concussed Denis Irwin – missed an inviting volleyed chance, then blazed over from close range on the rebound. Within five minutes, those passed opportunities would haunt United.

The home support cheered ironically as Stefan Effenberg slipped and scuffed his corner, but Bayern laughed last as the ball somehow ricocheted to Salihamidžić for a simple, bundled finish. Bayern's dander was up and Alex Ferguson's response was to replace

Yorke with Nicky Butt to shore up his midfield. The move worked, with United regaining a foothold in the game and almost moving back into the lead when Cole headed Beckham's superb cross just wide.

The tempo slowed as both camps realised results elsewhere meant progress was assured with a draw. That was little more than a source of confusion to those in the stands, who watched on disconcertedly as United declined to chase victory, including three bizarre minutes of injury time in which neither side coveted the ball.

Only the away supporters cheered the final whistle as United's fans endured ten agonising minutes before a stadium announcement confirmed the Reds' progress. 'We can settle down now until March,' said Ferguson. 'With our imagination and playing ability, I feel confident for what lies ahead.'

Manchester United: Schmeichel; Brown, G.Neville, Stam, Irwin (Johnsen h-t); Beckham, Keane, Scholes, Giggs; Yorke (Butt 64), Cole
Subs not used: van der Gouw, Sheringham, P.Neville, Blomqvist, Berg

Bayern Munich: Kahn; Matthaus (Linke 61); Babbel, Kuffour; Strunz, Jeremies, Effenberg, Lizarazu; Salihamidžić, Elber (Jancker 81), Zickler (Basler 81)
Subs not used: Scheur, Tarnat, Helmer
Booked: Lizarazu

Man of the Match: Jaap Stam
The big Dutchman was at his unflappable best, coping with Bayern's assorted attributes of pace, power and trickery and looking every inch a rock at the heart of the Reds' back line.

Saturday 12 December 1998 | Premiership | White Hart Lane |
Attendance: 36,079

TOTTENHAM HOTSPUR 2 Campbell 71, 90
MANCHESTER UNITED 2 Solskjaer 11, 18

A winless December run continued as ten-man United squandered a two-goal lead over Tottenham in a brilliant, bruising encounter at White Hart Lane. Ole Gunnar Solskjaer's clinical first-half double had the Reds in full control, only for the dismissal of Gary Neville to tip the balance back in Spurs' favour, before Sol Campbell headed home twice in the final 20 minutes to wrest a point for the hosts. Even though the draw temporarily put his side top of the Premiership table, Alex Ferguson fumed at full time, declining his post-match media duties and whisking his side onto the team coach.

In a bid to stave off the sluggishness which often afflicted his side after midweek European exertions, Ferguson made five changes to the side which drew with Bayern Munich, most notably including Solskjaer and Teddy Sheringham in place of Dwight Yorke and Andy Cole. The Norwegian needed only 11 minutes to justify his inclusion and remind Tottenham why they were so keen to enlist him earlier in the year. A quickfire counter-attack led to Ryan Giggs's header being parried out by Ian Walker, only for Solskjaer to lash home the rebound.

Soon enough, as the rain-slicked turf continued to host a high-octane spectacle, United's No.20 struck again, this time volleying home brilliantly from a typically accurate David Beckham delivery. Once again, a quick counter-raid had done for Spurs. 'I warned my players how good United were on the break, and that's exactly how they scored – with their pace and movement,' lamented George Graham.

The Spurs boss saw events turn in his favour just before the break. Referee Uriah Rennie had already cautioned four players, including Gary Neville for a lunge on Allan Nielsen, when the United defender hauled down David Ginola. Though the Frenchman's fall was theatrical, Rennie quickly brandished another yellow card and followed it with the obligatory red.

The numbers might have been evened up after the break when Andy Sinton exacted crude revenge on Beckham for an earlier foul, but the Tottenham winger was merely cautioned, prompting a huge melee involving both sets of players. With tempers flaring, Spurs halved the arrears as Campbell rose highest in a packed penalty area to thump home Darren Anderton's floated free-kick. Nevertheless, United appeared to ride out the storm – until injury time, when Anderton whipped in another free-kick and Campbell was left unmarked to guide another header past Schmeichel's sprawling dive.

Though the point briefly took United to the top of the pile, the following day brought Aston Villa's comeback victory over Arsenal at Villa Park, a result which relegated the Reds to second and underlined another missed opportunity.

Tottenham Hotspur: Walker; Carr, Young, Campbell, Sinton; Fox (Allen 83), Anderton, Nielsen, Ginola; Ferdinand, Armstrong
Subs not used: Baardsen, Calderwood, Clemence, Dominguez
Booked: Ferdinand, Sinton

Manchester United: Schmeichel; G.Neville, Johnsen, Stam, P.Neville; Beckham, Butt, Keane, Giggs (Blomqvist 87); Sheringham (Cole 75), Solskjaer (Berg h-t)
Subs not used: van der Gouw, Cruyff
Booked: P.Neville, Beckham, Butt, Sheringham
Sent off: G.Neville

Man of the Match: Roy Keane

A rain-sodden turf and a white-hot atmosphere set the scene perfectly for the United skipper. He stampeded about the field and set the tone for the Reds' aggressive approach, doing the work of two men in Gary Neville's absence.

Wednesday 16 December 1998 | Premiership | Old Trafford | Attendance: 55,159

MANCHESTER UNITED 1 Cole 45
CHELSEA 1 Zola 83

For all their traditional inconsistency, Chelsea had established themselves as a perpetual pest at Old Trafford, and Gianluca Vialli's Blues once again turned on the style to deny United a return to the Premier League summit. The Londoners had gone undefeated since the opening day of the season, underlining their menace in spite of travelling north without central defensive pairing Frank Leboeuf and Marcel Desailly.

Indeed, having levelled late on as Gianfranco Zola negated Andy Cole's opener, Celestine Babayaro came within a lick of paint of winning the match in injury time for the visitors. Had the Nigerian's 30-yard scorcher flown the other side of Peter Schmeichel's post, the Reds could have had few complaints, after being gradually ground down in the latest instalment of a fractious rivalry. Heavy challenges and tunnel bust-ups had punctuated recent meetings, and referee Graham Barber again had to contend with a spate of the former as he brandished his cards with festive regularity.

The game's competitive nature might have panned out differently had Cole not failed to convert Dwight Yorke's knockdown in the sixth minute. Instead, a cagey, bitty affair meandered towards half time, although Cole displayed phenomenal speed of thought and feet to give the hosts a spring in the step as they trotted towards the dressing room. The striker initially and inadvertently blocked Nicky Butt's goalbound shot, but Cole's lightning reactions allowed him to instantly locate the ball and drill it low into Ed de Goey's bottom corner.

One up by the break, United ought to have made the game safe in the second half. Alex Ferguson's stifling gameplan of fielding Butt, Paul Scholes and Roy Keane coagulated the visitors' creativity, and both Scholes and Jesper Blomqvist spurned inviting chances when confronted only with de Goey.

Conversely, Chelsea's patient passing gradually found holes in the United system, and the introduction of substitutes Ryan Giggs and David Beckham for Blomqvist and Yorke ultimately gave the Blues enough room to make a breakthrough.

The goal, which arrived with six minutes remaining, was simple yet intricately executed as Gus Poyet capped a patient move by releasing Zola, who lifted a sublime finish over Schmeichel. For the fourth game in a row, United surrendered a lead. That solitary point would also have been snatched away if Babayaro's effort hadn't whistled wide in injury time. As the *Independent*'s Jon Culley opined: 'Had Chelsea won, then United could not have put forward any serious complaints, such was the superiority of the London side in the closing stages.'

There was now no questioning Chelsea's title credentials. Sandwiched between league leaders Aston Villa and jockeying champions Arsenal, a four-way fight for the title had formed.

Manchester United: Schmeichel; Brown, G.Neville, Stam, Irwin; Butt, Keane, Scholes (Sheringham 85), Blomqvist (Giggs 77); Yorke (Beckham 61), Cole
Subs not used: Johnsen, P.Neville
Booked: Brown, G.Neville

Chelsea: De Goey; Duberry, Lambourde, Le Saux (Poyet 44); Ferrer, Petrescu, Wise, Di Matteo, Babayaro; Zola, Flo
Subs not used: Hitchcock, Goldbaek, Nicholls, Morris
Booked: Lambourde, Ferrer, Di Matteo, Petrescu, Wise

Man of the Match: Andy Cole
Aside from his early squandered chance, Cole was razor sharp all evening, troubling the Chelsea defence regularly and demonstrating his predatory prowess with a sharply taken opening goal.

Saturday 19 December 1998 | Premiership | Old Trafford | Attendance: 55,152

MANCHESTER UNITED 2 Butt 62, Scholes 70
MIDDLESBROUGH 3 Ricard 24, Gordon 31, Deane 59

If there was a price to pay for the dizzying highs which would punctuate the end of the 1998-99 season, then much of it was settled by this horrifying, slapstick home defeat to Middlesbrough. United would not taste defeat again all season – little wonder after the bitter taste which lingered long after Bryan Robson's side had plundered three easily avoidable goals and extended the Reds' winless run to six games.

'The entertainment is glorious, it is just the results that are a problem,' wrote Guy Hodgson, of the *Independent*. Worryingly, Alex Ferguson's men had now won only twice in the last ten games and for an hour of this match were far too easily outplayed.

Boro deserved their first win at Old Trafford since 1930, racing into a three-goal lead inside 60 minutes before a late United fightback almost pilfered a most undeserved share of the spoils. For the Reds, the afternoon was a study in absence; with Alex Ferguson away due to a family bereavement and Jaap Stam nursing an ankle injury, and between them all defensive sensibilities also failed to attend.

Striker Hamilton Ricard signalled that he was attuned to the occasion with an early blockbuster which required a fingertip save from Peter Schmeichel, and the Colombian opened the scoring in the 23rd minute with a simple tap-in after both Gary Neville and Schmeichel might have intercepted Dean Gordon's cross or Brian Deane's pull-back respectively.

Robson brought his side to Old Trafford on the back of a ten-game unbeaten run, and lurking just four points behind United. The Reds legend had identified a weakness in United's defence at set-pieces, which was spectacularly exposed after the half-hour as Gordon doubled United's deficit.

The excellent Andy Townsend picked out Deane with a cross-field free-kick and, though Ronny Johnsen was able to head clear, the Norwegian failed to do anything other than tee up Gordon for a thunderous, first-time volley across Schmeichel and into the bottom corner. Old Trafford's frustration turned to stunned silence, the annoyance of again missing a chance to move top of the table made way for genuine concern about the unfolding nightmare.

United limped in and out of the interval with little change in their fortunes, with no way to be found through the Boro defence, spectacularly marshalled by former home favourite Gary Pallister, back at Old Trafford for the first time since his summer transfer to Teesside. The difference between the two sides was highlighted in the visitors' third goal, which stemmed from a fine Steve Vickers interception to snuff out a half-chance for Andy Cole.

Though Boro lost the ball to Johnsen deep inside his own half, the Norwegian's inexplicably slack pass infield to Gary Neville only found Ricard. The striker's pass for Deane was too heavy, but ricocheted off Phil Neville and back into the Deane's stride and, to cap off a horrific concession, the ensuing shot was saveable by

Schmeichel's standards, but merely squirmed under the Dane's grasp and rolled into the Stretford End goal.

With half an hour to go, finally United were awoken, quite possibly by the mirth of the away supporters, who were singing 'We're gonna win the league' as Nicky Butt leapt to head home a fine, deep cross from David Beckham. Paul Scholes replaced Beckham, who had been booked, and caretaker manager Jim Ryan's move soon paid off, as a goalmouth melee culminated in the substitute sliding in to prod a finish past Mark Schwarzer. Just over 20 minutes remaining and, somehow, it was game on.

Boro, to their credit, rode out the storm, with their five-man defence coping admirably with a forward line now comprising Cole, Teddy Sheringham and Ole Gunnar Solskjaer. The former almost saved the day, pouncing on Schwarzer's slack pass to Pallister and charging through on goal, but the Australian recovered to take the sting out of Cole's shot and Vickers cleared to preserve his side's victory.

With one win in nine and a porous defence shipping goals, United's situation looked far from rosy. Fortunately, the afternoon would prove a launchpad from which the Reds would scale new heights.

Manchester United: Schmeichel; P.Neville (Solskjaer 79), Johnsen, G.Neville, Irwin; Beckham (Scholes 64), Keane, Butt, Giggs; Sheringham, Cole
Subs not used: van der Gouw, Blomqvist, Brown
Booked: Beckham

Middlesbrough: Schwarzer; Festa, Cooper, Vickers, Pallister, Gordon; Mustoe (Moore 72), Maddison (Beck 83), Townsend; Deane, Ricard
Subs not used: Roberts, Blackmore, Stockdale
Booked: Festa

Man of the Match: Nicky Butt

One of very few to give a sustained account of his true self on a dire afternoon. Butt was up for the fight and put his body on the line throughout, and also led the ill-fated comeback with a neat header.

Saturday 26 December 1998 | Premiership | Old Trafford | Attendance: 55,216

MANCHESTER UNITED 3 Johnsen 28, 60, Giggs 62
NOTTINGHAM FOREST 0

Hardly a festive miracle, but nevertheless an oddly straightforward afternoon for United, who emerged from almost a month of frustration to sporadically rediscover the free-flowing form of earlier in the season. A victory plus a clean sheet represented a timely confidence boost for Alex Ferguson's men ahead of a daunting trip to face title challengers Chelsea. Ronny Johnsen bagged an unlikely brace, while Ryan Giggs clipped home only his second league goal of the season, as the fixtures computer kindly served up struggling Nottingham Forest on a platter.

Dave Bassett's visitors equalled their own then-record run of 16 Premiership games without victory, and rarely looked like troubling the hosts, who dominated proceedings with comfort. Even minus Dwight Yorke, Andy Cole and Jaap Stam through injury, plus the suspended Gary Neville, United's control was almost total. After Dave Beasant had fended away a Giggs header, Johnsen rose highest to direct David Beckham's subsequent corner through a crowd of players and past the Forest stopper.

Even with Ferguson back in the dugout, United's performance meandered towards the interval. The manager's influence was apparent in the approach adopted by the hosts after the break, however, as

Forest were pinned back in their own half for long periods. Teddy Sheringham hesitated when well placed and allowed the visitors to clear, but there was no reprieve when Henning Berg headed Beckham's free-kick to Johnsen, whose thunderous volley rocketed past Beasant to all but tie up the victory.

Three minutes later came the surest sign of the afternoon that United were slipping back into character, as Giggs netted a sublime third goal. 'I don't think you will get a better piece of football anywhere in the country,' purred Ferguson, of a slick passing move involving Sheringham and Beckham, and beautifully finished off by Giggs's casual lob over the onrushing Beasant.

Job done with half an hour remaining, United stepped off the gas to save themselves for a trip to Stamford Bridge while Forest sought to avoid an embarrassing scoreline – an approach they would not be able to reprise when the sides reconvened in Nottingham six weeks later. That said, Beckham thudded a shot against the post and Peter Schmeichel almost conceded a consolation goal to Neil Shipperley, but United clung to a first clean sheet in 12 games. Overcoming the division's bottom team may not have seemed like much of a warm-up to a title battle against Chelsea, but at least it put the Reds back on track.

Manchester United: Schmeichel; P.Neville, Johnsen, Berg, Irwin; Beckham, Keane, (Greening 66), Butt, Giggs (Blomqvist 75); Scholes (Solskjaer 63), Sheringham
Subs not used: van der Gouw, Brown
Bookings: P.Neville

Nottingham Forest: Beasant; Louis-Jean, Armstrong, Chettle (Doig 68), Rogers; Bart-Williams (Bonnalair 54), Stone (Hodges 77), Johnsen, Quashie; Freedman, Shipperley
Subs not used: Crossley, Darcheville
Booked: Chettle, Quashie, Rogers

Man of the Match: Paul Scholes

The liveliest attacker on show all afternoon. Shunted forward alongside Sheringham to compensate for the absence of Yorke and Cole, Scholes spent 90 minutes tormenting Forest with his movement and intelligence.

Tuesday 29 December 1998 | Premiership | Stamford Bridge | Attendance: 34,741

CHELSEA 0
MANCHESTER UNITED 0

Fortune traditionally favours the brave, but on this rare occasion where United opted against a gung-ho approach, it was Chelsea's scattergun finishing which allowed a defensive Reds display to go unpunished.

Gianluca Vialli's side, as they ought to have done at Old Trafford earlier in the month, should have won, but this time found their finishing compass awry as a spate of chances went begging. Norwegian striker Tore Andre Flo was the principal culprit for the hosts, regularly chancing his arm but never once testing Peter Schmeichel, who was most meaningfully employed to thwart Gianfranco Zola in a trio of one-on-ones.

United had lost only once in seven league visits to Stamford Bridge, and less than a year earlier had served up one of the finest displays of Alex Ferguson's Old Trafford tenure with a swaggering 5-3 FA Cup triumph. But when Zola blazed off target after a fine Roberto Di Matteo pass in the opening seconds, a long evening beckoned.

In the 12th minute, Flo met Zola's deep corner but firmly headed wide. The Norwegian then should have converted Dan Petrescu's inviting centre, before firing wide after Schmeichel denied Zola. For all the hosts' dominance, the returning Andy Cole might have struck the opener when he rounded Ed De Goey, only for Michael Duberry to clear the striker's effort from a tight angle.

Flo twice more missed the target before half time, and Schmeichel again rescued his side by plunging at Zola's feet after an uncharacteristically slack pass from Roy Keane. Having somehow reached the break level, United emerged in the second half with greater purpose, grasping occasional control in midfield where they had previously been overrun – though there was one genuine scare when Duberry headed a Zola corner wide from close range.

Teddy Sheringham's introduction for Scholes after an hour gave United's attack greater cohesion, with Chelsea gradually pulled about by the visitors' growing movement and incisiveness. As the game meandered to a close, a rare opening was cynically halted when Frank Leboeuf brought down David Beckham as the winger charged beyond the home defence. Referee Mike Riley declined to show the Frenchman his second yellow card of the game, prompting Leboeuf to later admit: 'I think I deserved a red.'

A minute later, Chelsea almost heightened United's ire when Zola latched onto Petrescu's pass, only for Schmeichel to once again deny the little Italian with a sprawling save. Time remained for one last heart-stopping moment, as De Goey fumbled then recovered Ryan Giggs's harmless last-minute strike.

Chelsea had earned good fortune, having dominated for long periods. For United, it was another draw, another curiously under-whelming performance, and little sign of what would unfold in the remainder of the season.

Chelsea: De Goey; Ferrer, Duberry, Leboeuf, Le Saux (Goldbaek 88); Petrescu, Di Matteo, Morris (Desailly 73), Babayaro; Zola, Flo
Subs not used: Hitchcock, Nicholls, Forsell
Booked: Di Matteo, Leboeuf

Manchester United: Schmeichel; G.Neville, Stam, Johnsen, Irwin; Beckham, Keane, Butt, Giggs; Scholes (Sheringham 60), Cole
Subs not used: van der Gouw, P.Neville, Berg, Blomqvist
Booked: Cole

Man of the Match: Peter Schmeichel
The great Dane had come under intense scrutiny throughout the autumn, but prepared for his personal mid-season break with a timely return to form, repeatedly frustrating Zola and preserving a huge point.

December in statistics

Premiership table (29 December 1998)

	P	W	D	L	F	A	GD	Pts
Aston Villa	20	11	6	3	31	20	+11	39
Chelsea	20	9	10	1	31	17	+14	37
Manchester United	**20**	**9**	**8**	**3**	**39**	**23**	**+16**	**35**
Arsenal	20	9	8	3	22	11	+11	35
Leeds United	20	8	9	3	34	19	+15	33
6West Ham United	20	9	5	6	24	23	+1	32
Liverpool	20	9	4	7	36	25	+11	31
Middlesbrough	20	7	9	4	32	26	+6	30
Wimbledon	20	8	6	6	27	32	-5	30
Leicester City	20	7	7	6	23	21	+2	28
Derby County	20	6	10	4	20	18	+2	28
Tottenham Hotspur	20	7	6	7	28	30	-2	27
Newcastle United	20	6	6	8	24	28	-4	24
Everton	20	5	8	7	13	21	-8	23
Sheffield Wed	20	6	4	10	21	22	-1	22
Blackburn Rovers	20	4	6	10	20	28	-8	18
Coventry City	20	4	5	11	16	29	-13	17
Charlton Athletic	20	3	7	10	23	31	-8	16
Southampton	20	3	5	12	16	38	-22	14
Nottingham Forest	20	2	7	11	18	36	-18	13

Champions League, Group D table (9 December 1998)

	P	W	D	L	F	A	GD	Pts
Bayern Munich	6	3	2	1	9	6	+3	11
Manchester United	6	2	4	0	20	11	+9	10
Barcelona	6	2	2	2	11	9	+2	8
Brondby	6	1	0	5	4	17	-3	3

December form (all competitions): LDDDDLWD

Goals scored: 11   **Goals conceded:** 11

Most appearances: David Beckham, Nicky Butt, Ryan Giggs 6 starts and 2 as sub each

Players used: 23

Most goals: Ronny Johnsen, Paul Scholes, Ole Gunnar Solskjaer 2 each

Most assists: David Beckham 4

Different goalscorers: 8

Quickest goal: Ole Gunnar Solskjaer, 11 mins [v Tottenham (a)]

Latest goal: Teddy Sheringham, 71 mins [v Tottenham (a)]

Watched by: 365,724

Average attendance: 45,716

Chapter 6

January – New Beginnings, Happy Endings

The Treble season would become synonymous with late drama, and it was in January that United's penchant for nerve-shredding theatre really ramped up. Alex Ferguson's side won all five games in another goal-laden month, but three of the quintet were won in the last ten minutes to display the growing resolve and steel among a squad for whom the memories of 1997-98's collapse were still painfully fresh.

Fresher still was the embarrassment of December's shocking home defeat to Middlesbrough, and the flashbacks were hardly stymied when the Teessiders were quickly sent back to Old Trafford in the third round of the FA Cup. Bryan Robson's side were in understandably chipper mood ahead of their return. Dean Gordon, a scorer in December's upset, explained: 'We went to United last month and, against all the odds, we won. So we'll be going there in a positive frame of mind. To win the cup, you've got to beat the best – and there would be nothing better than beating United at Old Trafford.'

When Andy Townsend turned home the opening goal against the run of play, it looked like Boro were on course to repeat the previous month's victory, which had been their first at Old Trafford in almost 70 years. Instead, a sublime assist from Ryan Giggs allowed Andy Cole to level, before controversy reigned as Nicky Butt tumbled under a challenge from Neil Maddison to win a penalty that Denis Irwin converted. Giggs's scorching late clincher settled the debate, but all post-match talk was about the award of Irwin's penalty.

'Unfortunately, the referee buys a decision where Nicky Butt has dived,' lamented Robson. 'But you get some and you lose some. Neil said straight away that he didn't touch him and it's unfortunate to go out of a cup with a decision like that.' While Boro continued to stew over the manner of their exit, United's attentions quickly switched to the fourth round, where a sumptuous home draw against Liverpool instantly earned 'tie of the round' status.

Excited chatter of the draw gripped the Cliff's changing rooms, where other hot topics included Peter Schmeichel. Having jetted off to Barbados for the ten-day break he had been granted by Alex Ferguson in November, the Dane still managed to pop up on the pages of the British tabloids, snapped by sea-faring paparazzi. 'I wasn't even aware of their presence until I saw a picture of myself in swimming trunks filling the back page of the *Sun*,' he lamented. That irritation aside, the Caribbean jaunt would prove a seminal spell in Schmeichel's season.

'The really good thing was that he pulled himself together,' says Raimond van der Gouw. 'He had a little break where the manager sent him away and then he came back and he played better and better. After the break, you could see in training that he was playing like we knew he could; the real Peter Schmeichel was back.'

Firstly, however, Dutch understudy van der Gouw would need to keep goal for the Premier League visit of West Ham. Though the Hammers were just three points behind the Reds ahead of kick-off, they posed less threat to United's victory than the pre-match power failure which delayed the game by 45 minutes. 'It was a little disruptive,' shrugs van der Gouw, 'but we stayed focused and put in a really good performance.'

The stand-in stopper might as well have joined Schmeichel on the beach, so underemployed was he throughout the game. By the time van der Gouw was called into any meaningful action – being beaten by Frank Lampard's late consolation goal – two strikes from Andy Cole and a goal apiece for Dwight Yorke and Ole Gunnar Solskjaer had long since assured the Reds a comfortable victory.

By a curious quirk of fate, van der Gouw sustained an injury in training ahead of the following week's trip to face Martin O'Neill's Leicester City, presenting Ferguson with a choice: field reserve team goalkeeper Nick Culkin, or throw Schmeichel straight back into the team two days after touching down in Manchester.

'I came straight back into training on the Friday, and Raimond was injured and we were playing Leicester the next day at Filbert Street,' recalls the Dane. 'The boss said: "Good holiday?" I said: "Yep, I'm fresh now," and he asked: "Can you play tomorrow?" "Yes, no problem," I said, and that was it. From that point on, I never thought about being tired.'

Once again, however, United turned in an attacking display so irresistible that a goalkeeper was barely required. Leicester did muster a pair of goals – a howitzer from Theo Zagorakis and Steve Walsh's late consolation – but a Yorke treble, a pair from Cole and Jaap Stam's first (and only) goal for the club sealed a memorable triumph when once again all the post-match talk centred around United's deadly strike duo.

Though it was Yorke who took home the match ball, that honour could just as easily have gone to Cole. With each striker already boasting a pair, Yorke sealed his hat-trick by converting the rebound when Cole had hit the crossbar. While they laughed among themselves on the field, Cole insists that there was never a duel for goals between the pair.

'We didn't compete for goals,' he stresses. 'It wasn't like we were racing to get the hat-trick. When he had a brace and I had a brace, if he had a good opportunity to slip me in then he would have done it and vice versa. That is why that partnership worked. If he was in a better position than me, then I would have given it to him all day long. That is why it worked so much. People were looking at that partnership and thinking: "This is unbelievable, they must be working so hard together in training." But that wasn't the case at all. It was natural. We didn't even play in the same team in training, because on Fridays we used to play England versus the Rest of the World, so we'd be on opposite sides. We never played on the same team; we never played functional eleven-a-side together. The Rest of the World always won, by the way!'

Regardless of nationality, United's players were firing on all cylinders in the opening weeks of the new year. According to skipper Roy Keane, that stemmed from a policy of honesty behind the scenes, with December's lull in form examined in forensic detail by the players and their manager.

'We're our own biggest critics and we don't need anyone else to point out the problems,' said the Irishman. 'We don't hide from facts and we knew how bad we had been. We tell each other and I believe we would not have been so successful if we weren't honest in the dressing room.

'We had been a bit lethargic and the manager told us he wanted things to get back to normal. He isn't slow to remind us. We've all had a chat and it was about trying to cut out the mistakes. We had been poor compared with our normal high standards. Maybe some of us weren't going at it the way we should. It might be impossible to play at ninety miles per hour all the time, but we had definitely slowed down.

'We're better playing at a higher pace. Now we seem to be at high tempo again. There is definitely another championship within this team. We have a team capable of winning the championship, but you have to be able to prove that, week in week out.'

Though their meeting would come in the FA Cup, Liverpool would certainly test United's credentials in a tie billed as a battle of the strike partnerships: Cole and Yorke against Michael Owen and Robbie Fowler. United's main men had already plundered 31 goals between them in all competitions, but that was just one more than their Anfield counterparts, and the visitors' menace was underlined in just the second minute at Old Trafford when Owen headed the opening goal to send 8,000 travelling supporters wild.

Amassed in the Scoreboard End, it was the visitors who crowed for the vast majority of the game as United created and spurned chances aplenty against a Liverpool team defending as if their lives depended on it. In typical style, however, Alex Ferguson rolled the dice and hit the jackpot.

'The manager was used to risk in those days,' says Denis Irwin. 'He brought me off, put Ole [Gunnar Solskjaer] on and went three at the back, which he did quite regularly, to put an extra man up front. The manager was never afraid to gamble. Even in a league match, we have gone three at the back to get a result and even more so in the cups – we had thrown the kitchen sink at it and taken a risk. We were an attacking side, so sometimes it was the best way to go – particularly in a cup game – and that embodied what spirit there was in the team. It kicked us on and what happened after that didn't surprise me.'

Roy Keane might have had a hat-trick, twice hitting the post and having another effort deflect millimetres wide of David James's goal, but inevitably it was United's leading scorer who hauled his side back on terms with just two minutes to go. As Liverpool protested the award of a free-kick against Jamie Redknapp, David Beckham picked out Cole, whose vital knock-down was turned home by Yorke at the back post.

'We had some magical moments within that season, but that was incredible,' grins Yorke. 'We were one-nil down with two or three minutes to play, we were just pushing and thought it was one of those days and we weren't going to score at all. But then everything changed. Liverpool had played well, defended well and they thought they'd won, but then we snatched it from them.'

And, for all the pre-match chatter devoted to the four first-choice strikers, it was another forward, Solskjaer, who would have the final say of the afternoon. In his ten minutes on the field, the Norwegian hadn't once touched the ball, yet he would need only the most fleeting involvement to alter the course of the entire season.

'I had three touches of the ball, I think. That's all I had,' says Solskjaer. 'After we'd equalised, we just go straight up again. Jaap hoofs a ball up in behind, Scholesy gets it, so I run into his path, really, and just take the ball off him. I use one touch to take it off him, one touch to set myself, and then another to shoot through Jamie Carragher's legs. Those are the only touches I had in that game, I think.

'Sometimes you've just got to make the most of it as a sub. That was my job whenever I came on: to be in and around the box. I wasn't there to create chances for everyone else, I was just there to smell where the ball was going to land and that's where I was probably better than most. Finishing like that, through the defender's legs, came from my former coach, Age Hareide. He coached me at Molde and he was a defender himself. He said one of the worst places for a defender is when it's hit through the legs. For the goalkeeper it's impossible because he's got to cover the other angle and trust his centre back or defender to block the shot.'

Solskjaer's United career had been a curious tale. Plucked from obscurity with Molde, the totally unknown prospect had top-scored in his first season at Old Trafford, and had further endeared himself to United supporters in 1997-98 with a deliberate self-sacrifice; clattering Newcastle's Rob Lee to the ground rather than allow the midfielder to reach the penalty area after racing through on goal. Having turned down the advances of Spurs to stay and fight for his place in Ferguson's team, Solskjaer was heavily in credit. After sending every single United fan into delirium with his last-gasp turnaround against Liverpool, his stock rose even further – but it was a goal which still holds a special meaning for him on various levels.

'It's the best feeling you can imagine, there and then,' he beams. 'It's pure euphoria. It was a big goal for me as well, because I was a Liverpool supporter when I was young, so scoring that goal was very important for me. It was a massive, massive goal for me. You can see it in the celebration as well, when I was grabbing the United badge. You learn as long as you live, I've always said, and because when I was young Liverpool used to win things, that's where it stemmed from. You support the winning team in Norway. But coming over to England and scoring that goal, it was a brilliant, brilliant feeling. You could see how much it meant in the celebrations.'

The delights were layered: FA Cup progress, having come back from the brink of exit, at the expense of Liverpool. The squad was flooded with a collective high, and the afternoon is regarded by almost the entire squad as the result which kick-started the season's historic run-in. 'After Christmas, it all started to click,' says Gary Neville, 'but the season really started with the Liverpool game. Coming back against them in the last minute in the FA Cup was massive. You can forget about the first half of the season – you always do at United, you never remember anything – but that was the game that started everything. From then on, everybody was right and everybody was at it.'

Match-winner Solskjaer was the embodiment of Ferguson's squad rotation policy at its best. Ever a consummate professional, the

Norwegian knuckled down, trained harder and ensured that every time he was called upon, he was ready. With a sizeable squad full of such levels of professionalism, the United manager was delighted to see his approach bearing fruit.

'This is the kind of pool we need,' he said. 'It's good for competition and it's also for the long-term benefit of the club if we are to stay in the league, FA Cup and European Cup. There's still a lot of football to be played and they will all play their part. They all want to play and it's unfortunate that some of them have to be left out. But I hope they recognise the qualities of this club and the nature of football nowadays means they will all get their turn.'

Ferguson opted against making any personnel changes to his team as the Reds rounded off the month with what had looked likely to be a comparative cakewalk, but instead became another exercise in resolve and patience as struggling Charlton were overcome at the Valley. The second-bottom Addicks stifled United's game for an hour and looked to have ridden out a furiously one-way finale, only for Yorke to head home Paul Scholes's injury-time cross to take the Reds to the top of the table.

After back-to-back injury-time wins, United's pluck and moxie had been laid bare as a warning to their title rivals – most notably Arsenal, now two points behind and gathering momentum. As far as Yorke is concerned, it was January when United developed a season-defining knack for feeding off drama and pressure. 'After beating Liverpool the way we did, we played Charlton and won in the last minute and people forget all of those little things. It was dramatic. It was never-say-die. It was on a knife-edge, and that's how we liked it,' says the striker.

'The whole concept of not giving up and coming back from the dead was phenomenal. It was an incredible time for us, it really was special and I suppose those are the things that make the Treble year a memorable one. We had our backs up against the walls and things didn't look so good on a number of occasions, but somehow we always dug deep and got it back.'

Though his side were well placed on three fronts and Ferguson had no cause to dip into the transfer market, he still had one major recruitment to make: a new assistant manager. Jim Ryan had deputised ably and Ferguson had absorbed many of Brian Kidd's duties on the training pitch – 'We'd never run so many laps of the pitch midway through a season,' recalls Gary Neville – but the time had come to select a permanent incumbent. On face value, hardly an appointment of great importance, but the manager's choice would prove one of the key signings of the Treble season.

Sunday 3 January 1999 | FA Cup third round | Old Trafford | Attendance: 52,232

MANCHESTER UNITED 3 Cole 68, Irwin 82 (pen), Giggs 90
MIDDLESBROUGH 1 Townsend 53

It took almost 30 attempts on goal and the deployment of all four senior strikers, but United overcame Middlesbrough's dogged challenge to stage a rousing fightback and advance to the FA Cup fourth round.

There was more than a hint of controversy about the game's denouement, however. After Andy Cole had thrashed home an equaliser to cancel out Andy Townsend's opener, Nicky Butt fell under a challenge from Boro rookie Neil Maddison inside the penalty area. The youngster's incensed reaction made it clear that he felt Butt had dived, but Denis Irwin shrugged off Middlesbrough's protestations to fire United into the lead from the spot. Ryan Giggs capped a superb display with a fine solo goal in injury time, lending a fair reflection of the game's balance to the scoreline.

For over an hour, though, victory was far from certain. Mark Schwarzer produced two breathtaking saves from Cole and Dwight Yorke, while a series of blocks from Boro's hemmed-in back five spared the Australian stopper an even busier afternoon.

Peter Schmeichel was almost totally unworked, with his defence – boosted by the return of Jaap Stam – suitably wise to Boro's dangers just three weeks after their Premier League horror show at Old Trafford. Yet Robbie Mustoe went close with a first-half header that flashed past the upright, serving notice of the perils of profligacy. They were further underlined shortly after half time when Bryan Robson's men opened the scoring. Three awful concessions punctuated December's upset, and the ease with which Townsend rolled home his shot was alarming.

The small band of travelling supporters revelled at the prospect of a cup upset, but just as it appeared that lightning might strike twice, a thunderbolt from Cole levelled matters with 22 minutes remaining. Giggs's slide-rule pass fed the striker, who lashed an unstoppable finish into the roof of Schwarzer's net.

Desperate to avoid crowbarring a replay into an already packed fixture list, Ferguson threw on Ole Gunnar Solskjaer and Teddy Sheringham for Jesper Blomqvist and Cole, shifting to a 4-3-3 set-up to exploit the visitors' tiring defence. The game's decisive moment arrived when Butt crumpled under Maddison's attentions. The youngster later revealed: 'As soon as Nicky went down I went to him and said, "I didn't touch you, I can't believe you've gone down like that." But I've no arguments with him because he's a good honest lad and things like this happen in football.'

Gary Pallister advised Schwarzer which way his former team-mate was likely to direct the ensuing penalty, but Irwin still sent the Australian the wrong way to put United ahead. The fourth round draw had already paired the winner of this tie with Liverpool, and by the time Giggs crashed home an injury-time third goal, Old Trafford had already chorused: 'Bring on the Scousers.'

Manchester United: Schmeichel; Brown (P.Neville 75), Stam, Berg, Irwin; Blomqvist (Solskjaer 73), Keane, Butt, Giggs; Cole (Sheringham, 84), Yorke
Subs not used: van der Gouw, Cruyff

Middlesbrough: Schwarzer; Fleming, Cooper, Maddison, Pallister, Gordon; Gascoigne (Beck 74), Mustoe (Stamp 62), Townsend; Ricard, Deane
Subs not used: Beresford, Stockdale, Blackmore
Booked: Deane

Man of the Match: Andy Cole
Having missed the chance to pinch a point from United's Premiership defeat to the Teessiders, Cole seemed hell-bent on righting those wrongs, and he capped a superb display with a devastatingly clinical equaliser.

Sunday 10 January 1999 | Premiership | Old Trafford |
Attendance: 55,180

MANCHESTER UNITED 4 Yorke 10, Cole 40, 68, Solskjaer 81
WEST HAM UNITED 1 Lampard 89

On an afternoon when a pre-match floodlight failure stole all the headlines, United illuminated Old Trafford with a devastating dismantling of a lacklustre West Ham side. The blackout occurred shortly before kick-off and, although a stadium announcement was required to unearth a Norweb electrician, the game eventually went ahead after a 45-minute delay. 'I did my team talk in the dark,' Alex Ferguson grinned, 'and I think the players enjoyed it a bit more. A few of them could go to sleep.'

The pre-match furore certainly caught the imagination of the assembled press. 'Only an electricians' strike could have denied United a comfortable victory,' crowed the *Guardian*'s David Lacey, who added: 'West Ham simply could not hold a candle to their opponents.'

The encounter was a foregone conclusion from the moment Dwight Yorke blasted United in front after ten minutes, and the point was further bludgeoned home by an Andy Cole brace and Ole Gunnar Solskjaer's measured header during the course of a lopsided contest. 'At times United appeared to be forming an orderly queue for more goals,' noted Lacey.

Ferguson was even able to rest Gary Neville, Paul Scholes and David Beckham, in addition to the vacationing Peter Schmeichel, but the tone was set for a dominant performance inside the first minute, as Cole pounced on a Rio Ferdinand mistake to force Shaka Hislop into a smart stop. Ryan Giggs's curling effort was deflected wide as United continued to press, and the visitors' resolve buckled before ten minutes were up, as Cole slipped the ball through for Yorke to power a finish past his fellow countryman.

Conducted by a trademark non-stop display from skipper Roy Keane, United's tempo rarely dipped below breathless in the first period and, though the Hammers were initially spared embarrass-ment by wayward efforts from Cole and Giggs, the striker struck tellingly just before the break. Nicky Butt's deflected effort spun away off Hislop's post and fell perfectly for United's No.9, who thrashed the rebound into the untended goal.

There was more subtlety about Cole's second, scored midway through the second period, when he was cleverly released by Yorke and clinically side-footed a low, left-footed effort into Hislop's far corner. But for a fine stop from the Hammers goalkeeper to thwart a deflected Keane effort and another Cole shot, United might have romped to an even more emphatic victory. As it was, substitute

Solskjaer rounded off the scoring with a looping header ten minutes from time. And although Frank Lampard slotted home a late consolation, there was no way the hosts could be outshone after a dazzling display.

Manchester United: van der Gouw; Brown (Johnsen 78), Stam, Berg, Irwin; Blomqvist, Keane (Cruyff 84), Butt (Solskjaer 78), Giggs; Yorke, Cole
Subs not used: Culkin, Beckham

West Ham United: Hislop; Ferdinand, Ruddock, Pearce; Potts, Lazaridis, Lampard, Berkovic, Lomas; Sinclair (Cole h-t), Hartson
Subs not used: Forrest, Abou, Breacker, Iriekpen
Booked: Sinclair

Man of the Match: Roy Keane
Deprived of any meaningful competition in midfield, the skipper directed his limitless energy to driving his team forward throughout the game, while also unpicking locks with a succession of key passes.

Saturday 16 January 1999 | Premiership | Filbert Street | Attendance: 22,091

LEICESTER CITY 2 Zagorakis 35, Walsh 75
MANCHESTER UNITED 6 Yorke 10, 64, 86, Cole 50, 62, Stam 90

The Dwight Yorke–Andy Cole axis had shown signs of powering up against West Ham after a disjointed, injury-hit December, and the United strike pairing turned in a scintillating display to ravage Leicester City at Filbert Street. Yorke hit his first hat-trick for the Reds and Cole bagged another double, and though Jaap Stam volleyed home the solitary goal of his United career in the dying seconds, the headlines belonged to Alex Ferguson's strikers.

'They could have scored five each,' the boss said. 'Their understanding is so good.' Martin O'Neill could only agree, while stressing that his injury-hit side were never legitimate contenders for anything other than defeat. 'You can't tell me that Andy Cole is not a top-class finisher or that United are anything but exceptional,' said the Foxes' manager, 'but we had only sixteen players to choose from today. I could have done with a couple of Alex's subs!'

Leicester manfully coped during the first half, riding out a storm of wasteful finishing from the visitors to somehow go into the interval on level terms. Yorke opened the scoring after only ten minutes, rifling home Denis Irwin's cross after steadying himself, seemingly for an age, deep inside the Foxes' box, but total dominance yielded nothing but a scorching long-range equaliser from Theo Zagorakis.

Though carelessness allowed Leicester back into the game, the menace in United's play – and in Ferguson's body language as he strode to the dressing room at half time – hinted at an eventful second half. So it proved. The Foxes' injury-ravaged defence kept a curiously high line throughout, and it took just one searching pass from Ryan Giggs to release Cole in the 49th minute and he fired a clinical finish under Kasey Keller.

The American was soon besieged. Again exposed after Yorke bypassed Steve Walsh, Keller was able to get a touch on Cole's shot but was unable to stop his third concession. A fourth quickly followed. Irwin's long punt landed in space behind Leicester's defence and when Keller missed the ball Yorke somehow steered it home from an unforgiving angle.

The notion of a contest briefly resurfaced when Walsh kneed home Steve Guppy's errant shot, but it was buried again when Cole took advantage of more shoddy defending by motoring into the area.

His powerful effort thundered against the underside of the crossbar and Yorke finished it off to secure the match ball.

Both Yorke and Cole beamed in tandem, but Stam's elation was even greater in injury time when he reached David Beckham's cross to sidefoot home his first United goal as the Reds' title charge gathered pace. As the *Independent*'s Norman Fox put it: 'United are no longer tip-toeing back into championship contention but are stamping on the heels of Chelsea.'

Leicester City: Keller; Kaamark (Campbell 71), Taggart, Walsh, Ullathorne; Izzet, Lennon, Zagorakis, Guppy; Wilson (Parker 71), Cottee (Fenton 89)
Subs not used: Arphexad, Oakes
Booked: Walsh, Lennon

Manchester United: Schmeichel; Brown (P.Neville h-t), Berg, Stam, Irwin; Beckham, Keane, Giggs, Blomqvist; Cole, Yorke
Subs not used: van der Gouw, Johnsen, Scholes, Solskjaer
Booked: Keane, Blomqvist

Man of the Match: Dwight Yorke
Simply unplayable all afternoon. Quite aside from his hat-trick and his assist for Cole's second goal, the Trinidadian had the Leicester defence running scared all match with his speed of thought and vision.

Sunday 24 January 1999 | FA Cup fourth round | Old Trafford | Attendance: 54,591

MANCHESTER UNITED 2 Yorke 88, Solskjaer 90
LIVERPOOL 1 Owen 3

Even in a campaign so replete with seminal moments as the Treble season, there is no understating the importance of this victory over Liverpool; it was an epochal comeback which spawned all the history made by Alex Ferguson's team over the remainder of the campaign.

Trailing Michael Owen's header inside three minutes, United battered away at the visitors, straining every sinew and wringing every last drop of hope until, finally, Dwight Yorke tapped home an 88th-minute equaliser. Then, rather than consolidate and settle for an Anfield replay, United pressed on for more and duly received it when Ole Gunnar Solskjaer struck an injury-time winner that shook Old Trafford to its foundations.

The added gloss of *schadenfreude* capped an incredible day for Ferguson, his players and their supporters, but a mood of frustration had gripped Old Trafford for most of the game. It took Liverpool under three minutes to move ahead, as Vegard Heggem picked out Owen, who had strayed from Gary Neville and was free to nod home a simple opener.

'It was a terrible start,' lamented the United manager. 'God almighty, you wouldn't think a five foot, six inch striker would score with a header in the first minutes at Old Trafford. I wasn't too pleased about that.'

Stunned by their lackadaisical start, United's players took time to warm to the occasion. When the cohesion required to create a chance finally arrived, it was thwarted by a combination of David James's goal frame and ex-Reds midfielder Paul Ince. After James helped on David Beckham's cross, Roy Keane directed his header against the inside of the near post, only for the ball to bounce across the line, strike Ince and rebound to James.

Liverpool's 8,000 travelling supporters revelled in the near miss, and were almost in a state of pandemonium shortly afterwards when Robbie Fowler's speculative right-footed curler arced fractionally past Peter Schmeichel's top corner.

The visitors continued to threaten on the counter-attack, as Gerard Houllier allowed his side to sit deep for long periods – although, in fairness, they were often penned back by United's breathless attempts at forcing a way into the game. Keane came agonisingly close twice more, first with a shot that struck Jamie Carragher and bounced inches wide, then with a low, left-footed effort which pinged the base of James's post.

Owen's pace continued to prove problematic at the other end, but as the game entered its final ten minutes his touch let him down after Jason McAteer put him through on goal. By that point, Ferguson had repeatedly rolled the dice, introducing Solskjaer and Paul Scholes for Denis Irwin and Nicky Butt, while Henning Berg made way for Ronny Johnsen.

Liverpool continued to defend heroically, but were undone by their own passion two minutes from the end when they vehemently protested the award of a free-kick against Jamie Redknapp for a debatable foul on Johnsen. 'It was a crucial moment,' Houllier opined. 'I didn't think it was a foul and Jamie told me it wasn't. That broke our concentration.'

With Liverpool's players slow to resume their defensive positions, Beckham ignored the chance to shoot and clipped a ball to Andy Cole at the back post, and the striker headed perfectly into the path of Yorke for the simplest close-range conversion.

Old Trafford erupted, and was still abuzz when, midway through the second of two added minutes, Jaap Stam's long ball exposed Liverpool's deep defensive line, landing at the feet of Scholes. Before the midfielder could shoot, however, Solskjaer – with his first touch of the game – nicked the ball, shaped to shoot into James's far corner and instead drilled it through Carragher's legs and into the Stretford End goal.

It was bedlam in the stands as fans bounced and bellowed in undiluted joy, while Liverpool's players dropped to the turf, spent.

'Liverpool have every reason to be gutted,' puffed Ferguson. 'They defended fantastically but sheer determination got us through.'

Between the two goals lay the substance of United's season; a sense for momentum. They harnessed the impetus, the wave of emotion and relief that had greeted parity, and rode it all the way to victory over their fiercest rivals.

Manchester United: Schmeichel; G.Neville, Berg (Johnsen 81), Stam, Irwin (Solskjaer 81); Beckham, Butt (Scholes 68), Keane, Giggs; Yorke, Cole
Subs not used: van der Gouw, P.Neville
Booked: Butt, Keane, Giggs, Scholes

Liverpool: James; Carragher, Matteo, Harkness; Heggem, Redknapp, Ince (McAteer 71), Berger, Bjornebye; Owen, Fowler
Subs not used: Friedel, Kvarme, McManaman, Leonhardsen
Booked: Matteo, Owen

Man of the Match: Ryan Giggs
The surest sign yet that the winger was back to his best after returning from a broken foot. Never gave Heggem a moment's peace and was constantly probing for a route back into the game.

Sunday 31 January 1999 | Premiership | The Valley | Attendance: 20,043

CHARLTON ATHLETIC 0
MANCHESTER UNITED 1 Yorke 89

The feel-good factor generated by United's thrilling fightback against Liverpool was almost extinguished over the course of 88 spirit-sapping minutes at the Valley, only for Dwight Yorke's late winner to ignite it once again as the Reds moved top of the Premiership table.

In a spluttering display, Alex Ferguson's side gradually clunked into gear, reserving their best play for the second half, when the relegation-threatened Addicks manfully kept their visitors at bay until Yorke rose to direct Paul Scholes's cross in off the post. United's frustrations owed much to Alan Curbishley's gameplan of having his three-man central defence sit deep, while his wingbacks and midfielders hustled and harried United in the centre of the park, cutting off the supply line to Yorke and Andy Cole at source.

That restricted the Reds' first-half attacking output to a pair of volleys from Ryan Giggs – both saved by Simon Royce – and a shot from Nicky Butt which skirted past the upright. Charlton had held their own in the first period and were let down in several promising situations by a poor final ball, but in the second half they concentrated fully on weathering a United storm.

Butt went close again, as did Gary Neville's speculative effort, while heroic blocks from John Robinson and Steve Brown thwarted goal-bound shots from Giggs and Roy Keane. As time ticked away, Ferguson took chances, as he had against Liverpool, by introducing Ole Gunnar Solskjaer and Paul Scholes. Once again, fortune favoured the brave.

After Butt stabbed the ball wide of the post following a neat one-two with Yorke, only a superb challenge from Carl Tiler deflected the United's striker's effort narrowly over the bar. Yorke had the last laugh, however, on the cusp of injury time as he rose above Tiler to reach Scholes's floated cross and powered a header off the inside of Royce's post and into the net.

Further heightening United's sense of triumph, Chelsea's defeat at Arsenal put the Reds top of the table at the end of a completed weekend for the first time all season – not that Alex Ferguson was getting carried away. 'Being top doesn't matter at the moment,' he said. 'But it's always a sign that you're doing something right and, as a team, we're doing a lot right. It's a good result in context of winning the championship. Charlton defended well and handled our two strikers as well as anyone this season. They sat deep so there was no space behind them and we had to find another way through. Sometimes you have to dig in to find a result. This was one of those games.'

Charlton Athletic: Royce; Rufus, Brown, Tiler; Robinson, Kinsella, K.Jones, Redfearn, Powell; Hunt (Bright 78), Pringle (Parker 83)
Subs not used: Ilic, Newton, Konchesky

Manchester United: Schmeichel; G.Neville, Berg, Stam, Irwin; Beckham (Solskjaer 71), Keane, Butt (Scholes 82), Giggs; Cole, Yorke
Subs not used: van der Gouw, P.Neville, Johnsen

Man of the Match: Ryan Giggs
Confronted with massed ranks of Charlton defenders, Giggs was up to the task throughout and shone as United's most menacing attacking outlet for long periods of the afternoon.

January in statistics

Premiership table (31 January 1999)

	P	W	D	L	F	A	GD	Pts
Manchester United	23	12	8	3	50	26	+24	44
Chelsea	23	11	10	2	34	19	+15	43
Aston Villa	23	12	7	4	35	22	+13	43
Arsenal	23	11	9	3	24	11	+13	42
Leeds United	23	9	9	5	36	23	+13	36
Liverpool	23	10	5	8	44	28	+16	35
Wimbledon	23	9	8	6	29	33	-4	35
Derby County	23	8	10	5	23	20	+3	34
West Ham United	23	9	6	8	25	31	-6	33
Middlesbrough	23	7	11	5	32	28	+4	32
Tottenham Hotspur	23	7	9	7	29	31	-2	30
Leicester City	23	7	9	7	25	27	-2	30
Newcastle United	23	7	7	9	28	32	-4	28
Sheffield Wed	23	7	5	11	25	23	+2	26
Everton	23	5	9	9	13	25	-12	24
Coventry City	23	6	5	12	23	32	-9	23
Blackburn Rovers	23	5	7	11	22	30	-8	22
Southampton	23	5	5	13	23	46	-23	20
Charlton Athletic	23	3	8	12	26	37	-11	17
Nottingham Forest	23	3	7	13	19	41	-22	16

January form (all competitions): WWWWW

Goals scored: 16   **Goals conceded:** 5

Most appearances: Henning Berg, Andy Cole, Ryan Giggs, Denis Irwin, Roy Keane, Jaap Stam, Dwight Yorke 5 each

THE IMPOSSIBLE TREBLE

Players used: 20

Most goals: Dwight Yorke 6

Most assists: Andy Cole 3

Different goalscorers: 6

Quickest goal: Dwight Yorke, 10 mins [v West Ham (h) and v Leicester (a)]

Latest goal: Ole Gunnar Solskjaer, 90 + 1 mins [v Liverpool (h)]

Watched by: 204,137

Average attendance: 40,827

Chapter 7

February – Foundations for Success

February carried an air of the calm before the storm, albeit with a shower of goals against Nottingham Forest and lashing rain against Fulham and Arsenal, which continued to muddy Old Trafford's playing surface. Nevertheless, there remained a growing sense, for manager and players, that they were gathering themselves for a mission that went beyond their domestic challenges and that they had to come to terms with the very real possibility that a unique Treble truly was on.

Alex Ferguson was already beginning to anticipate that his squad might have to play in excess of 60 matches before the season reached its climax and was making it his mission not to expend the energy reserves of key players too hastily, and he clearly had one eye on the looming Champions League quarter-final encounter with Internazionale in early March. Squad rotation was a more novel concept in 1999 than it is today, but it would prove critical, if controversial at times. He decided that players would be rested where possible and to avoid the muscular injuries that can be so prevalent on late winter pitches, he would remove a player from action at the slightest tweak or tightness of hamstring or calf as a precaution against it getting any worse.

Meanwhile, wins over Derby, Fulham, Coventry and Southampton in February were all attained by one-goal margins. It wasn't that United didn't work hard, it was more akin to seasoned steeplechasers holding something back for the final laps. 'The picture is quite clear now,' Ferguson stated mid-month, shortly after a somewhat frustrating 1-1 draw with Arsenal at Old Trafford. 'I feel we can go all the way in Europe, we are in the quarter-final of the FA Cup and we are top of the league. I picture about sixty games for us, so we must pace ourselves and it's a matter of trying to keep all the players fit.'

The month started badly in that regard when Ryan Giggs pulled up with a hamstring injury 11 minutes into February's first test, against Derby County. The initial prognosis was four weeks on the sidelines and was painfully reminiscent of the Welshman's absence in the 1997-98 run-in. The sinewy winger suffered a hamstring problem early in 1998 – again in February, Derby once more the opponents – and United won only two of the eight matches he missed and exited the FA Cup, to Barnsley, and the Champions League, to Monaco. No wonder, then, that when asked why his side ended up potless in May that year, the Reds boss's answer consisted of two words: Ryan Giggs.

'We are monitoring Ryan all the time,' counselled Ferguson after his No.11's quicker-than-expected return as a substitute against the Gunners on 17 February. 'He is such an important player for us, especially in the Champions League. But he came on against Arsenal and changed the way we played. At Coventry, his display emphasised his value as his goal won the game. He finished off a marvellous move, which started with a corner at our end. Schmeichel caught it and by the time Yorke and Beckham had moved the ball along, Ryan, who had been defending the front post, had arrived in their goalmouth to score. It was a brilliantly exciting goal and I knew straight-away that it had won the game for us.'

Giggs epitomised United's counterattacking culture, but he was more than a mere pacy outlet for the Reds' pinball breakaways. He made even the coolest continental defenders look cumbersome and timid – domestic back lines didn't much like facing him either – his clever positional play, jinking runs and underrated deliveries con-stantly put teams on the back foot for fear of what he might do. His susceptibility to hamstring strains made the foresight of signing the unfashionable but effective Jesper Blomqvist in summer 1998 all the more prudent in these moments of need. Giggs's freshness and sharp-ness could be preserved, the inconvenience of any spell on the sidelines assuaged.

That's nothing new, of course. Ferguson always had a keen eye for the bigger picture. While some managers get bogged down in the details of today, the 'Govanor' cast his gaze towards many more tomorrows, widening his scope to see what broader impact the minu-tiae of the present might have on a more significant future. February was exactly that for United: groundwork for the run-in, the period in the season when trophies are won and places in history are secured. Ferguson had to ensure United's foundations were rock-solid.

Deeming a January signing on the field unnecessary, the boss was still searching for a replacement for Brian Kidd, who departed his assistant manager post for the top job at Blackburn Rovers in December. United plumped for Steve McClaren, Derby County's up-and-coming 37-year-old coach. Preston's David Moyes and former club captain Steve Bruce were reportedly on a three-man shortlist, but McClaren got the job, much to his surprise.

'Everything has happened so quickly – I'm in a bit of a whirl and can hardly think straight,' said a dizzied McClaren having just been offered the position. 'Alex Ferguson asked Jim Smith for permission to speak to me after Derby's game at Old Trafford. When that was granted, it was just a case of putting our heads together to finalise a few things. It didn't take me long to decide I wanted the job. I've not had that many dealings with Alex in the past and have only really been involved with him during matches between the two clubs. He has taken his time since Brian Kidd left and done his homework, and it's a big compliment that he came to me. Now I can't wait to get started.'

Phil Neville recalls McClaren's appointment as surprising yet seamless. 'We played Derby one night and the day after he was United's assistant manager,' he recalls, while team-mate Andy Cole jokes: 'Steve was up and down on the touchline for Derby two days before and we just looked at him and thought, "What a weirdo!" A couple of days later, he was at Old Trafford and we wondered if this was the same geezer.'

His task in replacing a popular and established member of the United backroom team must have been a daunting one for a relatively inexperienced coach arriving into an enormous set-up at a top club with established international stars. Kidd's connection to the club ran deep as a former player and scorer in the 1968 European Cup final. More pertinently, he had developed a trust, connection and camaraderie with the players on the training ground.

'Steve was a different kind of coach to Kiddo,' adds Cole. 'I loved Kiddo as a coach; for me he was fantastic both on and off the training pitch. He was really good and we were naturally disappointed when we lost him and we wondered who would replace Kiddo because he was an integral part of the team.

'When Steve came in, as the weirdo from the match the other night, he was very different. He was very buoyant, very jolly, he changed a few things in training and the warm-up, he entertained and had a laugh and joke, had a few games in the warm up. The boys took to him very well and Steve was a very good coach, most probably a better coach than a manager because you get people like that.

When it came to coaching, he was very good and you couldn't knock him for that.'

For a team with a compulsion to attack and, at times, leave its defensive door ajar – especially in the first half of the season and, in particular, in December when United won just once and conceded 11 goals – the organisation and fresh ideas that McClaren brought to training sessions at the Cliff could not be underestimated.

Henning Berg remembers an almost instant impact. 'When Steve came in, it made a big difference in terms of how we prepared and how we prepared the team pattern,' states the Norwegian defender. 'You noticed that especially in Europe. In England, player-for-player we were better than most teams so we could get away with not being tactically one hundred per cent, but you can't in Europe. I think the changes we made and what we started practising – making sure that we played better as a team and that everybody knew tactically how to be in the right position – made a massive improvement. That was one of the reasons why we managed to keep that winning streak going and not lose any games after Christmas that year. It made a huge difference and so for Steve to come in at that time was vital.'

The new focus and defensive discipline came from hours of work on the training ground not just dedicated to the back four, but the midfield and forwards as well. 'I think we became more focused on how we defended as a team instead of as individuals,' adds Berg. 'Having been surrounded by so many good players, we were able to get away with things in the Premiership, because individually we were more or less better than most players we played against. So we could play man against man at the back, which gave us an advantage when we had the ball because we had more attacking options. But when Steve came in we worked more on the back four and midfield and joining them together, as well as the positional play of the strikers. And we needed it, because you have to have that against the top teams otherwise they will cut through you.

'We improved that little bit in our organisation, which we practised on the training pitch. We had said a lot of these things before and certain things had been spoken about, but when you actually work on it in training it is so much easier to understand because the players know exactly what is being talked about. When you get down and practise, the learning is so much better and I think it was a big contribution to us having that run in the second half of the season.'

McClaren wouldn't be so bold as to claim any credit for what happened in his first game at the club, an 8-1 hammering of beleaguered bottom-placed club Nottingham Forest. 'I'll never forget Steve's first game, against Forest,' says Phil Neville. 'He wasn't doing much, just looking at what was going on for a couple of days beforehand. He was in the dressing room after we'd won at Forest and you could see the smile on his face was from ear to ear. I thought to myself that it must have been like Christmas Day for him.

'Then on the Monday morning it was an international break, so the reserves and the rest of the lads who weren't on duty stayed behind to train in the indoor gym at the Cliff and Steve took the session. You could tell from the first minute that he was a special coach, because it was fun, it was hard work, it was enthusiastic and it was everything you'd want from an assistant manager.

'I think that was probably the biggest turning point in our season, when Steve came in, because it was a different voice, a different way and I think he won the respect of the players probably quicker than he thought he was going to do. The players loved him. First and foremost, you've got to deliver on the training ground, and Steve delivered in training because he put on fantastic sessions. His communication with the players was as good as I've ever known.'

Jim Ryan had stood in as assistant manager between Kidd's departure and McClaren's arrival. He remained with the squad for the trip to Forest, and Ferguson earmarked a new role for his fellow Scot rooted in dressing-room communication. 'I had been aware of a weakness in our set-up,' the boss explained. 'If I have to tell a player he is not playing, invariably I don't have much time to spend discussing it with him. I always try to be sensitive, stress his value to us and his importance in the squad. But prior to a game there are a lot of other things to do. My job has grown so big with so many demands on my time. I can see a role here for Jim, talking things through with players, explaining in detail. He does it well.'

If ever Ferguson felt a pang of guilt for leaving a player out of his starting line-up, it was most likely that Ole Gunnar Solskjaer was the cause of it; he was a consummate professional who would rarely complain and instead went dutifully about his business. 'Ole's an intelligent lad and I think there is a realisation that he is up against two fantastic, in-form strikers,' said the boss. 'I'm sure he hates being called a super sub, and it's unfair, but the fact is . . . he is!'

That Solskjaer had the ability to read a match and make an impact on it was undoubted, as he so brilliantly exhibited with a quite remarkable performance as a substitute at the City Ground. With Andy Cole and Dwight Yorke already bagging braces, Ole emerged from the bench with instructions to 'keep things simple and see out the win' as he replaced Yorke, who had himself been desperately seeking a hat-trick.

Even Cole was surprised at the ruthlessness of United's finishing that day. 'We absolutely steamrolled them,' he said. 'It was frightening because it was one-one at one point and we still won eight-one. Yorkie scored first, then they equalised. I made it two-one and it stayed that way until half time, but after that the floodgates opened.

'The gaffer took Yorkie off at four-one and brought Ole on and he got four in fourteen minutes. I remember thinking to myself, "That is some going." People say it was against a bad team, but if you get four goals in fourteen minutes as a substitute, it says a lot about you. But Ole was a connoisseur of the game. He used to watch from the bench to see how he could hurt people. He used to get in great positions because he watched the game and realised the centre-halves were tired, or maybe he would work one individual more than the other. Ole was ridiculous from the bench, absolutely ridiculous.'

If that astonishing victory highlighted one trait, it wasn't the sheer brilliance of Ferguson's attacking options but, when placed in competition, just how devastating an impact that could have on the performance, individually and collectively. 'You have to be on your toes all the time here,' Yorke said after the win. 'If you want to understand that idea, then it was all there against Forest. You would think Andy and I had done all we needed to, and then Ole comes on and scores four goals. We can bring players in. Take them out. There's competition all through the squad. It's beautiful when you think about it. Lovely, in fact.'

Jesper Blomqvist, himself a beneficiary of the rotation system, particularly in support of Giggs, could also appreciate Solskjaer's true value. 'He is like a goal machine,' said the Swede. 'What he does actually helps Andy and Dwight, because it makes sure they stay alert. All the talk is about Andy and Dwight, but it's the three of them. The other two know that the slightest slip and Ole is waiting to come in. But the great thing about this side is that it's the same all around the pitch. We have players who can come in for anyone.'

After navigating past giant-killing Second Division leaders Fulham with a 1-0 FA Cup fifth-round win, United faced up to Arsène Wenger's Arsenal. The Gunners had notched four consecutive wins over the Reds, including the home and away games in the league on their way to 1997-98's Double, as well as August's 3-0 Charity Shield defeat and September's Premiership loss by the same scoreline at Highbury.

With a four-point advantage over Arsenal, who had been on the march since December and hadn't conceded a league goal in 1999,

United were determined not to cede ground at this stage of the campaign, as had been the case the previous season. It was a typical United–Arsenal affair, no quarter given, although Cole, United's equalising goalscorer on a rain-soaked evening at Old Trafford, recalls feelings of frustrations after a late Reds onslaught.

'Yorkie missed a penalty that day and I think he tried to dink it,' he says with a smile. 'Only Yorkie could do that and get away with it! But we should have won the game. I don't know how we went a goal down in the first place. [Nicolas] Anelka's goal was certainly fortunate. Arsenal was always a tough game for us. They were a really strong and powerful team, but skilful and attractive as well, and we always knew it was going to be a tough game. So when we went a goal down, having bossed the game, it was frustrating. I got the equaliser with a header and then we battered them. We just couldn't find a way through.'

Yorke did have a golden opportunity to atone for his earlier miss and, inexplicably given his form, he poked his shot wide from eight yards. Nevertheless, Chelsea's 1-1 draw with Blackburn Rovers, which saw Blues player-manager Gianluca Vialli sent off at Stamford Bridge, meant nothing changed among the three clubs at the top. Ferguson's men finished February with a 1-0 smash-and-grab win at Coventry and a late, nerve-racked 2-1 triumph over Southampton back at Old Trafford. That took United's unbeaten run in 1999 to 13 matches and set the Reds up for an almighty run-in and the resumption of the Champions League.

'We have made the most of the break from Europe,' the Reds boss concluded at the end of a tough month. 'When I think back to December and the difficult period we went through, I marvel at what the team has achieved since the turn of the year. The players have done everything I have asked of them and pulled off some notable successes in the league and FA Cup. They've taken games by the scruff of the neck and struck a level of form that has hardly wavered. It's not always possible to deliver an extravaganza, but we have ranged from scoring sprees to games where we have simply ground out a result.'

February may have offered only a sprinkling of this season's stardust in the form of that magnificent win at Forest but, then again, there was plenty of that to come.

Wednesday 3 February 1999 | Premiership | Old Trafford | Attendance: 55,174

MANCHESTER UNITED 1 Yorke 65
DERBY COUNTY 0

As Derby boss Jim Smith faced the press in his post-match conference at Old Trafford, Alex Ferguson was carefully composing a speech of his own outside in the corridors that burrow beneath the stadium's South Stand. The United manager was intent on pinching Derby's highly rated young coach, Steve McClaren, and approached Smith to ask permission to speak to his soon-to-be new assistant manager, which was duly granted.

The previous 90 minutes had been spent on pick-pocketing of different kind: nabbing three points from an eighth-placed Derby side who had, at that point, conceded fewer goals than United, had already held the Reds to a 1-1 draw in October and arrived in Manchester with an overloaded midfield in a suffocating 3-6-1 formation that readily became 5-4-1 in defensive situations. The loss of Ryan Giggs after just 11 minutes to a hamstring injury didn't help matters either.

In the face of Derby's stifling tactics in the first half, United could muster only a handful of long-range shots, although Jaap Stam's blockbusting effort after four minutes had Rams goalkeeper Russell Hoult struggling to see it off. The Reds remained patient, not lured into gung-ho gallivanting – a sign of the team's growing maturity, perhaps. That or it was the thrill of living dangerously following FA Cup drama against Liverpool and the previous game's last-gasp win at Charlton.

Dwight Yorke had broken Liverpool's resistance to equalise after 88 minutes and then headed an 89th-minute winner at The Valley, making him the prime suspect to strike again. As the clock ticked beyond the hour, and with the home crowd growing increasingly uneasy, the relief was palpable when Nicky Butt lifted a pass over the Derby defence and Yorke controlled the ball before calmly steering it past Hoult.

Yorke might have doubled the lead late on from Jesper Blomqvist's pinpoint cross, but this time he was halted by Hoult from close range. Nevertheless, Yorke's trademark grin remained, and with good reason amid his most prolific spell in an incredible season – he'd notched seven goals in five games and would extend it to nine in six. 'It seems that I'm making a habit of scoring winners,' he beamed. 'But it doesn't matter who scores and I really don't know how many I've scored. I just hope we carry on from here.'

Even having opened up a four-point gap to second-placed Chelsea, it wasn't all smiles as fears abounded that Giggs might miss the resumption of the Champions League in a month's time. 'He'll be out for several weeks and is very doubtful for the Inter matches,' Ferguson said gravely. Yet acting quickly after he 'felt a wee tweak' proved very prudent.

Manchester United: Schmeichel; G.Neville, Johnsen, Stam, Irwin; Scholes, Butt, Keane, Giggs (Blomqvist 11); Yorke, Solskjaer
Subs not used: May, Beckham, Cole, P.Neville

Derby County: Hoult; Laursen, Carbonari, Prior, Stimac, Dorigo; Powell (Hunt 80), Carsley, Harper (Burton 70), Bohinen; Wanchope
Subs not used: Knight, Schnoor, Christie

Man of the Match: Dwight Yorke

The irrepressible Reds front man continued his seemingly unstoppable scoring streak with another key goal to get United through a tricky league encounter against a stubborn Derby side who boasted the third best defensive record in the league.

Saturday 6 February 1999 | Premiership | City Ground | Attendance: 30,025

NOTTINGHAM FOREST 1 Rogers 6
MANCHESTER UNITED 8 Yorke 2, 67, Cole 7, 50, Solskjaer 80, 88, 90, 90

'In a nutshell, we got murdered.' That was the pithy parlance used by Nottingham Forest boss Ron Atkinson in summing up his team's obliteration from the merciless magnificence of United's attacking talent at the City Ground and, perhaps slightly less obviously, given the scoreline, the brilliance of David Beckham.

Even a cursory glance at the Premiership table indicated a huge gulf between pace-setters United on 47 points and bottom-of-the-table Forest with a paltry 16, but the Reds' biggest win of the campaign was an irresistible example of what the team's competitive forwards were capable of; Dwight Yorke and Andy Cole grabbed two apiece, but were outdone in 14 incredible minutes in which substitute Ole Gunnar Solskjaer grabbed four goals – and the headlines, too.

In-form Yorke got the party started when he scored after just two minutes. Beckham's centre overran, but Roy Keane retrieved the ball and pulled it back for Paul Scholes, who crossed for Yorke to make it 1-0. Forest's full-back-turned-winger Alan Rogers equalised on six minutes from a breakaway attack; however that was a brief and quickly forgotten flirtation with joy for the home side, as a minute later Cole restored the lead, racing onto Jaap Stam's searching ball forward, rounding Dave Beasant and slotting home.

Considering that blistering start and the eventual scoreline, it's surprising that United took until the 50th minute to extend the advantage. Cole reacted quickly and finished neatly on the rebound after Beasant saved a shot from Yorke, who then added a fourth on 67 minutes when Jesper Blomqvist's cross hit John Olav Hjelde and the post before United's No.19 tapped gratefully into an open goal.

At that point, Solskjaer admits: 'I was sitting on the bench thinking, "I'm not coming on today, Andy and Dwight are on fire." But the manager told me to get changed and Jim Ryan had a few famous last words: "We don't need any more goals, just keep the ball. Pass it and play it nice and simple." But, of course, I don't like to do it that way, do I?'

With 18 minutes to play Solskjaer replaced Yorke, whose smile Alex Ferguson later admitted looked 'a little fixed', having been on a hat-trick himself. But what came next from Solskjaer was simply stunning. On 80 minutes, Gary Neville scampered to overlap Beckham and crossed for the simplest of Solskjaer's goals at the far post. Then with two minutes of normal time left, Beckham set the Norwegian running through a Forest defence stood still as trees, and while his attempted lob was stopped by star-jumping Beasant, Solskjaer dropped a shoulder, rounded the keeper and arrowed a shot into the top corner.

United's players were in their element, and so was Solskjaer. Scholes teed up the substitute's hat-trick, the striker pulling down a dinked pass and volleying pitilessly past Beasant. His fourth – 13 minutes and 49 seconds after the first – came after Nicky Butt's pull-back and Scholes's scuffed shot and Ole just guided the ball into the far corner.

Nobody could deny Solskjaer his moment, nor United the fully warranted praise for an outstanding team display. 'United are a magnificent side and proved it today,' Atkinson conceded. 'We contributed a bit towards it as well, but they were quality all over the field.' Of Solskjaer, he quipped: 'Good job they didn't put him on earlier!'

Nottingham Forest: Beasant; Harkes, Hjelde, Palmer, Armstrong (Porfirio 74); Stone, Johnson, Gemmill (Matsson 57), Rogers; van Hooijdonk, Darcheville (Freedman 26)
Subs not used: Crossley, Bart-Williams
Booked: Porfirio

Manchester United: Schmeichel; G.Neville, Stam, Johnsen, P.Neville; Beckham, Keane (Curtis 72), Scholes, Blomqvist (Butt 76); Yorke (Solskjaer 72), Cole
Subs not used: van der Gouw, May
Booked: Keane, P.Neville

Man of the Match: David Beckham
The goal-getters grabbed all the headlines, but Beckham's passing was utterly sublime and underpinned much of United's attacking play. He did it in the face of yet more abuse from the stands, too, though he soon helped silence Forest fans.

Sunday 14 February 1999 | FA Cup fifth round | Old Trafford | Attendance: 54,798

MANCHESTER UNITED 1 Cole 26
FULHAM 0

Kevin Keegan's first return to Old Trafford since that infamous rant as Newcastle boss, when United were chasing a double Double three seasons previously, was an open invitation for the press to dredge up the moment he appeared to crack under the title-race pressure live on TV, even though Alex Ferguson insisted there were no hard feelings between the pair.

'Managers have their arguments, like couples in a marriage,' the boss commented. 'Kevin was upset at the way we were gaining ground on him for the championship and I have always understood his reaction. I could have done without the matter being dragged up by the press for what was, in the end, a peaceful cup tie.'

Keegan's circumstances had certainly changed since those heady days. His Fulham side, backed by Mohammed Al Fayed's millions, were en route to a rampant second-tier title win and they had knocked out top-flight Southampton and Aston Villa to tee up a fifth-round visit to Old Trafford. That form put Keegan in the frame to be the next manager of England, a role he would take a few days later.

United were without Roy Keane and Paul Scholes through suspension – Phil Neville joined Nicky Butt in midfield – while Ryan Giggs's absence due to that hamstring strain meant Ferguson was reluctant to risk Jesper Blomqvist until the final few minutes, with the crucial league clash against Arsenal just three days away.

Instead, he picked Ole Gunnar Solskjaer, Dwight Yorke and Andy Cole, figuring that 'putting three strikers out meant there was every chance of one of them scoring!' He also gave 20-year-old Jonathan Greening a run-out for the second half.

There was nothing like the fluency of the 8-1 win over Nottingham Forest on show. Midweek internationals, eyeing up the imminent clash with Arsenal, and Fulham's ebullience all contributed – but the Reds didn't hit full flow. Even Cole's solitary strike on 26 minutes, though neatly crafted by Butt's arcing cross and Solskjaer's cut-back, benefited from a slice of luck as the shot deflected off Chris Coleman to beat Maik Taylor, who was otherwise in fine form.

At the other end Schmeichel did well in the second half when he parried Steve Finnan's speculative 30-yard drive and smothered John Solako's rebound, though the Fulham winger could have done better. Results acquired simply via necessity often make for forgettable affairs. This wasn't a lovingly crafted triumph, but United got through it and gladly progressed.

Manchester United: Schmeichel; G.Neville, Stam, Berg, Irwin (Greening h-t); Beckham, Butt, P.Neville, Solskjaer (Blomqvist 68); Yorke, Cole (Johnsen 88)
Subs not used: van der Gouw, May

Fulham: Taylor; Finnan, Symons, Coleman, Brevett; Collins (Uhlenbeek 87), Smith, Hayward, Salako (Trollope 74); Lehman (Betsy 59), Hayles
Subs not used: Arendse, Brazier

Man of the Match: Andy Cole
A banner in the away end, 'Andy Cole – Fulham reject', referenced a Craven Cottage loan spell eight years previously yielding four goals in 15 games. Times change; Cole's 18th strike of the season was sweet not simply for the win it secured.

Wednesday 17 February 1999 | Premiership | Old Trafford | Attendance: 55,171

MANCHESTER UNITED 1 Cole 61
ARSENAL 1 Anelka 48

Forget for a moment the skill and craftsmanship at the disposal of these great rivals; if United and Arsenal are capable of anything it's an epic, blood-and-bruises slugfest. Perfectly suited, then, to a rain-soaked, floodlit night at Old Trafford. Chelsea continued to separate the two in the league table – United were top on 50 points, Arsenal third with 45 and a game in hand – but few doubted that these heavyweights would be slogging it out to the final bell in May. This particular bout was decided on points – one apiece.

'It was magnificent entertainment,' wrote John Dillon in the *Daily Mirror*, 'even if the purists sneer that the finishing was off-key. There wasn't a minute when you weren't spellbound by full-blooded action.'

Arsenal started brighter in the pouring rain on a pitch resembling a ploughed field. Peter Schmeichel saved well from Ray Parlour early on, while it took 28 minutes of toil for Roy Keane to test David Seaman. United should have led a minute later when Parlour fouled Ronny Johnsen and referee Gary Willard awarded a penalty. Usual spot-kick taker Denis Irwin was out with a groin injury, so Dwight Yorke stepped up, but it wasn't his night. He fluffed his kick, sending it wide of Seaman's post.

The Gunners goalkeeper then summoned an excellent stop from Andy Cole, who brilliantly turned Steve Bould before getting a low shot away. Three minutes into the second half, however, Nicolas Anelka gave Arsenal the lead. The Frenchman's rubber-legged partner, Nwankwo Kanu, adroitly turned Jaap Stam and darted into the box where Phil Neville's thudding block inadvertently fizzed the ball out to Anelka, who fired his shot into the roof of the net.

The younger Neville's misfortune was soon allayed. Cutting in from the left flank, Neville floated an inch-perfect cross to Cole, who nodded past Seaman for his 19th goal of the season and 100th Premier League strike. It was also the first time Arsenal's defence had been breached in the league since 13 December.

That was all the encouragement United needed, finishing the final 30 minutes on the rampage. Yorke again could have made the difference but suffered once more in a head-to-head with Seaman.

Substitute Ryan Giggs – returning from injury – burst down the left and Cole helped on the Welshman's cross to Yorke, who toed the ball wide under pressure from Arsenal's keeper. The striker sat muddied, perplexed, shaking his head.

Wenger certainly felt relieved. 'If we'd lost it would have been very hard to catch United,' he said. 'By the end United were closer to winning two-one than us. It's not a bad result for us.' Ferguson agreed: 'Arsenal will look back on this more fondly than us and they worked hard for the result.'

Manchester United: Schmeichel; G.Neville, Stam, Johnsen, P.Neville; Beckham, Keane, Butt (Giggs 77), Blomqvist (Scholes 61); Yorke, Cole
Subs not used: van der Gouw, Solskjaer, Brown
Booked: Keane, Yorke

Arsenal: Seaman; Dixon, Bould, Adams, Winterburn (Vivas 77); Parlour, Vieira, Hughes, Overmars (Diawara 84); Kanu (Garde 62), Anelka
Subs not used: Manninger, Grimandi
Booked: Vieira, Bould, Parlour

Man of the Match: Roy Keane
The Irishman never shirked a midfield battle, especially against his old foe Patrick Vieira, and with the match so delicately poised United's skipper stood out in driving his team forward to recover a one-goal deficit.

Saturday 20 February 1999 | Premiership | Highfield Road | Attendance: 22,596

COVENTRY CITY 0
MANCHESTER UNITED 1 Giggs 79

Ending a week in which United booked an FA Cup quarter-final berth against Chelsea and came out unscathed from a potentially tectonic top-of-the-table clash with Arsenal – and with a whiff of Europe's knockout stages in the air – a trip to a mud-bobbled Highfield Road against a Coventry City side seeking another great escape from the clutches of relegation would not have topped Alex Ferguson's wishlist.

Neither did risking Ryan Giggs, starting for the first time since his hamstring injury at Derby. 'Giggs needed the game,' insisted the United boss. 'There's no point coming to the match [against Inter] in eleven days and finding he doesn't have the stamina for it.'

In the event, it was as well the Welshman did play as he scored the decisive goal after 79 minutes of battling and squandered chances. 'Sometimes you just have to grind out a result,' Ferguson added. Giggs had the best chance of a disappointing first half, after a sweeping counterattack involving Dwight Yorke, David Beckham and Andy Cole, but he missed the target with Magnus Hedman and the Coventry goal at his mercy.

Jaap Stam was forced off at half time as a precaution after he felt his hamstring tighten, and so Henning Berg took up the task of dealing with big, awkward centre-forward Noel Whelan. Berg sidled up next to the impressive Ronny Johnsen and immediately set to work with a thunderous challenge that left Whelan in a heap. The challenge was fair – just – but an awkward fall forced Whelan off clutching his shoulder.

Seven minutes into the half, Cole, on a run of four goals in three games and nine in his last eight, had an effort harshly disallowed for offside having headed Giggs's cross past Hedman. United continued to rap on the door: Paul Telfor blocked Beckham's goal-bound shot, Paul Scholes fizzed an effort wide, while Giggs, who shot over in either half, sent a tame header wide. However, United's No.11 took one chance and that was all it needed.

The move started from a Coventry corner. Peter Schmeichel had already punched the ball clear when he claimed Gary McAllister's second attempt and launched a clinical break, throwing long to Yorke. Giggs, who was on the front post for the corner, bounded forward and took on possession to feed Beckham, whose cross skimmed Richard Shaw's head and fell to Giggs at the far post. It wasn't a clean hit, but Shaw couldn't keep it out.

Schmeichel did enough to deny Darren Huckerby at the death and caused huffing, puffing Sky Blues boss Gordon Strachan to lament: 'Their goalkeeper made saves but ours did'nae. Then the one time we're not focused, they score.' It wasn't a classic match, but the win was classic United.

Coventry City: Hedman; Nilsson, Williams, Shaw, Telfer, Burrows (Soltvedt 86); Boateng, McAllister, Froggatt; Huckerby, Whelan (Aloisi 65)
Subs not used: Ogrizovic, Konjic, Quinn
Booked: Boateng, Burrows

Manchester United: Schmeichel; G.Neville, Stam (Berg h-t), Johnsen, Irwin; Beckham, Keane, Scholes, Giggs; Yorke (P.Neville 87), Cole (Solskjaer 74)
Subs not used: van der Gouw, Blomqvist
Booked: Scholes, Stam, Cole

Man of the Match: Peter Schmeichel
The Dane drew criticism earlier in the season, but several key saves, most notably late on from Huckerby, and his ability to set United on a rapid counterattack with a long throw were crucial to the Reds getting through this tricky fixture.

Saturday 27 February 1999 | Premiership | Old Trafford |
Attendance: 55,316

MANCHESTER UNITED 2 Keane 80, Yorke 84
SOUTHAMPTON 1 Le Tissier 90

During Sir Alex Ferguson's 26-year reign, team selections rarely failed to raise eyebrows – even once sparking debate in Parliament. So it was little surprise, though nonetheless a talking point, that he rested four key men for Southampton's visit four days before Inter were due in town for a Champions League quarter-final first-leg tie, a game United eyes were focused on ever since the draw was made in December. Jaap Stam was left out altogether after a tight hamstring at Coventry, while Roy Keane, Andy Cole and Denis Irwin settled for places on the bench, although all three would be beckoned to rescue a lacklustre display.

'I was surprised; it was a careless performance,' said Ferguson. 'By half time my patience had worn out. We want to win the league and dropping points against Southampton is hardly the right recipe. So I brought Roy off the bench and the improvement was instant.'

That said, the breakthrough didn't arrive until the 80th minute, with nerves noticeably frayed and by which time Cole and Irwin had joined their captain's cavalry. David Beckham's corner was nodded down by Henning Berg and teed up by Dwight Yorke for Keane to drive a shot through a mass of bodies and over the line, despite the efforts of Patrick Colleter.

With the pressure off, Yorke quickly grabbed United's second as he tiptoed around Saints keeper Paul Jones to finish off a move that started when Beckham took down Irwin's high clearance and delivered a sumptuous cross into Yorke's feet. Matt Le Tissier's thumping header from Jason Dodd's late free-kick caused a brief wobble, but proved a mere consolation.

The press pondered the significance of the performance ahead of

Inter's visit, with the *Guardian*'s Ian Ross writing: 'United were so poor that those members of Inter's managerial team present must have felt they were victims of an elaborate hoax.' The *Daily Mail*'s Jeff Powell countered the selection debate, saying: 'The cynical wisdom whispered that Ferguson was throwing another glorious season straight out of the window by resting part of his dream team four days before United's big night – until they beat Southampton, of course. United are mature enough to change gear when required.'

There were no complaints about the manager's tinkering from inside the camp. 'It wasn't pretty but we got the points,' was Keane's assessment. 'The manager told me that he was resting me. I wanted to play, but you have to look at the system and I realise it has worked for us. I'm not arrogant enough to think I'm exempt from the rotation system. I was just happy to get on and do something.' That he certainly did.

Manchester United: Schmeichel; G.Neville, Berg, Johnsen, P.Neville (Irwin 79); Beckham, Butt (Keane h-t), Scholes, Giggs; Yorke, Solskjaer (Cole 68)
Subs not used: van der Gouw, Blomqvist

Southampton: Jones; Dodd, Lundekvam, Monkou (Benali 51), Colleter; Oakley, Hughes, Marsden, Bridge; Ostenstad (Le Tissier 68), Beattie
Subs not used: Moss, Hiley, Bradley
Booked: Colleter, Le Tissier

Man of the Match: Roy Keane
When the skipper was sent on at half time, it wasn't his goalscoring Alex Ferguson had in mind. Yet it was fitting that his game-changing introduction garnered a fourth goal of the season and his first in three months.

February in statistics

Premiership table (28 February 1999)

	P	W	D	L	F	A	GD	Pts
Manchester United	**28**	**16**	**9**	**3**	**63**	**29**	**+34**	**57**
Chelsea	27	14	11	2	41	22	+19	53
Arsenal	27	13	11	3	35	13	+22	50
Aston Villa	27	12	8	7	38	31	+7	44
Leeds United	26	11	9	6	39	25	+14	42
West Ham United	27	11	7	9	31	38	-7	40
Liverpool	27	11	8	10	50	34	+16	39
Derby County	27	9	11	7	26	25	+1	38
Wimbledon	26	9	10	7	30	36	-6	37
Sheffield Wed	26	10	5	11	34	25	+9	35
Newcastle United	27	9	8	10	35	36	-1	35
Tottenham Hotspur	26	7	12	7	30	32	-2	33
Middlesbrough	27	7	12	8	34	39	-5	33
Leicester City	25	7	9	9	25	34	-9	30
Everton	27	6	10	11	20	29	-9	28
Charlton Athletic	27	6	9	12	31	37	-6	27
Coventry City	27	7	6	14	28	38	-10	27
Blackburn Rovers	27	6	8	13	27	38	-11	26
Southampton	26	6	5	15	26	50	-24	23
Nottingham Forest	27	3	8	16	22	54	-32	17

February form (all competitions): WWWDWW

Goals scored: 14   **Goals conceded:** 3

Most appearances: Peter Schmeichel, Gary Neville 6 each (540 mins)

Players used: 18

Most goals: Dwight Yorke, Andy Cole, Ole Gunnar Solskjaer 4 each

Most assists: Scholes 3

Different goalscorers: 5

Quickest goal: Dwight Yorke, 2 mins [v Nottingham Forest (a)]

Latest goal: Ole Gunnar Solskjaer, 90 mins
[v Nottingham Forest (a)]

Watched by: 273,080

Average attendance: 45,513

Chapter 8

March – Big Steps Forward

In the latter stages of the Champions League, competence is simply not enough and brilliance alone carries no guarantees of success. Sometimes it requires a poker-faced front or outright bravado to battle through. More pertinently, confidence and experience are the currency of choice in European competition, and by spring 1999 Alex Ferguson's men had more than paid their dues.

Two years previously, a host of missed chances resulted in a painful semi-final defeat to eventual European champions Borussia Dortmund; while a mere 12 months had passed since a humbling quarter-final exit (on away goals against little-fancied AS Monaco) had led to United's season, at home and abroad, falling apart.

Mircea Lucescu, the Romanian coach in temporary charge of the Reds' latest quarter-final opponents, Inter Milan, sought to expose any lingering uncertainty in the character of Ferguson's players. 'Italian football, tactically and psychologically, is far superior to the English game,' he boasted, while defender Francesco Colonnese and midfielder Diego Simeone wilfully dubbed Jaap

Stam and Ronny Johnsen 'too slow' to deal with the quick feet of Youri Djorkaeff, Roberto Baggio, Ivan Zamorano and, should he recover from injury, the 1997 and 1998 World Player of the Year, Ronaldo.

Ferguson, himself a canny proponent of managerial mind games, waived his invitation to Lucescu's psychological warfare, with good reason. A year previously against Monaco, there had been no Ryan Giggs or Roy Keane (due to injury), no Jaap Stam or Dwight Yorke (as neither had yet signed up at Old Trafford), while the younger members of his squad were still learning one of knockout football's oddest quirks: a fall comes before pride.

'This time I'll be able to pick the side I want,' said Ferguson as he readied himself for Inter's visit to Old Trafford. 'We're in the best shape we've been in and hopefully we've got all those silly goals we give away at bad times out of our system. We've learnt from previous experience in Europe.'

The *Nerazzurri* were renowned underachievers back home and hadn't won a major trophy in a decade. Nevertheless, club president Massimo Moratti had reached for the stars and aligned a galactic squad. They clearly fancied themselves as favourites in the tie, as did many observers, even though Italian football was teetering on the precipice of a millennial downturn. Still, Serie A sides had appeared in nine of the previous ten finals in Europe's premier competition and their country's clubs were rich with wily know-how. Their swagger wasn't without foundation, while United's continental credentials remained unproven, even though group stage draws with Barcelona and Bayern Munich pointed to the team's growing pedigree.

Ferguson may have neglected the pre-game war of words, but he couldn't resist one of his most famous barbs when Ronaldo, following discussions with Lucescu and his personal physiotherapist Nilton Petroni, confirmed his decision not to travel to the game in

Manchester, saying: 'I'm staying in Italy to carry on training, it's the best thing to do.'

'I'm not convinced,' Ferguson retorted. 'Italians are innovators of the smokescreen. When I order a plate of pasta, I look underneath the sauce just to make sure it's there! I want to know why Ronaldo played in a practice match on Friday for an hour. I think they want him to play and it is just up to him and his doctor. In fact, I will just wait until I see the teams.' Ronaldo didn't make the match, although the contest wasn't left wanting for entertainment or drama in his absence.

'The atmosphere was electric at Old Trafford that night,' recalls Andy Cole. Champions League knockout nights fire the synapses, but Peter Schmeichel acknowledges an added undercurrent: 'The atmosphere that night was because of Becks and Simeone.' David Beckham faced Inter's Argentina midfielder Diego Simeone for the first time since the infamous incident in the previous summer's World Cup, where the United and England midfielder had kicked out and earned a red card. He shouldered the blame for his country's tournament exit and there was no danger that he would not be up for it.

Beckham dealt with the occasion as he had done all season: producing a brilliant performance on the field. After six minutes, he teed up United's opener for Dwight Yorke and just before half time the pair combined for a second goal. While the Beckham–Yorke combination had proven deadly all season, their understanding had required some early-season fine-tuning.

'That year, I really worked it out with Becks,' reveals Yorke. 'When I was at Villa you would take a touch, have time and then make your run. When I first came to United, in the first couple of games and in training with Becks, I thought, "F***** hell, this guy just whips it in and docs so with such pace that if you go in too late then you are nowhere." I thought, "Right, this going here and coming back there isn't going to work." By the time I'd done that, the ball was whizzing past me. It just wasn't working. So I stopped going too far that way; I'd feint to go forward, then come back with pace and I kept doing that because I knew what Becks was going to do.

'He was such a brilliant deliverer of the ball and if you weren't on cue, it was going to fizz past you. That's all it was, working out in your head that you need to go a fraction early to get on the end of the cross. If you go a fraction late, then you are going to miss the boat. I had missed the boat on a few occasions earlier on in the season, so I thought I was just going to go to the middle and the near post, where he delivered most of his crosses. Becks would hit them flat with power, or low with power and it was a tap-in every time or it was on my head. I never thought of myself as a great header of the ball, but when you look at the amount of goals Becks put on my head I had no choice but to head the thing . . . and they kept hitting the net.'

Beckham's crosses to Yorke's head yielded a 2-0 half-time lead. United's attackers had caused maximum damage at one end, although the Reds needed a couple of heroes at the other end, too. Schmeichel produced one of his most iconic saves in the second half: a typically unorthodox starfish stop from Ivan Zamorano's diving header. 'That save stands out because, ultimately, if he scored there then the tie changes completely,' remarks Cole. On reflection, the importance of the save at that particular point in the tie, rather than its athleticism and anticipation, is what leads Schmeichel to rank it among his finest ever. 'People ask me: "What's your best save?" I always say that one because if we'd taken a two-one score to San Siro then that's a hell of a job waiting for you.'

Schmeichel may have been approaching the end of his United reign, but he was part of a squad that was nearing its collective peak; and dawning belief added to primed ability makes for a potent mix.

'To put the Inter game in context, you have to look at nineties foot-ball history, really. We had a hard time finding out how to play teams in Europe. When we played in the Premier League, we just played how we played naturally. We had to make changes in Europe. We had to be more cautious because away victories were very hard to come by. It was a long, long way off what we had in the Premiership, where we won everywhere. It was difficult, and in that game against Inter – because they had such a good team, because they would come to Old Trafford not being scared – they had a really good go at us. They had a very good side.

'It was important for us to keep it tight, make sure we took our chances without having to compromise our way of playing. So that game at Old Trafford was *the* big change for us. Don't forget we'd played Barcelona and Bayern Munich that year and we'd managed only two draws and conceded five goals – Brondby didn't have the quality of those other two teams – so that Inter game was very impor-tant. We still gave away chances, though, which sometimes you can't avoid if teams are good.'

Before the job was complete, the Dane saved well again from Nicola Ventola in the second half, and Henning Berg, who was out-standing all night, cleared Francesco Colonnese's shot off the line late on. United held on and there was a realisation – like breaking through a glass ceiling to see out onto the horizon – that the team could step beyond previous limitations in Europe. 'It was a great night, absolutely phenomenal,' adds Yorke. 'Those are the games that will live with you forever.'

The celebrations couldn't last too long as Chelsea were knocking on Old Trafford's door that weekend for an FA Cup quarter-final tie. Ferguson understandably had to make changes to his team – five in total – and among them Phil Neville was handed the tricky task of marking Gianfranco Zola. It was a role that the dutiful 22-year-old relished.

'It was great,' enthuses Phil. 'I used to love playing midfield but never got the opportunity, and then the gaffer asked me to man-mark Zola because he'd played really well against us in the league game. He always caused us problems and he was a world-class player, but I marked him and marked him well. It was a great learning experience for me and it was another string to my bow.'

Neville's nullifying man-marking job epitomised this as a contained contest, with a wealth of chances created by United but none taken. Instead, the two teams resumed battle at Stamford Bridge a few days later. The younger Neville sat on the bench this time, as Ferguson opted for a more front-footed approach, which quickly paid dividends. After four minutes, Yorke guided the ball past Ed de Goey following good build-up play from Cole and Beckham, the latter's recent new arrival prompting a special goal celebration.

'We said we would do the baby celebration whoever scored, because Brooklyn was born a couple of days before,' says Yorke. 'So it was a perfect scenario for us to do it. I remember that Becks really wanted to score that day, but we decided before we went out on the pitch that whoever scored we would do the celebration as a gesture to Becks and Victoria.'

Yorke had reason to celebrate again in the second half when Cole's hard work in regaining possession put him through on goal. Yorke's lob over de Goey looked like it was the most instinctive, natural thing for any striker to do. It wasn't; it was something special and highlighted Yorke's unburdened character as well as his undoubted class. Another example of Yorke's quirky temperament came in the 2-1 win over Newcastle at St James' Park – United's first league action of the month.

Cole twice found the net in a relatively routine but nevertheless important victory after a hard couple of weeks of cup football. Yet one man was missing from the post-match revelry. Ferguson recalled: 'The players were on a high, hugging each other and clapping, shaking hands and having a fantastic time in the dressing room. It was an important league win for us. I noticed Dwight wasn't there and when he finally strolled in I asked where he had been. "Oh, I've just been talking to someone," he replied. What a personality, a ray of sunshine and you'll never change his cool Caribbean temperament. He misses a chance and smiles at the crowd. He doesn't smile at me, though. He's not that laid back.'

Smiles were quickly replaced with focused faces for United's San Siro trip that week to take on Inter and the returning Ronaldo, who, while still lacking match fitness, possessed enough ability and an aura that could undo even the sturdiest defence. 'We'd scored twice in the first leg and kept it at two-nil,' reiterates Schmeichel. 'That gave us an incredible advantage, a cushion for the second game.' But Ronaldo's return was a concern. 'We had played Inter the season before in a pre-season game; it was Ronaldo's first appearance for them and just from that match, a pre-season game, we knew what could be waiting for us. Fortunately, the result at Old Trafford gave us that all-important advantage.'

Of all the star names in United's ranks, however, an unlikely hero stepped forward for another spell in the limelight. Henning Berg had turned in one of his finest displays in the first leg against the Italians and he was at it again. Berg was constantly alive to the danger of Inter's other attackers. One flying clearance in the first half took the ball right off Zamorano's head, who must have been plotting his celebration such was the seeming inevitability that he would convert Javier Zanetti's cross. Berg had other ideas.

'Most United fans, when thinking about my name, remember me for the two games against Inter,' he says. 'The fans remember the clearances, especially the one at home when it was a goal-line clearance, but also the one in the second leg. I had two good games against Inter. Even if I hadn't played the league games, Ferguson felt that I was more suited to play in Europe and in the big games. But those two games were where I did some decisive things for the team.

'In the away match, I had a really good game. I remember a fantastic cross from Zanetti and I knew Zamarano was behind me and he was a good header of the ball, so I had to stretch to reach it. It was a gamble, because the danger is that it's possible to score an own goal in that position, but I knew that if I didn't get anything on it then he would have scored. I just concentrated on touching it, getting something on it that would take the ball away from him, and I was lucky enough to do so. It was a good interception and I was surprised that I connected the way I did because it was the right connection and I'd really had to stretch for it.'

Ronaldo was replaced after an hour having shown only flashes of his brilliance. 'He wasn't at his very best, far from it, but he still wasn't bad,' adds Berg. 'I had played against him before for Norway against Brazil and I think that helped. We beat Brazil four-two in 1997, and Ronaldo and Romario were up front. You don't get much better than that! Me and Ronny [Johnsen] played together and it was a fantastic game, the best home game we had ever played. I played against him in 1998, too. So I knew what he was like and sometimes I found it easier to play against well-known players because I knew what they could do. You could study them and hopefully read them. Players you didn't know could do something you didn't expect. But it was a great feeling coming off the pitch that night.'

The final 30 minutes were no stroll in the park, though. Ronaldo's replacement, Ventola, scored within three minutes of his substitution, and it was from a rare Roy Keane error of judgement, as he let the ball bounce in the area, that was ruthlessly punished. 'It was the only mistake Roy made in the whole of that year,' says Schmeichel.

Keane explained afterwards: 'I tried to read the bounce and it went higher than I expected. I was disappointed, but I always felt we'd score.'

'We knew it was going to be difficult – the referee [Gilles Veissiere] was very good,' continues Schmeichel. 'We knew what the Italians could get up to with a bit of diving, but the ref was up for it and we were delighted with him. Our whole defence was great and the standard of defending throughout the team was really good – even Yorkie and Coley were closing down defenders. We always thought we'd get chances and fortunately Scholesy popped up near the end.

'Inter still had to score. They still had to commit players forward and with the players that we had, we knew that we only needed one or two chances and that would be it, and we got them. Of course we got them. Every game, we created chances.'

Substitute Paul Scholes capped off United's first triumph against Italian opposition over two legs in the 88th minute although, typical of the man, he eschews praise for his close-range finish through Gianluca Pagliuca's legs. 'Coley knocked it down and I totally mis-kicked it, to be honest with you,' recalls the scorer. 'It came off my shin and went straight down the middle of the goal. The keeper dived one way and it went in. Bottom middle, you don't save them! That said, it was a great feeling because it was a big night for us. Inter were a brilliant side, they really pinned us back and had chance after chance after chance, it seemed. They went ahead and they were a hell of a team, so we had a really difficult night. We managed to get that away goal and it virtually killed the game.'

Schmeichel concludes: 'It was a great game, what an atmosphere that night in Milan. Christ, fantastic game!'

With each new advance United made, the looming prospect of a potential Treble grew ever larger. The question was: could United actually pull it off? 'That's the million-dollar question, isn't it?' said Keane. 'We've used a few excuses over the last couple of years – injuries, suspensions, a lack of luck. Hopefully this year we can go all the way.'

As United moved into the Champions League last four – with Bayern Munich, Dynamo Kiev and Juventus also in the draw – and continued to look convincing in the FA Cup and the Premiership, with a month-concluding 3-1 win over Everton which Ferguson cited as being more important than any other match played in March, belief within the dressing room was becoming increasingly unbreakable.

Gary Neville perfectly sums up the mood in those heady days. 'From March onwards, every game felt like the best one you've ever played in. We played Inter Milan, Chelsea in the FA Cup, then Arsenal, Juventus in April. Against Chelsea, I remember driving forward and took a shot, and I thought, "Bloody hell, I feel good." Playing away at Inter, the ball came to me, the crowd were up for it, I controlled it and took it around Roberto Baggio and I remember thinking that everything felt right.

'I'd just turned twenty-four years old and was so full of confidence in that team. I never feared any opponent. Nobody was going to get the better of me, no matter who it was. That was that point in my career. There were other moments when I felt great – the mid-2000s with England and with United, when I became captain, that was a good time – but in that season everything felt spot on. I could go forward and back, everything felt really good. I think the whole team felt like that. Each player felt it individually and everybody came together at the perfect time.

'Inter Milan couldn't handle the speed and intensity of our play, of Keane, Beckham and Scholes and so many others. We weren't carrying anybody, there wasn't a character who didn't work as hard as the others. The defending from the front was brilliant, the midfield were the best attackers and defenders, and then you had two massive characters at the back in Jaap and Ronny. Me and Denis would fly forward and support at every opportunity, and we had a great goalkeeper too. Then you've got Nicky Butt in midfield, a warrior, and my brother Phil would come in for me or Denis.

'It wasn't the biggest squad, but the quality, effort, attitude and intensity was unbelievable. Teams couldn't live with Beckham's crosses or Giggs running at their defence. They couldn't live with the power of Keane and Scholes, they couldn't live with our running ability in the last fifteen minutes of games. People could stay with Beckham for seventy-five minutes, but he would wear them out and then whip in a cross. It was the same on the other side with Giggs, running at somebody fifty times, then the fifty-first run killed them. The runs from the midfield killed them in the latter stages. Teams couldn't stay with us, which is where we got so many of our late goals from. We attacked with eight men because the two at the back were one-on-one. As full-backs, me and Denis detached ourselves from the back four and flew forward.

'We had a great spirit between us as a group. Most of us had come through the ranks, but we had a good sprinkling of foreign players too – not too many, the right balance. Everybody was in a perfect moment.' With belief like that, who was going to stop United?

Wednesday 3 March 1999 | Champions League quarter-final, first leg | Old Trafford | Attendance: 54,430

MANCHESTER UNITED 2 Yorke 6, 45
INTERNAZIONALE 0

On critical European nights in seasons past, United were accused of naivety and lack of concentration, but with quality, belief and focus – and luck, too – Alex Ferguson's men were about to show the requisite ruthlessness for Champions League knockout football.

Inter boasted stellar names: Roberto Baggio, Ivan Zamorano, Youri Djorkaeff and Ronaldo, although the latter was left at home nursing his troublesome knees. Even without the Brazilian, and despite a creaking instability epitomised by the temporary contract of their boss, Mircea Lucescu, Inter would test United's confidence and conviction to progress. Steely-eyed skipper Roy Keane summed up the growing confidence: 'It's important we blank them out in defence, because we're capable of scoring against the world's best. We've proved that in Europe this season.'

'The emphasis against Inter was twofold,' Ferguson explained of his gameplan. 'We had to defend the centre of midfield and get our crosses in. We watched them several times and I felt sure we'd score from our centres.'

That tactic formed the basis of the careful preservation of Ryan Giggs's hamstrings throughout February, but it was on the opposite flank, from the majestic right boot of David Beckham, that Inter would be undone.

All eyes were on United's No.7 before a ball was even kicked. As the Champions League music blared out, he awaited a first reunion with Diego Simeone, the Argentina midfielder whose theatrical reaction to the Englishman's petulant kick at France '98 earned Beckham a red card and the unforgiving wrath of a nation. Simeone offered a firm handshake by way of reconciliation; Paul Scholes drily teased his team-mate, who simply smiled. And well he might, Beckham would soon savour a form of redemptive closure.

Beckham was a whippet out of the traps from the off, chasing anything that moved, especially Simeone. Yet it was his excellence on the ball, as much as his endeavours off it, that shone through. After six minutes United gleaned the perfect start when Yorke beat Aron Winter in the air, nodded the ball out to Beckham and then met his cross, unmarked, to beat Gianluca Pagliuca.

United's passing turned a tad sloppy as Inter probed forward, and it got feisty too as Scholes went in full-blooded outside Inter's area. In the ensuing scuffle, Zamorano was booked and when he returned to the front line, feeling aggrieved, he attempted to barge into Jaap Stam. The Dutchman stood still as a wall and gave the Chilean a stone-cold stare.

The Italians niggled and aggravated but United bit back, too. Keane, who was outstanding, was mostly controlled aggression, although a cheap booking was the groundwork for later heartache, as it was for Scholes, also yellow carded. In contrast to the *Nerazzurri*'s grizzled old pros, United possessed an air of untainted innocence – possession wasn't cynically or lovelessly hoarded, if anything it was too frequently surrendered as the Reds always sought to be positive.

Beckham's deliveries were certainly that. A glorious cross to Cole ten minutes before half time was toe-poked goalwards and Pagliuca turned the ball past the post with an outstretched boot. However, Inter had no answer to Beckham and Yorke. On the stroke of half time, Yorke attacked Beckham's near-post cross and again beat Pagliuca to make it 2-0.

Giggs could have added a third after the restart when he headed wide from Yorke's cross, but minutes later at the other end Peter Schmeichel produced a save of stunning improvisation and agility to keep out Zamorano's diving header. That chance apart, United blitzed Inter on the break early in the second half. But the Italians simply wouldn't give in. Simeone had the ball in the net, but the effort was disallowed and the night's pantomime villain crumpled to the floor – again – as the home crowd crowed.

In the dying embers of a night that crackled with intent and incident, Schmeichel saved from substitute Nicola Ventola, who escaped Henning Berg's attentions. The Norwegian redeemed himself in stoppage time after Schmeichel again denied Ventola and

Berg blocked Francesco Colonnese's rebound on the line. 'It's a great result,' beamed Ferguson, adding confidently: 'We'll score over there.'

Manchester United: Schmeichel; G.Neville, Johnsen (Berg h-t), Stam, Irwin; Beckham, Keane, Scholes (Butt 69), Giggs; Yorke, Cole
Subs not used: van der Gouw, P.Neville, Brown, Blomqvist, Solskjaer
Booked: Keane, Irwin, Scholes

Internazionale: Pagliuca; Galante, Bergomi, Colonnese; Zanetti, Cauet, Djorkaeff, Simeone, Winter; Baggio, Zamorano (Ventola 68)
Subs not used: Frey, West, Milanese, Gilberto, Pirlo, Ze Elias
Booked: Zamorano, Winter

Man of the Match: David Beckham
Classy on and off the field – Beckham even swapped shirts with his nemesis Simeone at the final whistle. 'David was magnificent,' said Ferguson. 'They couldn't handle him or Yorke.'

Sunday 7 March 1999 | FA Cup sixth round | Old Trafford | Attendance: 54,587

MANCHESTER UNITED 0
CHELSEA 0

After United's exertions on a highly charged Champions League night against Inter Milan four days previously, Ferguson sought freshness with five changes to his team for Chelsea's visit to Old Trafford in the FA Cup quarter-finals. As well as a reshuffle in personnel, there was also a rejigging of team formation. Phil Neville was tasked with tracking Chelsea's little Italian, Gianfranco Zola, a player of whom Ferguson made no secret of his admiration. With United's own feared front men, Andy Cole and Dwight Yorke, taking a breather on the bench, Ole Gunnar Solskjaer led the line alone.

Chelsea's Dutch goalkeeper Ed de Goey had endured a hellish afternoon at Stamford Bridge 14 months previously, when United won 5-3 in this competition's third round. 'United were five-nil up and cruising,' de Goey reluctantly recalled. 'That was one of the worst days of my career.'

Yet he was about to experience one of his better ones. The changes to United's starting line-up didn't diminish United's attacking creativity, as the Reds notched two dozen attempts on goal – Paul Scholes could have had at least a hat-trick, Gary Neville struck a post and David Beckham missed a very presentable scoring opportunity. But de Goey's goal still couldn't be breached.

United were initially aided by Paul Durkin's over-officious refereeing, as he dismissed Roberto Di Matteo before half time for a second bookable offence. He then evened things up by sending off Paul Scholes five minutes from time, prompting Ferguson to ask Durkin before the replay at Stamford Bridge if he had 'had a row with his wife before the last game. It was as if he was in a bad mood.' Gary Neville joined the debate, adding: 'It was a real shame that two players were sent off when it was never really dirty. There were no malicious tackles.'

There could be no disputing United's profligacy in front of goal. Otherwise there were positives to take from the game, like the display of 19-year-old Wes Brown, deputising for the injured Jaap Stam at centre-half, and Phil Neville's man-marking job on Zola, which resulted in the skilful Sardinian being replaced on 80 minutes. Still, Chelsea were the more satisfied team at the end. 'It's a great result for us,' said de Goey, clearly pleased with his clean sheet. 'The second half was difficult with ten on eleven, but now they have to come to us.'

United's task for the replay couldn't be clearer – a little fresher, the Reds would have to be much more incisive in the box.

Manchester United: Schmeichel; G.Neville, Brown, Berg, Irwin; Beckham, Keane, P.Neville (Yorke 73), Blomqvist (Sheringham 82), Scholes; Solskjaer (Cole 82)

Subs not used: van der Gouw, Curtis

Booked: Keane, P. Neville

Sent off: Scholes

Chelsea: de Goey; Ferrer, Lambourde, Desailly, Le Saux; Petrescu (Newton h-t), Di Matteo, Morris, Goldbaek; Zola (Myers 80), Flo (Forssell 61)

Subs not used: Hitchcock, Nicholls

Booked: Desailly

Sent off: Di Matteo

Man of the Match: Phil Neville

Zola was singled out as Chelsea's man to watch, so Phil followed him everywhere. The Italian playmaker was withdrawn before the end and young Neville had added another role to his broadening repertoire.

Wednesday 10 March 1999 | FA Cup sixth round replay | Stamford Bridge | Attendance: 33,075

CHELSEA 0
MANCHESTER UNITED 2 Yorke 4, 59

There was a perceptible feeling that Chelsea, having taken the tie back to Stamford Bridge, had given themselves the greater chance of clinching an FA Cup semi-final tie with Arsenal in April. However, while United's starting line-up at Old Trafford looked somewhat experimental – and subsequently lacking firepower – the Reds were now fully armed and came out all guns blazing in West

London. Gianluca Vialli's men didn't know what had hit them as Alex Ferguson's full-strength side played it perfectly on the counter-attack.

Dwight Yorke secured a 1-0 lead after just four minutes when Chelsea's French centre-back Frank Leboeuf failed to clear David Beckham's free-kick and Andy Cole nodded the ball down to his strike partner, who swivelled into shooting position and guided the ball past Ed de Goey. Yorke's baby-cradling celebrations heralded Beckham's latest delivery: baby Brooklyn.

Chelsea quickly found new life, too, and upped their intensity. Peter Schmeichel had to be sharp off his line to chase down the onrushing Gianfranco Zola and saved well with his legs, but Dennis Wise came closest to equalising when his unconvincing, but never-theless goal-bound, side-footed shot was inadvertently deflected wide by tumbling team-mate Tore Andre Flo.

United's ruthlessness had been evident already in 1999, so even despite Chelsea's 16 chances compared to the visitors' four, the Reds this time possessed an essential cutting edge. Yorke's 25th goal of the season at the start of the first half was followed by his 26th early in the second.

Cole again fed on scraps to tee-up his colleague as he dispossessed a dithering Marcel Desailly with a sliding challenge, poking the ball into Yorke's path. The first-time finish was truly special; Yorke barely broke stride before clipping an audacious outside-of-the-boot lob – a shot that only a striker high on confidence would even attempt – over a helpless de Goey. 'Dwight certainly is a character,' said his manager. 'He's some man. He's been fantastic for the place. He's brightened it up. He is also the premier striker in the country at the moment. Yorke has a gift; he can beat a man, he has pace, is good in the air and he is as brave and strong as a bull.'

His counterpart at Chelsea, Zola, added graciously: 'He's great. I'd put him in the "greatest" category. He's doing very well this season and has completed his game. Above all, he's in complete symphony with his team. That makes him very effective.'

Chelsea: de Goey; Lambourde, Leboeuf (Myers h-t), Desailly, Le Saux; Wise, Di Matteo, Morris (Goldbaek 72), Babayaro; Zola, Flo (Forssell 72)
Subs not used: Hitchcock, Newton
Booked: Desailly

Manchester United: Schmeichel; G.Neville, Berg, Stam, Irwin; Beckham, Keane, Scholes, Giggs (Blomqvist 76); Yorke (Solskjaer 85), Cole (P.Neville 71)
Subs not used: van der Gouw, Brown
Booked: Yorke

Man of the Match: Dwight Yorke
The Tobagan's second goal summed up his breezy, infectious attitude; confidence coursing through him, he took on an outrageous shot seemingly certain of its outcome and it spectacularly paid off.

Saturday 13 March 1999 | Premiership | St James' Park | Attendance: 36,776

NEWCASTLE UNITED 1 Solano 16
MANCHESTER UNITED 2 Cole 25, 51

While Dwight Yorke was busy grabbing headlines, Andy Cole hadn't scored in a month when he pitched up at St James' Park, his former stomping ground and a stadium in which he scored 47 goals in 45 matches as a Newcastle player. Having already netted there for United, he got back to scoring ways and took his Tyneside tally to half-a-century with a clinical brace.

Newcastle started brightest and Nolberto Solano gave the home side the lead on 16 minutes when he fired an unstoppable free-kick in off Peter Schmeichel's post. Alex Ferguson was preparing to leave his vantage point in the directors' box for a more favourable position from which to lambast his players' lackadaisical return to league action after two weeks on cup duties.

In the end, however, he didn't need to alter his position; Cole's movement did all the damage. On 25 minutes, Henning Berg flicked on Gary Neville's long throw and Yorke attempted an acrobatic volley. His shot was blocked and Cole pounced inside the six-yard box to level the scores.

Newcastle applied pressure but with little penetration and their fans' initial fervour soon dissipated. The United boss later described an agitated Alan Shearer's display as 'disappointing', the rumoured differences between star player and manager, Ruud Gullit, self-evident and self-destructive. United still had a job to do, and the team was led by its ubiquitous captain, Roy Keane, who made numerous key interceptions and tackles while tapping out a metronomic passing rhythm to bring the Reds back into control.

It was needed. Despite Newcastle's mid-table league position, they boasted just one defeat in 11 games and the task was made more difficult for United when Schmeichel had to be replaced at half time by Raimond van der Gouw. The press were told the Dane had flu, but he had strained his back in the warm-up. Ferguson didn't want Inter targeting any perceived weakness in the Champions League quarter-final second leg four days later.

With the European match in mind, Ryan Giggs was replaced on 74 minutes, only after teeing up Cole's second. Giggs controlled David Beckham's sweeping cross-field pass and curled his centre around Warren Barton. Shay Given was drawn to the ball like a moth to a flame and Cole nipped in first to poke his shot into the net.

Victory maintained a four-point lead at the Premiership's summit, and although Arsenal's 2-0 win at Everton kept them clinging onto United's coattails, it was offset by a third red card of the season for Emmanuel Petit and a subsequent three-match ban.

Newcastle United: Given; Barton (Maric 84), Charvet, Dabizas, Domi; Solano, Hamann, Speed, Georgiadis (Lee h-t); Ketsbaia (Saha 62), Shearer
Subs not used: Harper, Griffin
Booked: Georgiadis

Manchester United: Schmeichel (van der Gouw h-t); G.Neville, Berg, Stam, Irwin; Beckham, Keane, Scholes (P.Neville 87), Giggs (Johnsen 74); Yorke, Cole
Subs not used: Blomqvist, Solskjaer
Booked: Irwin

Man of the Match: Andy Cole
Cole's two-goal show edged Keane's excellent input and continued his good record against Newcastle. 'Andy was lightning today,' his boss enthused. 'He's getting better all the time. It's vital that he and Dwight team up so well.'

Wednesday 17 March 1999 | Champions League quarter-final, second leg | San Siro | Attendance: 79,528

INTERNAZIONALE 1 Ventola 63
MANCHESTER UNITED 1 Scholes 88

United had never beaten Italian opposition over two legs, never won on Italian soil and only Norman Whiteside had scored for the Reds in six contests in the country shaped like a boot. That doesn't fully contextualise the task facing United at a hostile Stadio Giuseppe Meazza; referee Gilles Veissiere had to contend with *Nerazzurri* theatrics, while Nicola Ventola's goal on 63 minutes threatened Alex Ferguson's side's 2-0 first-leg lead.

This was a performance in which United as a team came of age. Still, gratitude was due to individual contributions from Peter Schmeichel, Jaap Stam and Henning Berg, the latter once again standing tall against Inter, who had Brazilian star Ronaldo back from injury. Even lacking his scything sharpness due to knee problems, Ronaldo required close attention.

So too did the Italians' play-acting, although when Ivan Zamorano tumbled in the area in the first half after toeing the ball away from Schmeichel, Inter could have had a penalty. Zamorano then legitimately tested the Dane with a fierce shot from 12 yards, before the Chilean seemed destined to head his side in front when Javier Zanetti flighted an inviting cross to the far post. Fortunately, Berg's flying interception took the ball off Zamorano's head. Moments later, Zanetti struck a post with a swerving shot that had Schmeichel beaten.

Like the frame of the goal, United could have been rattled, but Ferguson counselled at half time: 'We've done well, now concentration is vital.' His prescience for potential danger was proven when Roberto Baggio played in Ronaldo after the restart and Schmeichel needed a strong right hand to keep him out. Frustrated, Ronaldo turned to darker arts as he beat Gary Neville with a stepover and crashed to the deck in the box. Lesser referees might have succumbed; Veissiere was having none of it.

Eventually Inter's pressure told after an hour, when Benoit Cauet drifted infield and lofted a pass to substitute Ventola. Roy Keane misjudged its bounce and Ventola pounced to beat Schmeichel. Now United's resolve would really be tested. Inter boss Mircea Lucescu attacked, replacing 35-year-old sweeper Giuseppe Bergomi with winger Francesco Moriero. United's substitutions were smarter still. Paul Scholes replaced Johnsen, selected in midfield to halt Ronaldo dropping deep, while Giggs was swapped for Phil Neville to stop Zanetti's marauding runs.

Ze Elias wasted a glorious late chance before Scholes killed the tie with two minutes left. Francesco Colonnese was drawn out of position and Dwight Yorke teed up Gary Neville, whose high cross was headed down by Cole for the unmarked Scholes to beat Pagliuca.

Red flares fumed amid the fervour of United's travelling support as Scholes celebrated and the home supporters streamed out of the stadium. Afterwards, Lucescu, who quit his job four days later, grumbled: 'They were clear penalties.' Ferguson countered: 'The referee was fantastic and called everything correctly.'

Internazionale: Pagliuca; Zanetti, Colonnese, Bergomi (Moriero 69), West, Silvestre; Cauet, Simeone (Ze Elias 32); Baggio, Ronaldo (Ventola 60), Zamorano
Subs not used: Frey, Galante, Winter, Djorkaeff
Booked: Bergomi, Ze Elias, Silvestre, Colonnese

Manchester United: Schmeichel; G.Neville, Stam, Berg, Irwin; Beckham, Keane, Johnsen (Scholes 77), Giggs (P.Neville 82); Yorke, Cole
Subs not used: van der Gouw, Brown, Blomqvist, Sheringham, Solskjaer
Booked: Johnsen, P.Neville

Man of the Match: Henning Berg
The Norwegian once again kept the Italians at bay and few moments summed up Berg's commitment to the cause more than his flying clearance to prevent Zamorano scoring.

Saturday 21 March 1999 | Premiership | Old Trafford |
Attendance: 55,182

MANCHESTER UNITED 3 Solskjaer 55, G.Neville 64, Beckham 67
EVERTON 1 Hutchison 81

With struggling Everton's massed ranks behind the ball, and the minds and legs of the men in red weary from midweek European exertions, the first half of this encounter was both predictably dire and instantly forgettable. That said, half of the Reds' dropped league points in 1998-99 had come in a post-European daze, so it was vital Alex Ferguson's men mustered victory at a key stage of the run-in before a two-week international hiatus.

Urgency was lacking in a flavourless first half, Peter Schmeichel saving Marco Materazzi's free-kick in the best of the chances, and it was only after the break that United emerged refocused. And how.

The Reds wrapped up all three points with three goals in a 12-minute second-half blitz. Ole Gunnar Solskjaer got the scoring underway when Gary Neville fizzed in a pass and the Norwegian followed a rapid-fire exchange with Dwight Yorke by lashing a shot past Everton keeper and fellow countryman Thomas Myhre.

For United's second, Yorke dropped a shoulder to receive Neville's pass and beat his man, then subtly disguised his return ball for the Reds' right-back on the overlap. Neville timed his run and shot perfectly, as he allowed Myhre to commit himself and at the last moment coolly slipped the ball under the keeper from a tight angle. It was Neville's first goal in almost two years. It showed in his celebrations.

United's quick-fire treble was completed with another drought-ending effort, this time from David Beckham. The Reds' No.7 hadn't scored since the 5-0 Champions League win over Brondby on 4 November – a dry spell spanning 25 appearances. This 25-yard free-kick was vintage Beckham, and although Myhre got a hand to the ball he stood little chance of keeping it out. Don Hutchison's consolation strike came with ten minutes left.

Above Champions League and FA Cup quarter-final wins over Inter Milan and Chelsea, Ferguson highlighted this fixture as the best barometer of United's Treble chances. March boasted more noteworthy results and April promised even greater highs, but reaching 19 matches unbeaten before an international break allowed the Reds' boss to admire just how far his team had come, and to ponder how far they could yet go.

'We're looking very powerful,' he said after beating Everton and heaping more misery on his friend and opposite number Walter Smith. 'We've come through six crucial games in eighteen days and the players have excelled. They're approaching games in the right way, focused on winning every game, and the evidence of how they are going about it is very encouraging.'

Manchester United: Schmeichel; G.Neville, Berg, Stam, P.Neville; Beckham (Greening 71), Johnsen, Butt, Solskjaer (Curtis 90); Yorke, Cole (Sheringham 71)
Subs not used: van der Gouw, Brown

Everton: Myhre; Weir, Short, Materazzi, Unsworth, Ball; O'Kane (Jeffers 61), Hutchison, Grant (Degn 68), Dacourt; Bakayoko (Cadamarteri 5)
Subs not used: Simonsen, Watson
Booked: Weir, Hutchison, Dacourt

Man of the Match: Gary Neville
United's No.2 had regularly proven his ability as an ultra-reliable defender, but here his probing forward passes – and, of course, that rare goal – highlighted what a useful attacking outlet he could be for the team.

March in statistics

Premiership table (21 March 1999)

	P	W	D	L	F	A	GD	Pts
Manchester United	**30**	**18**	**9**	**3**	**68**	**31**	**+37**	**63**
Arsenal	30	16	11	3	42	13	+29	59
Chelsea	29	15	11	3	44	23	+21	56
Leeds United	30	15	9	6	49	27	+22	54
West Ham United	30	13	7	10	34	39	-5	46
Aston Villa	30	12	8	10	39	37	+2	44
Derby County	30	11	11	8	32	32	0	44
Wimbledon	30	10	10	10	34	44	-10	40
Liverpool	28	11	6	11	52	37	+15	39
Tottenham Hotspur	29	9	12	8	34	34	0	39
Middlesbrough	29	9	12	8	39	40	-1	39
Newcastle United	30	10	8	12	38	42	-3	38
Sheffield Wed	30	10	5	15	35	33	+2	35
Leicester City	28	8	10	10	28	37	-9	34
Coventry City	30	8	7	15	31	42	-11	31
Everton	30	7	10	13	23	35	-12	31
Blackburn Rovers	30	7	9	14	32	42	-10	30
Southampton	30	8	5	17	28	56	-28	29
Charlton Athletic	29	6	10	13	33	40	-7	28
Nottingham Forest	30	4	8	18	27	59	-32	20

March form (all competitions): WDWWDW

Goals scored: 10   **Goals conceded:** 3

Most appearances: Peter Schmeichel, Gary Neville 6 each (540 mins)

Players used: 21

THE IMPOSSIBLE TREBLE

Most goals: Dwight Yorke 4

Most assists: Cole 3

Different goalscorers: 6

Quickest goal: Dwight Yorke, 4 mins [v Chelsea (a)]

Latest goal: Paul Scholes, 88 mins [v Inter Milan (a)]

Watched by: 313,578

Average attendance: 52,263

Chapter 9

April – Crossing the Rubicon

Manchester United, captured in all its splendour in April 1999, proved either that fate is capable of plotting the most peculiar path, or that destiny is not pre-determined at all, but rather grasped with both hands. Whether earthly or divine, this thrill-seeking month featured two of the greatest and most unforgettable performances in the club's history, and those games created a groundswell of momentum toward greater glory.

Alex Ferguson's men took so many knocks and body blows along the way that all the previous hard work and the talk of a historic Treble appeared as though it could so easily come tumbling down. The Reds had to face up to the daunting dominance of Juventus at Old Trafford in the Champions League semi-final first leg, when they were pitted against the otherworldly skills of Edgar Davids and Zinedine Zidane, as well as seeing Arsenal and Dennis Bergkamp on the brink of an FA Cup final place at the end of a monumental bout at Villa Park.

United's ability to push their fans to the precipice only to haul them back at the last has rarely been more evident. And in such scenarios, confidence feeds momentum and momentum fuels confidence in what amounts to a virtuous cycle.

The month started with a less-than-inspiring 1-1 draw at Selhurst Park against Wimbledon – in fact, United drew after 90 minutes in five of seven matches in April – and within a matter of days, Arsène Wenger's rallying Gunners had edged to within a point of the league-leading Reds. Regardless of that, the title race would have to be put on the backburner for two full weeks as United tackled what became four epic semi-final ties.

The Champions League last-four summit with Carlo Ancelotti's Juventus side carried a great level of intrigue, as United had for so long looked enviously upon the Italians' European eminence. Despite this, Ferguson's midfield four of David Beckham, Roy Keane, Paul Scholes and Ryan Giggs had been touted by many as the finest in Europe, which didn't go down well in Turin, of course, where Davids, the forthright fulcrum of the Juventus midfield, had teamed up with World Player of the Year Zidane, Didier Deschamps, Antonio Conte and Angelo Di Livio.

United went on the front foot at Old Trafford in an attempt to capitalise on home advantage in the first leg, yet Juve were smarter, calmer, less eager, wilier – and it showed. The *Bianconeri* swarmed all over the hosts in a rabid first-half display and, through Conte, went in 1-0 up at half time scratching their heads as to how their lead was still so slender. At times it was akin to a cat playing with its prey. United's eagerness was exposed, though nowhere near as ruthlessly as Juventus would have liked. So, even when the Reds fought back with Ryan Giggs's stoppage-time goal, Juventus had seen enough to feel confident of progress.

Davids told reporters in Italy: 'They are supposed to have the best midfield in Europe. Well, I didn't see too much of them at Old Trafford. We were like a steam train, overrunning them. I felt sick when Giggs equalised, even though he is a fantastic player. We would have settled for a one-one draw beforehand, but the longer I was out there, looking at opponents who had been described as such big stars, the more I realised just what was in it for us. I have no fears of them any more. I want to get at them again.'

'They were very sure of themselves – probably too sure of themselves,' added Conte, the goalscorer. 'They thought they would win, perhaps rather easily, but I think they understand now who is the better side. Juventus are not fading giants.'

A subtle but telling tactical switch at half time had rescued United, as Ferguson gave Beckham a narrower brief to bulk up the midfield, while Giggs, the Reds' surest threat in the second 45 minutes, attacked from a much deeper starting position.

The pitfalls of attacking too readily had been discussed beforehand, according to chief scout Mick Brown. 'Sometimes, being Manchester United, you need to be a bit defensive,' he says. 'When you discussed the opposition we were playing against, you'd say: "Listen, we can't be gung-ho because they're set up for counter-attacking," and this was especially the case against the Italian teams.

'You'd put in maybe four or five reports and that was a common theme. When you went back and put your reports in and had conversations about it, the coaches have got to factor in a league match and another cup game either side of the match, so they can't be as focused on the points you're making. Then it comes down to two days before the game, players need rest, need recovery and they can't be doing too much on the training ground prior to these big games, and the big games were coming thick and fast.'

United's plans were also hampered by the loss of Henning Berg just before half time – a big miss considering how well he had performed against Inter Milan in the previous round. 'It was at a corner and a really innocent thing, just jumping up with a player to defend, but when I landed I tweaked my knee and that was it,' says the Norwegian. 'I felt it just before half time and thought, "Whoops, this is painful." I played on until half time, but I went in and it was really sore. I tried to walk, but there was no chance and I couldn't play on.'

A scan revealed medial ligament damage and a rueful Berg did not play again that season. 'It wasn't the best time to get injured with those games coming up,' he admits. 'I wouldn't have played in all of them, but maybe a few of the semi-finals and finals. You never know, we had a few players out for the Champions League final and if my form was good, I probably would have played.'

There was little time for reflection or introspection on United's part, however, and Giggs's late intervention to salvage a draw offered more than a glimmer of hope in the tie. 'I have a gut feeling we're going to win,' said Ferguson. 'I feel the nature of our club is that they torture you so much, the only relief you can get is from winning. I hope I am right. It will be a great game in Turin and the feeling I have got is that we can go through to the final.'

Just four days later, United were at Villa Park for an FA Cup semi-final with Arsenal, with both sides chasing a domestic Double – the Gunners eyeing a double Double, having done it the season before. Keane's disallowed effort in the first half enraged United's fans, as one goal would surely separate two evenly matched teams, and referee David Elleray took a verbal battering afterwards. Even when Nelson Vivas was sent off for elbowing Nicky Butt in extra time, the two rivals could not be separated.

'It was a battle,' recalls Denis Irwin. 'I don't think the first game with Arsenal was bad, though. There was a lot at stake and they were trying to win the Double. They were a really good side, with a mixture of strength, pace and skill. They had Patrick Vieira, Emmanuel Petit, Nicolas Anelka and Dennis Bergkamp, who had great ability. Overmars and Parlour were good wide players and we know all about the lads at the back and the goalkeeper. So it was a big game with a lot riding on it.'

Peter Schmeichel adds: 'We had the disallowed goal in the first game and we were playing eleven against ten for quite a bit of that game. But if you look back, we had chances and they had chances, it was end-to-end stuff and it was still a nil-nil game. It speaks volumes about the quality of those two teams.'

The replay, however, was played at such a frenetic pace and with such abandon that a goalless draw simply wasn't an option. 'I still say to this day that the FA Cup semi-final replay was the best game of football I've played in. Ever,' says Phil Neville. 'People say about the finals, the international games I've played in, but that semi-final replay was incredible. It's hard to describe. I don't think there was anything to choose between the two teams, it was like a boxing match with two teams just punching the absolute hell out of each other. There was no let-up, and we were unbelievable that night, we were absolutely unbelievable.

'I gave away a penalty . . . but forget the penalty! It was just the most amazing game. They had Bergkamp, Anelka, Adams, Keown, Petit, Vieira, Overmars – a great team. Our manager made four changes that night and I was one of them. He left Coley, Yorke, Denis and Giggsy out and our freshness was telling. We came out of the traps and just battered them. Becks scored for us in the first half with a great strike, then they came back and we were under the cosh in the second half when Keano got sent off.'

Keane was dismissed for a second yellow card after fouling Marc Overmars five minutes after Bergkamp struck Arsenal's deflected equaliser, and it appeared that the tide had turned completely in the Gunners' favour when in stoppage time Phil Neville committed a tired foul on Ray Parlour to concede a penalty. The match – and, not to overstate the point, United's season, too – was at Bergkamp's mercy from 12 yards. But he had the towering figure of Schmeichel to beat.

'Honestly, and this is the truth, when Phil committed the foul, normally you'd be, "F***** hell!" but in my mind we had ten or twelve minutes left. I kept thinking, "If he scores, we've got time. We've got time, and we've been really good in that part of every game, particularly if we've been behind. Something happens to us. We can chase, and we can get a goal." And I was surprised, really, really surprised, when the game ended shortly after that. I was pleased and glad that I didn't know how long was really left.

'I don't know if he was put off by facing me, but if he was then it worked! I didn't even look at him. I didn't second-guess what he was going to try to do, I just made my mind up: "I'm going to do this, and I'm going to stick to it." So as soon as he hit the ball I knew I was going to dive to my left. Before he'd run up, I'd absolutely decided. With penalties it's a lottery for goalkeepers because you have no control. The ref blows the whistle, but the penalty taker actually makes the decision about when to start, when to hit the ball, where to hit the ball – so you've got no control. A guess is really good because you've made up your mind, you're going to cover most of that side and, fortunately for me, he put it there ... Fortunately for all of us he put it there.'

Schmeichel's recollections of that moment are somewhat self-effacing: he insists Bergkamp missed the penalty, rather than him saving it. Yet to everyone else it was an intervention as crucial to the galvanising effect this game would have on United's season as the match-winning moment that followed. With the clock counting 109 minutes of ceaseless slogging it out, a moment became etched indelibly in United folklore, which is where Phil Neville picks up the story. 'The ball got played square by Vieira and Giggsy cut it out. He hadn't started the game, so he was quite fresh. I was at left-back at the time and I was so tired, I just couldn't get on the overlap, so I was saying: "Go on, just run." I was shouting: "Keep going, keep going!" And it was like slow motion. Honestly, he just ghosted past Vieira, Dixon,

Roy Keane leads his troops into battle against a Juventus side aiming to reach their fourth consecutive Champions League final.

Joy unconfined grips the away dressing room at the Stadio delle Alpi, after the Reds roar back from two goals down to win 3-2 and reach May's final.

Alex Ferguson sets the champagne corks popping as the Reds fly home from Turin with three trophies moving into sharp focus.

Denis Irwin scores at Anfield, but his – and United's – evening worsens when he is sent off and Liverpool snatch a 2-2 draw to dent the Reds' title hopes.

A frustrating evening at Blackburn yields a goalless draw, but a priceless one-point advantage in the title race going into the final game of the league season.

In his final league appearance for the Reds, Peter Schmeichel leads the celebrations at the start of an incredible eleven-day spell for the club.

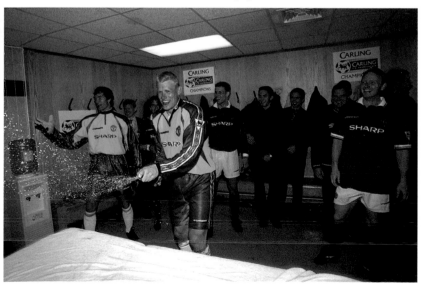

CARLING
CHAMPIONS 1998-99

CARLING
CHAMPIONS 19

That's two. Paul Scholes
is mobbed after putting
United 2-0 up against
Newcastle in the
FA Cup final and sealing
a domestic Double.

One down, two to go, as goals from David Beckham and Andy Cole give the Reds yet another comeback victory over Spurs to clinch the Premier League title at Old Trafford.

The star of the show at Wembley, however, is Teddy Sheringham, who bags a goal and an assist in a superb outing as an early replacement for the injured Roy Keane.

After 90 minutes of frustration, United finally make the breakthrough against Bayern Munich as Sheringham equalises from close range in the first minute of injury time.

In the third minute of injury-time, the Reds have flipped the Champions League final on its head. Goalscorer Ole Gunnar Solskjaer slides into club folklore.

United are kings of Europe again and, after an epic, undulating season of 63 games, they have won all three major competitions.

The Reds return home to an unforgettable welcome, as hundreds of thousands of supporters line the streets of Manchester to salute Alex Ferguson's history-makers.

The Impossible Treble: the FA Cup, the European Cup and the Premier League trophy.

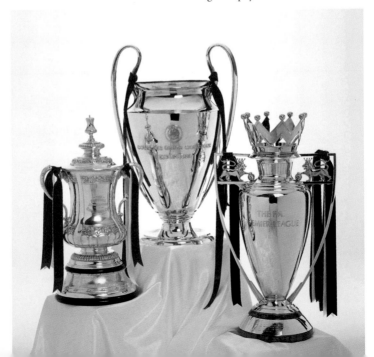

Keown, Adams, then bang, top corner and I went mad. I was the first one there on the scene.'

'I would say it's the greatest goal scored by a team-mate that I've played with,' continues Schmeichel. 'I've never experienced being part of a team and someone coming up with a goal like that. He actually beat Lee Dixon twice. I've worked with Lee and I play a lot of golf with Lee, and he still talks about that: "He beat me f***** twice!" It was great going all the way through, but he still had to beat one of the greatest goalkeepers the game has ever seen, from a very, very tight angle, and he did it.

'I think the only thing about the goal was the celebration; nobody wants to see that again! I think Giggsy wanted them to delete the footage once he watched it back. He was embarrassed, I think. But no, it was a good celebration; everything about the goal was brilliant. It was such a fitting end to those games and the battle that we had with Arsenal.

'I'm sure that, looking at it retrospectively, had we lost that game in a similar manner, we'd have accepted that it took something special like that to win it. It was a moment of genius. It's something you see very, very rarely in football. Those little moments of genius, when you create them, it's so much greater. But even when it hits you, you have to appreciate that this was just something out of this world, and for that game to end in that way was so fitting.'

Schmeichel makes a salient point about how easily momentum could have shifted in Arsenal's favour. 'I have to say, Arsenal had a team as good as ours. The semi-finals, for me, that is the point where everything turned our way. We came through them. And when you win a game with a goal like that, it's not something you carry in your conscious mind; your subconscious has that. You don't think about it, but it's there. You win a game like that, which is so fierce, you've tried to settle it twice and then you win it that way. It makes you feel invincible.'

The belief swirling through United's sails in the aftermath of the win at Villa Park propelled the team forward at speed. 'I've played in some great games, but that one had everything that was perfect about football,' reiterates Phil Neville. 'It was probably the night we won the Treble in many ways, because if they'd won then they'd have won the Double. We won, we went on and it was the momentum from that game that saw us through the rest of the season. It was then that we thought: "Something special's happening here."'

The celebrations at the final whistle are still spoken about now among supporters – they were even briefly mentioned that week in Parliament – as a sea of Reds poured onto the Villa Park pitch. For Schmeichel, it was a moment of trepidation as well as exhilaration.

'I have to say, it's a bit uncomfortable, because how do you know they're all United fans?' he says. 'We've seen examples of people running on the pitch where players are getting hurt and injured. So even though you're happy and you want to celebrate – you really want to celebrate with your fans – it frightens all of us, so all you're thinking about is getting off the pitch, getting to the dressing room and getting to safety. I'm not criticising our fans because it was some win. Our fans have been well behaved for so many decades, and for them to breach the code of conduct if you like, for that one game . . . Fine, because that was a good reason.'

How do you follow an act like that? Well, Ferguson kept largely the same starting line-up for the league match against Sheffield Wednesday, which followed quickly in the slipstream of that semi-final, ensuring that his top guns were fresh for the trip to Turin four days later. A trouble-free 3-0 victory, with goals from Ole Gunnar Solskjaer, Teddy Sheringham and Scholes, was a welcome pause for breath.

After the high of beating Arsenal, and given the way United had fought back against Juventus in the second half at Old Trafford, Andy Cole admits confidence was high ahead of the second leg against

Juventus. 'After that, we just went there and didn't fear them,' he says. 'We knew how good a team they were, we knew how tough it would be, but we didn't fear them. Then we went two-nil down inside eleven minutes.'

Pippo Inzaghi's quickfire brace put United ominously behind, 3-1 on aggregate. 'Nobody went to Juventus and got anything at all,' recalls Irwin. 'They had a marvellous team, with Zidane pulling the strings in midfield and Inzaghi up front. But anyone in our team that season will tell you there was a great belief that we could score goals. We had a great trust in each other and great camaraderie. We would always dig in, and we did.'

'Even going two-nil down,' explains Cole, 'we didn't really change the way we played. It was just a case of getting up, dusting yourself down and grafting: "Let's work our arses off," "Let's try to get a goal before half time." It took us going two goals down to liven up.'

That's when Keane stepped forward to deliver one of his most talismanic displays in a United shirt, grabbing the game by the scruff of the neck and scoring a glancing header after 24 minutes from Beckham's corner. 'Roy was unbelievable,' says Scholes. 'He scored that great goal to get us back in the game after we'd gone two-nil down in eleven minutes. Before that I just thought: "We've got absolutely no chance here," and then Roy got the header that got us back into the game.'

'When Roy got the goal, it really galvanised us,' continues Cole. 'For some reason, not long after that, I ended up on the right wing. They tried to head it clear and I took a touch and bent a cross in to Yorkie. It was a Becks-style delivery. Bang! It was two-two after half an hour.'

'At that point,' says Irwin, 'I remember thinking, "There's still a long way to go here." Two years prior to that, losing to Dortmund had been such a bad feeling, so you knew nothing was certain; 1997 hurt because we had been building and we thought that was a good chance for us, but it didn't materialise. So I knew that beating Juventus would be huge, and we were so determined to see it out.'

Irwin nearly clinched United's place in the final himself when he attacked down the left, cut inside and unleashed a shot that cannoned off the post, before finding the side-netting with his follow-up. 'I don't know what I was doing up there in the first place,' he says. 'It was two-two at the time so I shouldn't have been anywhere near there!'

Ironically, Irwin says, it had been United's tactical discipline and preparation that contributed to the turnaround in the team's fortunes that night. 'We played very well, particularly in the second half. We'd done our homework and the manager and Steve [McClaren] were ready. We knew where they were strong. We knew we could score goals, but we weren't very good at keeping clean sheets that year – it was the nature of how we played.

'In fact, the following year, we got beaten three-two by Real Madrid at home and the manager changed his tactics after that. He tightened it up when we travelled away from home because we couldn't keep getting away with it in Europe. But we did that season, we rode our luck at times and we knew we could score goals. The belief in the team and our camaraderie gave us a great chance. In the second half, we attacked them even at two-two when there was a chance of them stealing a goal, particularly with the likes of Zidane and Inzaghi. We won three-two in the end, and it was a great feeling when Coley stuck it in – it was relief, I know that.'

Cole, though, denies that his goal was influential at all. 'People say, "Oh your goal was so important," but I always say we were going through on away goals anyway,' he opines. 'My goal wasn't that important. When I went through on goal, I had nothing to think about because the referee should have given a penalty, but he didn't. I was just following in and I put it in the back of the net. People ask if I knew how close it was, but I knew nothing because I thought the referee was going to give a penalty anyway. When it went into the back of the net, though, we were ecstatic because we knew we were through.

'But even to this day, I don't think my goal was important. It was the away goals; we'd done it at two-two. We'd done it through our camaraderie and team spirit. We were in some really adverse positions that season. We went down to ten men quite a few times, but it made no difference. We always thought we could work it out. That's how we were as a team.'

That togetherness made the hit of losing Keane and Scholes, both booked in Turin and ruled out of the final, all the more difficult to accept. Scholes is typically forthright about the situation. 'It was a tackle where I think I got the ball. I just remember Deschamps making one of these loud noises that they do and I think that probably influenced the referee and that was that. I knew I was going to miss the final, but it didn't matter, you just had to carry on playing the game. It was a big, important game. That's just the way it goes.'

Gary Neville says the absence of Keane and Scholes from the Champions League final 'was a blight after Juventus'. He continues: 'There was a tempered enthusiasm after that, because we all knew that they couldn't play in the final. But it has happened to players before and there is always somebody every year. You go back to Milan in 1994 against Barcelona when Franco Baresi and Alessandro Costacurta were suspended. They weren't the first and they won't be the last. But it was a big thing for them and for us because we were in it together.'

United completed a testing month with a typically trying 11.30am Sunday morning kick-off at Leeds, with Cole rescuing an important point after Jimmy Floyd Hasselbaink found the net for the hosts. And even while temporarily slipping into second place in the league table, United had already set a course to achieving something special. The games against Juventus and, in particular, the replay win over Arsenal, revealed something to the players that, while nothing was yet won, it was there to be won.

'You only have to look at the games that came after the Arsenal match,' concludes Schmeichel. 'It just put something in our minds that if we do our job, if we all individually do what we're asked to do, and collectively we play with the same enthusiasm, the same conviction in our game, and we go out there and enjoy it, then nobody will beat us. That was the attitude. It was one of those teams you never forget playing in. You never, ever forget. Every position was great. You might argue we didn't have the best in the world in every position, but we had something that made that team the best in the world at that time.'

Saturday 3 April 1999 | Premiership | Selhurst Park | Attendance: 26,121

WIMBLEDON 1 Euell 5
MANCHESTER UNITED 1 Beckham 44

With all the potential rewards and indubitable excitement promised by April's jam-packed fixture schedule, a visit to Selhurst Park to take on Wimbledon presented the humblest beginning to an epochal month for Treble-chasing United.

It certainly wasn't an ideal start to the match, either, when Gary Neville's misjudged headed pass to Peter Schmeichel after five minutes allowed Jason Euell to put the Dons in front. United were hauled level by David Beckham's close-range volley before half time, but second-half chances were spurned when, with semi-finals in the offing against Juventus in the Champions League and Arsenal in the FA Cup, ruthlessness was requisite.

United were without Jaap Stam, who turned an ankle on international duty with the Netherlands, although Alex Ferguson insisted: 'I regard Jaap as my main central defender, but I am very confident if I go with Ronny Johnsen and Henning Berg.'

The big Dutchman might have been useful, as United were quickly undone by route-one football. Wimbledon goalkeeper Neil Sullivan caught Jesper Blomqvist's cross and hoofed the ball downfield. Neville's miscued header to Schmeichel allowed Euell to pounce and he poked the ball round the stranded Dane and beat Denis Irwin in a sprint to force it into the empty net. Euell could have had a quick-fire second, but Schmeichel held his powerful shot.

The Reds' performance was far from classic, but in Beckham's endeavours Ferguson's men always stood a chance of recovery. The midfielder quickly notched double figures for crosses but, for a player whose angles are ordinarily of mathematical precision, he kept getting his sums wrong. Unperturbed, the Reds' No.7 was persistence personified and took out his frustration inside the box instead, equalising just before the break when Dean Blackwell failed to deal with Irwin's cross and Beckham scissor-kicked a volley past Sullivan from close range. For a player who had gone five months without a Premiership goal, that was two in two.

That was the cue for United to kick on in the second half and, in terms of chances created, it was, but all of them went begging. Andy Cole, Dwight Yorke and Blomqvist all had good openings – the latter's left-foot shot deflected off Chris Perry but was still stopped by Sullivan's outstretched boot.

Paul Scholes had the best chance to win it when substitute Ole Gunnar Solskjaer teed him up 12 yards out, but Sullivan again denied United a win that would have ensured a six-point summit lead following second-placed Arsenal's draw at Southampton. More positively, this was a tricky encounter ticked off with no discernible domestic damage done.

Wimbledon: Sullivan; Thatcher, Perry, Blackwell, Kimble (Ardley 81); M.Hughes, Earle, C.Hughes (Roberts 83), Gayle; Euell, Hartson (Cort 68)
Subs not used: Heald, Ainsworth
Booked: Cort

Manchester United: Schmeichel; G.Neville, Johnsen, Berg, Irwin; Beckham, Keane, Scholes, Blomqvist (Solskjaer 73); Yorke, Cole
Subs not used: van der Gouw, P.Neville, Butt, Giggs
Booked: Berg

Man of the Match: David Beckham
Beckham's mantra for crossing persistence must be: 'If at first you don't succeed, try, try and try again.' That is until he decided it still wasn't working and got into the box to finish the job himself.

Wednesday 7 April 1999 | Champions League semi-final, first leg | Old Trafford | Attendance: 54,487

MANCHESTER UNITED 1 Giggs 90
JUVENTUS 1 Conte 25

Alex Ferguson and United's European Cup obsession could not have been depicted more accurately in the pre-match reverence shown to Juventus and the misplaced keenness to capitalise on home advantage in two contrasting halves.

Juventus, attempting to reach a fifth straight European final (and a fourth consecutive one in the Champions League), were the benchmark of European progress for Ferguson's team. Carlo Ancelotti's team read like an imposing who's who of continental excellence: Edgar Davids, Didier Deschamps and World Footballer of the Year Zinedine Zidane were among many gems in the Old

Lady's collection of jewels – even though Alessandro Del Piero was a missing diamond.

'Juventus have fantastic experience and have been over the course time and again,' said Ferguson. This was the third successive season in which the teams had met, and while the previous Old Trafford encounter ended in 3-2 group stage win for United, the other three games were all 1-0 defeats.

Jaap Stam returned from an ankle injury, boosting the Reds' rearguard, while Ryan Giggs was passed fit and seen as vital to United's plans. 'I wanted to get at their right-back through Giggs,' explained the Reds' boss. 'I wanted Ryan as our third attacker, making Juventus defend against three all the time.' David Beckham had the same role if play was on the other side.

In their eagerness, both wide men attacked simultaneously, leaving United exposed. The visitors swarmed through the midfield and scored after much pressure on 25 minutes via Antonio Conte's beautifully worked goal – Zidane's charge infield was taken on by Davids, who nutmegged Paul Scholes to find Conte's run, and he beat Peter Schmeichel.

The losing margin could have been far greater by the break. 'I was angry that the players hadn't grasped what we should be doing,' fumed Ferguson. Tactically, things changed. Beckham tucked in beside Roy Keane and Scholes, while Giggs joined United's attack from deep. The tide, and the tie, eventually turned in a frenzied finale to a night of almost unbearable tension.

Giggs, now far more potent, led United's best chances. A scrambled shot from the Welshman, after good work from Andy Cole on the left, was clearly handled by Mark Iuliano, yet no penalty was awarded. And the officials were berated again as Giggs's pass from Beckham's cross allowed Cole to lay the ball off for Keane, whose scuffed effort was diverted in by Teddy Sheringham. The late – but correct – offside flag was most unwelcome.

United's breakthrough finally came in stoppage time. Juve failed to clear their lines at several attempts before Beckham hooked a cross over his shoulder, and after flick-ons from Sheringham and Cole, Giggs lashed a shot into the roof of the net and Old Trafford erupted in relief as much as joy.

Not everyone was impressed. The *Daily Mail*'s Graham Hunter opined: 'Outplayed, outthought and utterly outperformed for 80 minutes, United were almost out of the competition.' But Ferguson added: 'Juventus are favourites and rightly so, but they may live to regret our late goal. Something tells me we're going to win in Turin.'

Manchester United: Schmeichel; G.Neville, Berg (Johnsen h-t), Stam, Irwin; Beckham, Keane, Scholes, Giggs; Yorke (Sheringham 79), Cole
Subs not used: van der Gouw, P.Neville, Butt, Blomqvist, Solskjaer

Juventus: Peruzzi; Mirkovic, Montero (Ferrera 68), Iuliano, Pessotto; Conte, Davids, Zidane, Deschamps, Di Livio (Tacchinardi 77); Inzaghi (Esnaider 88)
Subs not used: Rampulla, Birindelli, Tudor, Amoruso
Booked: Mirkovic

Man of the Match: Ryan Giggs
Italians have always feared the Welshman's searing pace and subtle nous. Repositioned and recalibrated for the second half, he finally had the platform to start causing damage, and he did so with that crucial late intervention.

Sunday 11 April 1999 | FA Cup semi-final | Villa Park |
Attendance: 39,217

ARSENAL 0
MANCHESTER UNITED 0

'I said to our players before the tie: "The last thing we want is a replay. Whatever you do don't come back in with us involved in an extra match at this busy juncture,"' Alex Ferguson said of this score-less semi-final. 'A fat lot of notice they take of me!'

In truth, United's players were not wholly to blame. While the Reds failed to convert a sizeable share of possession and scoring opportunities, one goal was always likely to win it against an Arsenal defence that had conceded just 13 goals in 31 league games. It arrived in the 38th minute.

David Beckham, temporarily on the left, slipped a pass out to Ryan Giggs, who flicked the ball past Lee Dixon to cross from the byline. At that point, Dwight Yorke – jogging back onside in the goalmouth – was flagged. Play continued, Giggs crossed and Yorke flicked the ball on to Roy Keane, who smashed his shot past David Seaman and wheeled away in celebration. Referee David Elleray stubbornly waved away protests at his decision to disallow the goal – even-tempered Denis Irwin was booked for dissent – yet it was plain to see he called it wrong.

However, even when Arsenal were reduced to ten men in extra time, as Nelson Vivas was dismissed for an elbow on the excellent Nicky Butt, United still came up short. The absolute dearth of goals wasn't for the want of trying. After just eight minutes Cole's cross was fired over the bar by Giggs. Then after Keane's cancelled-out effort, Yorke and Andy Cole teamed up to leave the latter with just Seaman to beat. Unfortunately, the finish was tame and Arsenal were off the hook again.

In the second half, Cole again failed to make proper contact, this time from Gary Neville's low cross, and the No.9 encapsulated United's frustration when he failed to make the most of good approach-play from Giggs and David Beckham.

Even in extra time, with Arsenal a man down – their tenth red card of the season and 22nd in three years under Arsène Wenger –

the Gunners' defensive resolve was merely accentuated. Dennis Bergkamp played in substitute Freddie Ljungberg late on, but his shot was well saved by Peter Schmeichel. Victory would have flattered Arsenal, especially as United remained incensed about the first-half incident that would have avoided a replay and further fixture chaos.

David Lacey of the *Guardian* wrote: 'A combination of poor finishing and an aberrant offside flag – a piece of retrospective legislation which stretched the game's statutes of limitation – conspired to deny United the place at Wembley that their sharper and more imaginative attacking play demanded.'

'It was absolutely ridiculous,' Ferguson barked. 'I point the finger at the referee. He had at least a minute to get it right and bail out his assistant. We should have won, but it wasn't a goal and we have to get on with it.'

Arsenal: Seaman; Dixon, Keown, Adams, Winterburn; Parlour, Vieira, Vivas, Overmars (Ljungberg 90); Bergkamp, Anelka (Kanu 100)
Subs not used: Lukic, Bould, Grimandi
Booked: Parlour
Sent off: Vivas

Manchester United: Schmeichel; G.Neville, Johnsen, Stam, Irwin (P.Neville 85); Beckham, Butt, Keane, Giggs (Solskjaer 99); Yorke, Cole (Scholes 113)
Subs not used: van der Gouw, Blomqvist
Booked: G.Neville, Irwin

Man of the Match: Nicky Butt
In the battlefield that is the middle of the park during United–Arsenal clashes, only strong characters survive – especially with Keane and Vieira duking it out. Butt was outstanding in a dominant display.

Wednesday 14 April 1999 | FA Cup semi-final replay | Villa Park | Attendance: 30,223

ARSENAL 1 Bergkamp 69

MANCHESTER UNITED 2 Beckham 17, Giggs 109

In a season already acquiring mythological status, no match equalled the constant intensity and blow-for-blow drama that this enthralling 120 minutes of football conjured; an epic heavyweight battle, packed with intrigue and incident, comprising every possible, yet implausible, plot-twist – and with a breathtaking winner to boot.

Matches of such significance can paralyse participants too focused on the consequences of defeat. But as Alex Ferguson's and Arsène Wenger's men duelled from the off, neither backed down or took stock even for a second. From David Beckham's sweet early opener to Dennis Bergkamp's opportunistic second-half equaliser; from Roy Keane's red card to Peter Schmeichel's last-gasp penalty save; and from extra time and United's fading energy to Ryan Giggs's moment of genius – it was breathless stuff.

On the team coach travelling back up the M6 after the initial semi-final stalemate, Ferguson confided in Steve McClaren and Jim Ryan that, with fixtures piling up, resting key men and placing faith in their trustworthy lieutenants – regardless of any backlash – was the only way to cope. Andy Cole, Dwight Yorke, Ryan Giggs and Denis Irwin were all benched for the replay, while Teddy Sheringham, Ole Gunnar Solskjaer, Phil Neville and Jesper Blomqvist got their chance.

The changes raised eyebrows inside and outside of the club. 'You hear the hush when directors come into the dressing room and see the line-up,' said Ferguson. 'It's written on their faces – what on earth is he doing now? Some of them have given up trying to understand my selections.'

Rolling the dice was the only option and Sheringham, one of the beneficiaries, quickly repaid that trust with typically subtle craft. He led Emmanuel Petit, Tony Adams and Nigel Winterburn astray before flicking the ball back to Beckham, simultaneously opening up the angle for the United No.7 to arc a brilliant shot past David Seaman's flailing dive to make it 1-0 after 17 minutes.

It was then up to Schmeichel to deny Dennis Bergkamp and Petit, while after the break Solskjaer scampered after Ronny Johnsen's towering headed clearance, but the Norwegian forward's shot was halted by Seaman. Arsenal kept coming back, and on 69 minutes Bergkamp beat Schmeichel with a 25-yard shot diverted off Jaap Stam.

The Gunners thought they had grabbed a second when Schmeichel spilled another long-range Bergkamp shot and Nicolas Anelka sneaked in to round the keeper and slot the ball home. Their delirious celebrations were cut short as Anelka eventually realised he was given offside.

Minutes later the tie really turned in Arsenal's favour when Roy Keane was dismissed for a second booking, his sliding challenge sending Marc Overmars tumbling at speed. The sudden change in fortune was compounded when Phil Neville's rash tackle felled Ray Parlour in the area as Arsenal secured a stoppage-time penalty. Bergkamp stepped up for his moment of glory, one kick from the final and the end of United's Treble dream, but Schmeichel looked huge in the goal frame and pawed the ball away like a grizzly bear swatting a leaping salmon.

Even with Giggs, Yorke and Paul Scholes off the bench, ten-man United looked leggy as Schmeichel again denied Bergkamp with a strong save. Yet on 109 minutes an energy-sapped loose pass from Patrick Vieira let in the man with the freshest legs on the park. Giggs slalomed through Arsenal's defence, dodging Vieira, dummying his way past Lee Dixon, eluding Adams and shifting away from Dixon again before arrowing his shot into the roof of Seaman's net. Giggs wheeled away in shirt-twirling, rug-chested, match-winning delirium.

Who could blame him? He left Villa Park on crutches, still buzzing. 'I don't remember much about it, really,' he said. 'I picked the ball up and I just took off, then I hit it. It's the best goal I've ever scored.'

Ferguson, ecstatic and astonished, said: 'You cannot separate genius from Ryan Giggs. We were hanging on for grim death before he scored. We needed something out of this world to get us through and he came up with that remarkable goal.'

The question was, at what cost emotionally and physically had victory come? Ferguson proffered the perfect answer: 'Look, it could all blow up in our faces, but can you forget a game like that? Our supporters and our players will talk about that for years. That's what football is about – trying to reach peaks and climaxes in the season. We're in the final against Newcastle. Now let's go and try to win this league.'

Arsenal: Seaman; Dixon, Keown, Adams, Winterburn; Parlour (Kanu 104), Vieira, Petit (Bould 119), Ljungberg (Overmars 62); Bergkamp, Anelka
Subs not used: Lukic, Vivas
Booked: Keown, Parlour

Manchester United: Schmeichel; G.Neville (Yorke f-t), Johnsen, Stam, P.Neville; Beckham, Butt, Keane, Blomqvist (Giggs 61); Sheringham (Scholes 76), Solskjaer
Subs not used: van der Gouw, Irwin
Booked: Stam, Beckham
Sent off: Keane

Man of the Match: Peter Schmeichel
Ryan Giggs's wonder goal won the tie, but Schmeichel made sure United didn't lose it. He stood tall all night and frequently denied Bergkamp, from whom the Dane's penalty save in the dying seconds of normal time was game-changing.

Saturday 17 April 1999 | Premiership | Old Trafford |
Attendance: 55,270

MANCHESTER UNITED 3 Solskjaer 34, Sheringham 45, Scholes 62
SHEFFIELD WEDNESDAY 0

After the drama of the previous ten days, United were grateful for a routine Premiership victory, and yet those very circumstances made the simplicity of this win against Sheffield Wednesday, one of only three teams to inflict a league defeat on United in 1998-99, all the more remarkable.

It was surprising, too, considering the energy expended in that mammoth semi-final replay with Arsenal, that Alex Ferguson made just three changes to his starting line-up. Peter Schmeichel, Ryan Giggs and Andy Cole were rested, while Denis Irwin, David Beckham and Dwight Yorke were on the bench, the latter an emergency goalkeeping option, who donned a broad grin and keeper gloves as he fielded shots in the warm-up.

Aware that United's weary troops might need a little help, Ferguson took to the microphone before the game to express his gratitude for the incredible support at Villa Park. 'I'd like to thank you for the magnificent support you gave the players on Wednesday,' he said. 'I ask you to get behind them today, because they deserve it.'

In the teeming rain, the visitors threatened to make the brightest start, as Benito Carbone twisted and turned to beat Wes Brown and force a good save from Raimond van der Gouw. Seconds later the baggy-shirted Italian volleyed over with a speculative 25-yard effort.

The rain turned into a deluge, and the goals soon flooded forth. On 34 minutes, Jesper Blomqvist's hopeful cross to the far post was clipped back by Roy Keane and Teddy Sheringham's vision and execution of his angled pass on the slide back to Ole Gunnar Solskjaer were sublime. The Norwegian rarely missed those sorts of opportunities, although his celebrations were curtailed as he had clashed boots with an opponent as he fired home his 17th goal of the season.

Solskjaer then returned the favour for Sheringham before half time when his curling cross allowed his strike-partner to glance a header inside the far post to make it 2-0. Paul Scholes completed the scoring after an hour, following a sublime move that started on the right with a throw-in from Nicky Butt and took in 17 passes from nine different players, with Brown and van der Gouw the only players not to touch the ball. The play flowed from right to left twice before Scholes combined with Sheringham to create space for a shot, which deflected off Des Walker to beat Pavel Srnicek.

Done and dusted, and with Juventus waiting in Turin, Ferguson replaced Jaap Stam and Keane with David May and Jonathan Greening. Old Trafford, meanwhile, launched into a resounding: 'We shall not be moved.' The men on the pitch, however, weren't being swept off their feet just yet. 'It is absolutely vital that it remains in the forefront of our minds we have as yet won absolutely nothing,' said a grounded Gary Neville.

Manchester United: van der Gouw; G.Neville, Brown, Stam (May 63), P.Neville; Scholes, Butt, Keane (Greening 63), Blomqvist (Irwin 75); Sheringham, Solskjaer
Subs not used: Beckham, Yorke

Sheffield Wednesday: Srnicek; Atherton, Thome, Walker, Hinchcliffe; Alexandersson (Scott 55), Jonk, Sonner, Rudi; Carbone, Booth (Cresswell 71)
Subs not used: Pressman, Briscoe, Stefanovic

Man of the Match: Teddy Sheringham

The Londoner made a telling impact against Arsenal and he put Sheffield Wednesday to the sword here. He made the first, scored the second and was involved in the third, repaying Alex Ferguson's pledge to put trust in valuable squad men.

Wednesday 21 April 1999 | UEFA Champions League semi-final, second leg | Stadio Delle Alpi | Attendance: 60,806

JUVENTUS 2 Inzaghi 6, 11
MANCHESTER UNITED 3 Keane 24, Yorke 34, Cole 84

When United arrived in Turin, Alex Ferguson told anyone who would listen that his team would score against Juventus – a very deliberate tactic to instil belief in his players, but also to put his opponents on the back foot. In the dressing room as his side prepared for the cauldron of the Stadio Delle Alpi, he urged his troops to play with freedom: 'It doesn't matter if Juventus score because after drawing one-one in the first leg, just one away goal puts the ball back in our court.'

Ferguson wasn't reckoning on the Italians – buoyed by a dominant first-half display at Old Trafford – going two goals up inside 11 minutes. The 3-1 aggregate deficit was made all the more formidable by the fact that the *Bianconeri* had not been eliminated from European competition since 1993.

The second of Pippo Inzaghi's double took a fortuitous deflection off Jaap Stam to loop over a helpless Peter Schmeichel. But Ferguson was riled by Inzaghi's first, after six minutes; Zinedine Zidane played a short corner and whipped in a cross for the Juve striker, who all-too-easily guided the ball over the line from four yards.

Yet this United team embodied entirely the gritty spirit of its manager; never more determined than when challenged to respond, never more dangerous than when backed into a corner and forced to come out fighting. If Juve's players were oblivious to it, they soon wouldn't be. After 24 minutes, Roy Keane leapt highest in the penalty area to glance a header inside the far post from David Beckham's corner. The skipper wasted no time celebrating, sprinting back into position, ready to go again.

From joy to despair: minutes later, Nicky Butt's loose pass gave Zidane possession and Keane, stretching to reach the ball, clipped the Frenchman and collected a yellow card that ruled him out of the final. That the Irishman's performance never wavered is testimony to his character. Ferguson said it was an honour to be associated with Keane, adding: 'Far from inhibiting him, it inspired him. It was a truly selfless contribution and everyone responded.'

Arguably Keane's most important work – not just scoring, but hauling United back into contention with rhythmic, aggressive passing – had already been done. Juventus weren't totally blunted, as Stam – excellent once settled after the early goals – cleared Antonio Conte's looping header off the line, but United had the momentum. Andy Cole and Dwight Yorke were blisteringly irresistible up front and the pair soon combined for United's second.

Cole received Beckham's knockdown from Gary Neville's searching ball forward and the Reds' striker arced an exquisite cross to Yorke, whose diving header found the bottom corner of the net. Juventus were shell-shocked. From absolute command at 3-1 up to 3-3 on aggregate – with United's two away goals to the Italians' one giving them the advantage – all inside 23 minutes.

Yorke struck a post as United's swagger became more pronounced, but a berth in the final wasn't yet won as the two teams traded second-half jabs. Inzaghi had the ball in the net but was ruled offside, while Denis Irwin hit the woodwork with a low shot and found the side-netting with the rebound. But as the Italians tired in the face of United's limitless energy, with Keane still rampaging and Beckham full of running, Juve were worn down.

There was nothing subtle about the winner. Schmeichel's punt had Juve's defence back-pedalling and Yorke skipped past two defenders and rounded Angelo Peruzzi, who brought him down, only for Cole to follow up from an acute angle. Against all odds – and yet somehow so typically – United were in the final.

The English press lauded United. Graham Hunter wrote in the *Daily Mail*: 'The Juventus crowd, every man, woman and child, rose to applaud United off the pitch. No wonder they clapped until their hands were sore. This was one of England's – never mind United's – best performances in Europe. Ever.'

In the joyous aftermath, the glorious outcome was unimpeachable, but progress was indeed tempered by the loss of Keane and Paul Scholes, also out of the final. 'This is a fantastic night for us,' said Ferguson. 'But what happened to Keane and Scholes is a tragedy. All I can say is that the only two players guaranteed a place [in the FA Cup final] are Scholes and Keane.' Keane, naturally, wasn't teary-eyed: 'I'm hurting but I'm not going to ponder on it. The most important thing is that we're in the final – Manchester United is bigger than any one individual.'

Even without two key men, the rush of victory could not dilute Ferguson's confidence: 'We have the strength to carry on, I know that.'

Juventus: Peruzzi; Ferrara, Iuliano (Montero h-t), Birindelli (Amoruso h-t), Pessotto; Di Livio (Fonseca 80), Conte, Zidane, Deschamps, Davids; Inzaghi
Subs not used: Tudor, Tacchinardi, Esnaider
Booked: Davids

Manchester United: Schmeichel; G.Neville, Johnsen, Stam, Irwin; Beckham, Butt, Keane, Blomqvist (Scholes 68); Yorke, Cole
Subs not used: van der Gouw, May, P.Neville, Brown, Sheringham, Solskjaer
Booked: Keane, Scholes

Man of the Match: Roy Keane
The famous commentary – 'a captain's goal' – couldn't have been more apt as Keane hauled United back into the game. And for a player as team-oriented as the Irishman, this engrossing display of self-sacrifice, in the face of a booking that ruled him out of the final, represented a curious blend of both the zenith and nadir of his playing career.

Sunday 25 April 1999 | Premiership | Elland Road | Attendance: 40,255

LEEDS UNITED 1 Hasselbaink 32
MANCHESTER UNITED 1 Cole 55

With places booked in the FA Cup and Champions League finals, it was back to league duty with bump: a hostile trip to Elland Road to face David O'Leary's youthful Leeds, a side on a run of nine matches unbeaten and chasing Champions League qualification. 'Leeds are always a challenge,' said Alex Ferguson, nonplussed by a post-Europe trek across the Pennines for an 11.30am start. 'The atmosphere is guaranteed, but we're accustomed to it these days. I believe it will inspire my players.'

Of broader concern, Arsenal had edged two points ahead of United (albeit having played two more games) by trouncing Middlesbrough 6-1 the previous day. That followed a 5-1 win over Wimbledon as Arsène Wenger's side all but wiped out United's advantage on goal difference and snatched top spot for the first time that season. Jaap Stam, outstanding in Turin, pulled out of the starting line-up in the warm-up with an Achilles problem. As Ronny Johnsen had joined Ole Gunnar Solskjaer on international duty with Norway and Henning Berg was out with a knee ligament injury, squad players David May and Wes Brown were thrown together at centre-half.

Leeds flew out of the traps, led by Harry Kewell, who gave Gary Neville the slip before crossing to Lee Bowyer at the far post and he headed over. Then Alan Smith tested Peter Schmeichel, who smothered the young striker's close-range shot. United's best chance came from a David Beckham corner, as Roy Keane narrowly failed to connect with a near-post header as he had in Italy, while May should have done better with a tame follow-up shot that Nigel Martyn saved easily, before he cleared Andy Cole's rebound off the goal line.

Leeds' feistiness and pressing was the last thing a leg-weary, injury-hampered United needed, and Kewell's pre-injury-plagued pace wasn't far behind on the list of undesirables. It was little surprise that the Australian created Leeds' opener. He capitalised on Nicky Butt's loose pass, raced forward and slipped the ball to Jimmy Floyd Hasselbaink, who delayed his shot then nicked it past Schmeichel in off the post.

Kewell went close before and after half time, but it was United who emerged more purposeful in the second half, and after ten minutes the Reds were level. Keane clipped the ball to the back post for Butt, and his header on the bounce was saved by Martyn, only for Cole to jab the ball home in front of United's ecstatic away support. That finish marked the 50th goal of the Cole–Yorke partnership.

The other half of the duo, however, endured a frustrating day against Lucas Radebe. Yorke's misery was summed up with a potentially match-winning last kick of the game, as he burst into the box following a one-two with Teddy Sheringham and launched his left-foot shot over the bar. He buried his head in the turf while Ferguson tore hair from his head on the sidelines. Nevertheless, a hectic, heady month was completed with a valuable point and United marched into May with the Treble still very much on.

Leeds United: Martyn; Jones, Woodgate (Wetherall 59), Radebe, Harte; Bowyer, Batty, McPhail, Kewell; Smith, Hasselbaink (Wijnhard 87)
Subs not used: Robinson, Halle, Ribeiro
Booked: Hasselbaink

Manchester United: Schmeichel; G.Neville, May, Brown, Irwin (P.Neville 71); Beckham (Scholes 84), Butt, Keane, Blomqvist (Sheringham 76); Yorke, Cole
Subs not used: van der Gouw, Curtis
Booked: May, Butt, Keane

Man of the Match: Roy Keane
Showing little if any after-effects or self-pity from the draining night in Turin, Keane commanded, once again, like a true leader and helped navigate United to a valuable point in a tricky away trip.

April in statistics

Premiership table (25 April 1999)

	P	W	D	L	F	A	GD	Pts
Arsenal	34	19	12	3	54	15	+39	69
Manchester United	**33**	**19**	**11**	**3**	**73**	**33**	**+40**	**68**
Chelsea	34	17	14	3	49	26	+23	65
Leeds United	34	16	12	6	54	30	+24	60
Aston Villa	35	15	10	10	47	39	+8	55
West Ham United	35	15	9	11	41	42	-1	54
Middlesbrough	35	12	14	9	47	48	-1	50
Derby County	34	12	12	10	37	41	-4	48
Liverpool	34	13	8	13	60	44	+16	47
Tottenham Hotspur	34	11	13	10	41	40	+1	46
Leicester City	34	11	13	10	36	41	-5	46
Newcastle United	35	11	11	13	46	50	-4	44
Wimbledon	35	10	12	13	39	56	-17	42
Sheffield Wed	35	11	7	17	39	40	-1	40
Everton	35	10	10	15	35	42	-7	40
Coventry City	35	10	7	18	35	48	-13	37
Blackburn Rovers	34	7	11	16	36	49	-13	32
Charlton Athletic	35	7	11	17	37	52	-15	32
Southampton	35	8	8	19	31	63	-32	32
Nottingham Forest	35	4	9	22	30	68	-38	21

April form (all competitions): DDDWWWD

Goals scored: 11   **Goals conceded:** 6

Most appearances: Gary Neville 7 (661 mins)

Players used: 21

April – Crossing the Rubicon

Most goals: David Beckham, Ryan Giggs, Andy Cole 2 each

Most assists: Sheringham 3

Different goalscorers: 8

Quickest goal: David Beckham, 17 mins [v Arsenal (n)]

Latest goal: Ryan Giggs, 109 mins [v Arsenal (n)]

Watched by: 306,379

Average attendance: 43,768

Chapter 10

May – The Promised Land

'This is a special season. No matter what happens on the last lap, you should enjoy it because you may never see the like again.' So said Alex Ferguson, with seven games separating his side from a unique achievement, or a second trophyless season, or various points of success in between. Assured of a berth in two cup finals, with a game in hand on Arsenal and the chance to move two points clear in a Premier League title race containing only five more hurdles, United began May on the brink of history.

In the league, home games against Aston Villa and Tottenham Hotspur bookended three tricky trips to Liverpool, Middlesbrough and Blackburn Rovers, while Newcastle United and Bayern Munich awaited in the FA Cup and Champions League finals respectively. Seven wins would guarantee a clean sweep, but that would hardly be United's style, would it?

In his *United Review* programme notes ahead of Villa's visit, the manager continued: 'Personally, I am elated and delighted to be challenging on three fronts at this stage of the season. I am enjoying every minute of it, and I can tell you that the players are loving it, too. I believe anyone watching Manchester United this season will remember it for the rest of their lives. It may prove impossible to repeat.

'On top of all that has been the manner of our getting to the top. We have scored 119 goals this season and I think even our critics would be hard put to nominate a more entertaining and exciting team to watch. This is not the end of the road, but at the same time, don't take anything for granted … enjoy these final three weeks, because this really is the pinnacle of football and what it is all about.'

Though it was hardly a free-flowing affair on an afternoon stifled by the baking Manchester sunshine, United's seven steps to glory started well enough, with David Beckham thundering home a phenomenal long-range free-kick against Villa, after Julian Joachim had briefly set hearts aflutter by cancelling out Steve Watson's earlier own-goal in United's favour.

'David's goal was a marvellous strike,' enthused Ferguson. 'He was practising free-kicks in training the day before and still works at them. Top players have to work hard. They are successful because of the hard work that they put in. I am now setting my mind on four victories in our remaining four league matches.'

Coincidentally, victory was the only thing United's next opponents coveted. Liverpool were still smarting from January's last-gasp FA Cup turnaround at Old Trafford, and Anfield manager Gerard Houllier was hell-bent on avenging that perceived injustice. 'This is an important game for the Liverpool fans, and the players know they will have to be at their very best if we want to beat United,' said the Frenchman. 'But after what happened in the FA Cup, this game is an ideal chance to put things right.'

In addition to the return of Roy Keane, Jaap Stam and Andy Cole for the short trip down the East Lancashire Road, United's sky-rocketing mood was handed another boost the day before the game, when Ferguson ended all uncertainty over his own future by penning a new, three-year contract to extend his tenure to 2002.

'I am delighted that the matter has been settled,' he said, 'and that I have a contract which will take me to sixty years of age. My hunger for success remains undiminished and I will be striving to ensure that the next three years are as successful as the last thirteen.'

Three points at Anfield would represent a huge step towards the first of those successes, but a balmy evening on Merseyside turned stormy through a controversial late climax. United led 2-0 through Dwight Yorke's header and a Denis Irwin penalty, earned by the outstanding Jesper Blomqvist, but the Swede was then bafflingly penalised for a fair challenge on Oyvind Leonhardsen inside his own area with 21 minutes remaining.

'So much happened,' smiles Blomqvist. 'I was having a great game, even though I got a bad kick in the chest for our penalty. I laugh about it now, but it hurt! Then I had that penalty against me and it was not as fun any more. When you come over as a non-English player, you don't realise how big Man United v Liverpool is and what kind of tension is behind those games, but you soon realise how much those encounters mean. That game was a great game, and I think I still got the Man of the Match award, which provided a tiny bit of comfort, but things just went wrong for us at a bad time.'

Jamie Redknapp smashed home the penalty to halve the Reds' lead, before referee David Elleray took centre stage once again. Irwin, who had already been booked, ran the ball fractionally out of play and carried on, in spite of the official's whistle. Taking this as a bookable offence, Elleray promptly dismissed the Republic of Ireland full-back to leave United defending with ten men for the final 15 minutes.

'Obviously I still think it was a harsh decision, because they had just scored from a penalty and the noise at Anfield was very loud,' recalls Irwin. 'Add in the fact that they were trying to stop us from winning the league and the Treble, and it was deafening. I remember the ball coming over from an over-hit cross, and I must have flicked it away and it was running out. I couldn't hear a thing, and I knew the ball had just gone out and I started dribbling up the field because I didn't hear the whistle or see the linesman's flag.

'It only went for ten or fifteen yards, but when I looked around and saw Elleray was looking at me, I knew it was curtains. It was disappointing, but I didn't think I would miss the Cup final. My first thought was just that we were two-one up in a massive game and we needed to get a result. I didn't hear the whistle, it's as simple as that.'

The Irishman again couldn't escape the noise from the home supporters when former Red Paul Ince – of all people – turned home an 89th-minute equaliser from close range to send Anfield into fevered joy and stun the travelling supporters, who had rejoiced at the apparent navigation of the United's toughest remaining league fixture. While Ince booted a cocktail of joy and rage into the advertising hoardings at the Kop, Irwin watched on in horror.

'The fact they came back and I had to watch the goal from the dressing room was not a nice feeling,' he admits. 'It was always a tough place to go, so to be two-nil up and not win ... We hadn't lost since December and, although we didn't lose at Anfield, it felt like a defeat in the dressing room afterwards. We were in a head-to-head with Arsenal, they'd won at Tottenham that night and you know every point counts.'

While disappointed in the short term, the Reds were by no means disheartened over their long-term goals, according to Phil Neville. United were aiming for a fifth title in seven years; the run-in was a well-trodden path for Alex Ferguson's men.

'Were we worried? No, not really,' says the versatile defender. 'By that point we were chalking games off, like a countdown, but we also knew that along the way there was going to be a hiccup, because that's what happens when you get to March, April, May. It's not that draw or defeat that you suffer, it's how you react to that. If you react badly and lose the next one, that's where the problem lies, but we knew we were probably going to slip up once. We did, but it didn't affect us and we moved on.'

In a perverse way, Phil Neville was perhaps the only United player to benefit personally from the events of Anfield. Even in spite of a plea from PFA chief executive Gordon Taylor on his behalf, Irwin's dismissal – the first of his career – was not rescinded and the Irishman knew in advance that he would be suspended from United's FA Cup final squad.

'Denis got suspended and I knew I was going to start the FA Cup final,' recalls Neville. 'But there was such a unique feel about the squad at the time that it didn't matter. Who cares who plays, we're going to make history here – that was the mood. Looking back, I think we were in a daze over everything going right. Honestly, we didn't want days off. We wanted to come in, to work, to be together, and we must have seen each other more than our wives and kids that year. It was just one of those special things.

'The good thing was that every big game we went to, all the wives, kids, mums and dads came with us, so they were generating spirit as well, and it was just a travelling circus that used to come into town, take over and get out. Even now I get goosebumps thinking back to it all.'

Following the setback at Anfield, Ferguson had vowed: 'We'll recover.' His team's 28-game unbeaten run would be tested next by their most recent conquerors: Middlesbrough. Even though the Teessiders were comfortably safe in mid-table and harbouring only the faintest ambitions of a late surge for European qualification, manager Bryan Robson insisted he would be gunning for victory, regardless of his legendary status with his opponents.

'The fact that I had such a long career at Old Trafford doesn't come into it,' Robson insisted. 'I've got to get on with my own job.

Alex Ferguson always used to say that nobody does you any favours in this game. If you win things, you win them off your own bat.'

And sure enough, the Reds mustered enough character and spirit to eke out a gritty 1-0 victory at the Riverside Stadium, with Dwight Yorke heading home his 29th goal of the season from close range on the stroke of half time. It wasn't pretty, but it was invaluable, as it took the Reds back to the top of the table, level with Arsenal on points and goal difference, but ahead by virtue of goals scored. The stylistic difference between the two title rivals was underlined by the fact that United had scored and conceded 20 more goals than the reigning champions, but still, with two games to go it became a staring contest between the pair. Fortunately for United, Arsenal blinked first.

A thrilling, nail-biting Tuesday night encounter between the Gunners and Leeds United at Elland Road could easily have gone either way, but was ultimately settled by Jimmy Floyd Hasselbaink's late diving header for the Yorkshiremen. Seldom has a Leeds goal been so well received in Manchester, and to continue the theme of skewed loyalties, the following evening gave United the chance to all-but seal the title at the expense of Brian Kidd.

'I couldn't watch Leeds and Arsenal,' recalls Irwin. 'I was probably watching *Emmerdale*, which will be the only time, but watching that game would have been agony. Thankfully Leeds won. We knew what we had to do and it was in our hands, so we needed a result against Blackburn. Kiddo was the manager, and if they didn't beat us then he and Blackburn were down, which wasn't very nice, but you have to look after your own destiny.'

Across an agonising 90 minutes at Ewood Park, United just about retained control of the title race, but missed the chance to virtually bury the issue. A goalless draw – which might have been worse, had Ashley Ward not missed a presentable late chance for the hosts – ensured a one-point lead and a similar margin on goal difference going into the decisive weekend of the season, when United hosted Tottenham and Villa travelled to Arsenal. Yet still, with 60 games played, 31 wins, 24 draws and five losses (none of which had come since 19 December), there was no guarantee that United would end the season with a single trophy – never mind three.

'That's what makes it so fantastic,' beams Teddy Sheringham. 'From an outside point of view, people probably thought: "Oh, United won the Treble, it was an easy season for them." No way. But that's how we liked it. That's how it felt good to us, that it was all so competitive. I think if we'd have won the league with three games to go, perhaps our form might have dipped at certain times. You never know, me and Ole might have got a couple more games! But that was how it was, it kept us on tenterhooks, kept us focused and the nerves were nicely balanced.'

Nerves had, according to Alex Ferguson, reared their head in stuttering to a draw at Blackburn, but the manager set a cool example when downplaying any concerns ahead of the final-day decider against Spurs. 'I think there are periods when maybe they're getting anxious,' he said. 'I made that point to them at half time [at Blackburn] not to force the game. I think they were trying to stampede their way through it, instead of playing with their normal patience and control.

'I think it's a test of nerve when you go into a big game anyway, but if they had any lack of nerve it would have shown itself in Juventus and they would have probably bottled it completely when they were two-nil down. But they kept their nerve; it's a matter of keeping it rather than showing it. I've got to look at what my players have achieved this season and how they've responded to the big-game situations. I mean the Juventus performance, and [Inter] Milan, and Arsenal in the semi-final were all against teams of the highest quality. And they don't come any bigger than Sunday now; the players know they're going to have to produce their best-ever performance and I said that in Juventus and I said it in Milan. That is the nature of progress.'

The manager's progressive nature had yielded a spectacularly successful rotation policy, to the point where he knew that he could rely on almost any of his players to step into the breach for the biggest game of the league season, if required. Keane declared himself fit, despite ongoing injury concerns, but Jaap Stam's damaged Achilles prompted the inclusion of David May at centre-half alongside Ronny Johnsen. There would also be, in typical Ferguson fashion, a selection gamble upfront as the Yorke–Cole partnership was temporarily disbanded.

Having spent much of the season on the periphery of the unfolding drama, Sheringham was suddenly centre stage. 'Sunday, an hour before the game on the final day of the season, I get the nod I'll be playing,' he remembers. 'I was very surprised, knowing that the FA Cup final wasn't until the following Saturday and the European Cup final the following Wednesday. But to get the nod against my old club, with the thought of winning the league, was a huge boost for me, especially given the season that Yorkie and Coley had had. Unfortunately, things didn't quite go according to plan!'

United began brightly enough, and almost took the lead in bizarre circumstances when Spurs goalkeeper Ian Walker's clearance rebounded off Yorke and spun against the inside of the post. 'The ball spun off the post the wrong way,' laughs the Trinidadian. 'What the hell? We hit the post, Scholesy had a couple of chances, it was going all over the place. There were near misses and the crowd were getting tense.'

That tension was cranked up to almost unbearable levels after 24 minutes, when a hopeful punt forward released Les Ferdinand, whose speculative toe-poke towards goal looped agonisingly up, up, up and over Peter Schmeichel, whose scrambling efforts weren't enough to prevent the ball crossing the line and, out of nothing, Spurs were ahead. 'When Les scored, it silenced everybody,' remembers Sheringham. 'I don't think Tottenham really wanted to be scoring, because it wasn't great for them for Arsenal to be winning the league.'

Despite the setback, however, United's response was positive, cranking up the production of chances, only to find Walker in top form and several players' radars askew. 'I could have scored five that day, but I didn't score any,' laments Paul Scholes, while May adds: 'It reminded me of 1997 against [Borussia] Dortmund in the European Cup. We had chance after chance after chance, but we just couldn't score.'

Until three minutes before the break. Having passed up a far easier headed chance minutes earlier, Beckham received the ball inside the Tottenham area, but at an unforgiving angle on the right hand side. No matter.

'Becks just pulled out one of those whipped, free-kick-type shots,' remembers Yorke. 'He was a class finisher and he loved scoring against Spurs ... What a wonderful goal it was.'

'It was a bit surreal to see some of the Tottenham fans celebrating, but I just thought: "That's it, we've broken them,"' remembers May. But though the momentum was firmly with United going into the interval, Alex Ferguson decreed that changes were required.

'I got booked in the first half,' explains Sheringham. 'I went to close down Sol Campbell, went steaming in, slipped and got booked for a challenge that I didn't really mean. I think it was one of those that looked clumsy, but I slipped at the last minute. Fergie came in at half time and changed it straight away, put Coley on. Whether it was because of that, I don't know, but he said to me: "Look, you've already been booked, I can't risk it, I've got to change it." In hindsight, from my point of view, it was a fantastic thing to do, because one more slip from my point of view and we're down to ten men. Changing it – a little bit of freshness putting Coley on – was the right thing to do.'

Straight away, Cole's fresh legs made the telling difference. Less than two minutes of the second half had been played when the striker latched onto Gary Neville's lofted pass and impudently lobbed Walker to set Old Trafford ablaze in celebration. 'I have always said to Nev that it was the best ball he ever played in his career,' grins the goalscorer. 'He lobbed it in behind the full-back and I took a touch – my first of the game – let it bounce and then I lobbed Walks with my first two touches of the game. After that, I was obviously trying to get myself over to the bench, but the lads didn't let me get that far. It was just a great feeling.'

Suddenly, United's gung-ho heroes had what they required. 'It was a long forty-odd minutes after that,' says May. There was no pressure on the Reds to force the issue, rendering the unfamiliar sights of self-control and pragmatism in the hosts' play. When news filtered through that Arsenal had taken the lead against Villa, the entire stadium – even the away support – was gripped by nerves.

'We didn't push on any more; we were kind of hanging on,' recalls Yorke. 'We didn't play as a driving force – we just thought: "F*** this! This is what we've got, keep it tight and keep the ball!" I remember the gaffer putting me on the right wing with five across the middle of the park with one up top to close up shop.'

Tottenham seldom threatened to make even a half-chance, yet still every second crawled by in agonising fashion until at last, after untold ado, referee Graham Poll blew the final whistle to light the fuse on almighty celebrations in Manchester – the first time United had clinched the title on their own turf under Ferguson.

'At the end of the game, the relief was unbelievable,' recalls Gary Neville. 'The stadium was full of colour – it felt red. Sometimes you go to the stadium and you just see black coats because it is winter, but you could feel the euphoria and the atmosphere and the tension, and the place just felt red. Old Trafford gets like that two or three times a season. You can't get like that for every game, it's impossible. You might not even get it once in a season, but that was just a massive day.'

One down, two to go. And, with six days to go until the second instalment of the historic chase, United's players were afforded an almighty win bonus: two days to party. 'The manager told us to make sure we enjoyed the moment,' recalls Yorke. 'But four days after we went back in we'd be at Wembley again, and we knew it was going to be the craziest week when we'd have to be here and there for all sorts of things like interviews.'

No one could have prepared for the unexpected blip to hit United's post-match celebrations, however. After being hit by a glass and provoked into a scuffle by three strangers in a city-centre bar, Keane was arrested for drunk and disorderly conduct. Though it was quickly proven that the skipper had been the victim of a set-up, so that the perpetrators could sell the story to a tabloid newspaper, and Keane was cleared of all wrongdoing, he wrote in his autobiography: 'Yes, it was a set-up, but that was no excuse. There was no excuse.'

Alex Ferguson arrived to collect the midfielder the following morning and quickly turned his focus back to more pressing matters. With the Cliff brimming with reporters for a scheduled media day, there was no escaping the incessant demand for news about United. 'I've never seen that many people at the Cliff before,' recalls Schmeichel, while Yorke adds: 'There was a huge buzz around. We couldn't walk the streets, we couldn't go anywhere because we were the centre of attention. It was mad, there were press people outside my house . . .'

Though the players were duly whisked down to London for the FA Cup final, there was one dissenting voice amid the clamour for the Reds. After overcoming Spurs, Ferguson had declared: 'I'm painting my team as the gods of the game.'

'Fergie's wrong, Manchester United are not gods,' countered New-castle manager Ruud Gullit. 'He made his comment in the right way, but gods . . . no, I don't think so.' Unfortunately for the Dutchman, his players would appear far more affected by United's growing aura. 'That FA Cup final was one of the easiest games I've ever played,' says David May. 'You'd have thought it would have been a lot more difficult, but I think we were just on a roll – we were flying at the time. We just thought: "Let's get this over and done with."'

While the final transpired to be a cakewalk in the baking Wembley sunshine, United once again had to overcome an unforeseen setback. For the second time in six days, it involved Keane. Unceremoniously crunched to the ground by Gary Speed, the Irishman – who carried an injury into the game – was unable to continue. Given his European suspension, Keane's season was over. Sheringham's, however, was about to begin in earnest.

'Before I knew it, I'd exchanged a couple of one-twos with Scholesy and put us one-nil up with a shot through the keeper's legs,' recalls the striker, sent on as Keane's replacement. 'Wasn't it a lovely goal? Six minutes, I'm not involved. Eleven minutes, I've scored to make us go one-nil up against Newcastle in the FA Cup final. What a dream!'

Sheringham's goal extinguished Newcastle's feisty start to the game, and thereafter United were able to dictate play in total comfort, even with a rejigged formation of Beckham in central midfield and Ole Gunnar Solskjaer on the right wing. Though out of position, the Norwegian comported himself admirably and played a key role in United's second goal, early in the second period, by winning the ball and feeding Sheringham to tee up Scholes who drilled in a simple finish.

'It was one of the proudest moments I've had, walking out at Wembley in the FA Cup final, because I'd watched all the FA Cup finals when I was a kid, and just being part of that experience was huge,' recalls Solskjaer. 'Then the game went well, too, so I have great memories of that day. The downside was that it was a hard pitch, though: dry, heavy, horrible. It was a horrible place to play, Wembley, because you were knackered whenever you came off that pitch.'

Safeguarding against Wembley's famed fatigue factor, United's manager had rejigged his side with one eye on the looming Champions League final just four days later. Aside from the suspended Irwin, Stam and Yorke were restricted to substitute cameos, while Blomqvist and Nicky Butt were not risked, as Ferguson weighed up the potential cost of losing more midfield bodies in addition to the suspended Keane and Scholes.

'It was quite surreal, really, that players were getting rested for a cup final,' admits Phil Neville. 'Nicky Butt couldn't be risked, cotton wool, not even a sub, and I remember going up to him after the gaffer named the team and said: "Butty, I'm sorry you're not playing, mate." He replied, "If another person says that to me! I'm missing an FA Cup final . . . You've got a European Cup final . . . No! Don't . . ." Everybody must have been saying the same thing to him. Everyone wanted to play. The FA Cup final was almost like a practice game, in a way. We played against a good Newcastle side, but they didn't turn up on the day and we strolled it. It was a perfect warm-up for the main event.'

With the Champions League final so close on the horizon, the post-match celebrations were, inevitably, muted in comparison to the two-day event prompted by the Premier League title. With two down and one to go, the stakes had never been higher, and the players were given fitting transport to such an occasion: Concorde.

'It was just brilliant,' remembers Yorke. 'We got the VIP treatment. We were all decked out, everybody was moving together, there were cameras, the airport was buzzing and we checked into the Concorde lounge . . . It was just mad. I don't think anybody had been on it prior to that. Everyone was excited, there was a pure buzz, everything was laid on for us – we were like rock stars. It took forty-five minutes to get to Barcelona!'

With two days to go before the final, against Ottmar Hitzfeld's Bayern Munich, the squad mingled at their hotel, with all conversation centring around the game. 'It was a fantastic atmosphere, it was absolutely brilliant,' says Cole. 'Then on Tuesday evening, we started to feel the nervous energy, because none of us had been there before. Everyone was looking at each other like we had done all season, but this ... it was the first time for everyone. When we got down for breakfast on Wednesday, everyone was asking: "How did you sleep?" Turned out nobody could sleep that night, it was unbelievable.'

Perhaps that was one of the reasons behind United's sluggish start to the game. In the fifth minute, Johnsen was penalised for a foul on towering Bayern striker Carsten Jancker, much to the Norwegian's ongoing chagrin. 'He came through, I was running past him. He put his leg out, I fell forwards and he fell backwards, and he got the free-kick,' shrugs the Norwegian. Mario Basler compounded Johnsen's ire at the time by threading the set-piece low, around Schmeichel's wall and into the back of the net.

'We jumped in the wall, but it went in the other corner and was such a bad goal,' remembers Cole. 'After just five minutes, we didn't know what it was. Having not won it since 1968, everyone kind of tensed up because we knew we needed to win. We knew we should have won it in previous years, maybe twice, but we never played the way we had all season.'

Hitzfeld's side had United precisely where they wanted them, and the Premier League champions lacked the threat of Beckham's presence on the right flank and Giggs's on the left, with the former joining Butt in central midfield and the latter shunted to the right. Blomqvist occupied the left wing, and spurned United's first proper opening of the game early in the second period, stabbing over the bar on the half-volley after a lightning sprint into the box.

'If I had scored I would probably have stayed on the pitch and wouldn't have been substituted,' suggests the Swede. 'I didn't perform as well as I could have done, but scoring a goal would have released everything in me. It was our best chance in the game until the very end, and I just couldn't reach it. Now, I think I prefer it like this anyway. If I had scored, maybe it would have ended one-one and they might have won on penalties!'

Blomqvist made way with 23 minutes remaining, as Ferguson introduced Sheringham. 'Get out there and make a difference, son,' the manager urged his veteran striker, who emphatically heeded the advice – though Sheringham insists: 'It wasn't until Ole came on [for Cole] with ten minutes to go that things really changed.'

The substitute duo entered the fray in a period when Bayern were seeking to kill off the game. Schmeichel was repeatedly tested, while Mehmet Scholl clipped a delightful chip against the Dane's post and Jancker crashed an overhead kick against the crossbar. 'You can't say you really knew we were going to win it, but the stars were on our side because they kept f****** missing,' recalls May.

For Solskjaer, however, the signs were glaring that Bayern had allowed carelessness to creep into their game, disguised as overconfidence. 'They were so confident that they had us beaten, that they were only thinking about getting the second goal,' recalls the Norwegian. 'I ran on and I was amazed to see that there were spaces everywhere. I hadn't seen that beforehand because it's a horrible place to sit, the dugouts at the Nou Camp, because you're so low and you can't see anything. When I got out there, it was a big, massive pitch with loads of spaces and my legs felt great, so I could run everywhere.'

Almost straight away, Solskjaer provided goalkeeper Oliver Kahn's first test of the evening, and the Bayern stopper would increasingly find his goal under siege in the final few minutes. 'It was probably our worst performance all year,' says Yorke. 'But there was belief in the team. We were missing two of our key players, which altered our team, but there was still crazy belief there. We didn't play great and everyone accepted that, but it is amazing what belief and courage we had. You look at the clock and see it's the ninetieth minute, but everyone was flying around and still trying their hardest. It would have been a travesty if we had not got back into the game.'

In the first of three added minutes, along came the equaliser. With Schmeichel granting himself dispensation to join the mêlée awaiting a Beckham corner, Bayern's defenders suffered an attack of the jitters and failed to deal with the situation decisively. A half-cleared ball was scuffed back towards goal by Giggs, and swept home by Sheringham.

'When someone was shooting, it was just in my make-up to be alive to where the ball could go,' says the striker. 'I'd been taught that at a very young age. Giggsy scuffed his volley towards the far post. I think it was just missing. There was one of their players on the line so I knew I was onside, and I got enough on it, got my sock on the top of my boot on it to scuff it into the empty net where the fella had been before he'd tried to go up for offside. You beauty!'

Half of the Nou Camp erupted with joy and flares lit a heaving, writhing mass of bedlam around Kahn's goal. It wasn't over. But within two minutes, it would be. 'Obviously you play a Champions League final and you get something back like we had, you expect to get the draw and go into golden goal in extra time,' reasons Schmeichel. 'That was my thinking. I was so happy. I was thinking: "I need to compose myself now, because we're playing golden goal and I've never been in that situation before." So I was taking deep breaths and composing myself, and I saw we'd got the corner, but it's not even in my mind that we're going to score. And we score.'

Simple as that. Another corner. Beckham into Sheringham, and Solskjaer has won it. 'I was going to go for goal, but realised that I needed to help it on,' remembers Sheringham, whose header fell perfectly for Solskjaer to prod a volley into Kahn's top corner. 'Pure instinct,' insists Solskjaer. 'Out of all the goals you score in your career, that's the one you don't ever practise in training.'

At 90 minutes, United were trailing. Three minutes on, referee Pierluigi Collina sounded his final whistle and crowned the Reds kings of Europe. Disbelief gripped all present. United's players cavorted and ran aimlessly about, circumnavigating the fallen carcasses of their beaten opponents.

'This was meant to be, how we were supposed to win it. It was our time to win and we did it,' insists Cole. 'Fate is a massive thing. Things happen for a reason and without them we wouldn't have a history. It was our time. We had played great football all season, but sometimes you have to win ugly. We were the best team by far that season, anybody who drew us in Europe was worried.'

'We had our backs up against the wall and came back from the dead all season,' continues Yorke. 'That was our mentality: never give in until that whistle is blown. That is what we did and that is what we needed to do to accomplish what we did. No matter how bad things may look, you can turn it around at any given time.'

For Alex Ferguson, the promised land had been reached. His and United's fixation on reclaiming the European Cup had been realised at last, and the match-winner sought out his manager afterwards to offer his own congratulations. 'I looked at him and I was more happy for him than for myself or anyone else, and I thought: "You deserve this,"' recalls Solskjaer. 'If you have that as a manager – when you win and you're successful and the players don't think about themselves, but rather about the manager, that he deserves it – then you know you've managed a club in the right way. And that's from a sub, from one who thinks he should have played more, that is probably more p***** off than anyone that he's put on the bench! But it's true: I just looked at him and said: "I'm so happy for you."'

That exchange came after an epic celebration between players and fans out on the field – orchestrated brilliantly by David May – and preceded the club's post-match, post-season, post-Treble party. 'Probably the best party I've ever been involved in,' grins Sheringham. 'It was one of those that just went on and on till five, six in the morning and that was only the start of it.'

There were a few more people keen to join the festivities – between 500,000 and a million, according to various reports – when the squad returned to Manchester the following day. An open-top bus meandered through Sale, Altrincham and Stretford before making its way into the city centre. To a man, all those on the bus remain flabbergasted by the scenes they witnessed.

'We were absolutely knackered,' admits Gary Neville. 'But I will never forget turning into Deansgate. It was unbelievable. They were hanging off lampposts and bus shelters. You could see what it meant to people – it was that unbelievable feeling. Those are the moments that you wish could last forever, because you know when you are having them that they are out-of-body experiences, they are like alien experiences. There is nothing that can repeat that.'

The same can still be said of United's Treble winners. Both the achievement and the manner of its attainment will forever be a study in the perfect marriage of skill and sheer, bloody-minded refusal to admit defeat. This was a team who stared down adversity time and again and never blinked first, a squad of players who will be asterisked in history as the finest ever to represent English club football.

Saturday 1 May 1999 | Premiership | Old Trafford |
Attendance: 55,189

MANCHESTER UNITED 2 Watson 20 (og), Beckham 47
ASTON VILA 1 Joachim 34

May began with the tricky hosting of Aston Villa, a side considered title contenders before they lost form at the turn of the year, and as United had become increasingly enchanted by the notion of an unprecedented Treble, it is in precisely these moments that nervousness grasps slender winning margins with a vice-like grip.

Alex Ferguson's side, missing Jaap Stam, Andy Cole, Ryan Giggs and Roy Keane, started the afternoon a point behind league leaders Arsenal and looked purposeful from the off, moving in front after 20 minutes when Steve Watson scored a scrappy own goal. The vibrant Villans struck back through Julian Joachim, but a stunning David Beckham free-kick at the start of the second half restored United's lead. However, after a rare Denis Irwin miss from the penalty spot with 20 minutes to go, John Gregory's side sensed the uneasiness inside Old Trafford – from players and fans – and cranked up the pressure for an almost unbearably tense conclusion.

United hadn't planned on a close encounter. Early on, Paul Scholes's diving header forced a good early save from Michael Oakes, while the Villa goalkeeper was beaten by a Beckham free-kick only for Gareth Southgate to head off the line. Oakes was included as the Villa No.1 only because Mark Bosnich had refused to extend his contract beyond its summer expiry and had reportedly agreed a deal to succeed Peter Schmeichel.

When Oakes was eventually beaten midway through the half, it was untidy stuff. Scholes received the ball from Jesper Blomqvist and appeared to be aiming for Dwight Yorke when Watson turned the ball over the line. But Villa edged their way back into the contest, and after 34 minutes Steve Stone crossed for Joachim to bag his second goal of the season against the Reds.

After the break, United won a free-kick 30 yards out and Beckham, on the eve of his 24th birthday, gift-wrapped an early present for United as he dispatched a shot via special delivery straight into the top corner. And it looked like the celebrations could start early when Stone pushed Phil Neville in the box and Irwin lined up the penalty. Oakes's one-handed save galvanised Villa and they pressed on in search of parity.

It felt like Ferguson's men were holding on at the end, yet that's exactly what they did to bag three points that temporarily put United top of the league, even if Arsenal returned to the summit the following day by beating Derby County. 'It's not torture, it's sheer bliss!' said Ferguson of the high-stakes intensity as the season reached its climax.

Manchester United: Schmeichel; G.Neville, Johnsen, May (Brown 79), Irwin; Beckham, Butt, Scholes, Blomqvist (P.Neville 63); Yorke, Sheringham
Subs not used: van der Gouw, Wilson, Greening

Aston Villa: Oakes; Watson, Southgate, Calderwood, Wright; Stone, Draper (Thompson 67), Taylor, Merson; Joachim, Dublin (Vassell 76)
Subs not used: Enckelman, Ehiogu, Barry
Booked: Taylor

Man of the Match: David Beckham
Beckham's stunning set piece at the start of the second half was a worthy winning strike, and yet brilliant as he was at making the ball do exactly as he wished, his work-rate, pressing and endeavour were all laudable attributes he put to good use once again here.

Wednesday 5 May 1999 | Premiership | Anfield | Attendance: 44,702

LIVERPOOL 2 Redknapp 70 (pen), Ince 89
MANCHESTER UNITED 2 Yorke 22, Irwin 57 (pen)

The season's third instalment of Manchester United versus Liverpool was every bit as enthralling as the previous two. Late goals, penalties, and Paul Ince playing the role of pantomime villain once again – the only shame was that the outcome didn't follow that of the Old Trafford encounters.

'We would have won the game had it not been for the referee,' said a furious Alex Ferguson, after watching a penalty given against Jesper Blomqvist for a supposed foul and Denis Irwin dismissed for perceived time-wasting. Those decisions, both of which were highly questionable, helped Liverpool recover from 2-0 down with 20 minutes remaining to claim a 2-2 draw. On a night when Arsenal registered a 3-1 derby victory over Tottenham Hotspur, the dropping of two points appeared a serious blow to the Reds' title aspirations.

The evening had started well for United. Against a backdrop of Liverpool fans waving Bayern Munich flags, Dwight Yorke had given the visitors the lead. It was a goal beautifully worked, with Roy Keane and David Beckham exchanging passes before the latter sent in a delicious cross for the Reds' leading scorer to head in at the far post.

Liverpool's first chance of note arrived early in the second half, Ince slicing a half-volley high into the Kop, but it was United who scored next. Blomqvist, still in for the crocked Ryan Giggs, raced onto a through pass in the home penalty area and attempted to get his head to the ball. Instead he got Jamie Carragher's boot full in the chest, leaving referee David Elleray the easy decision of pointing to the spot. Just as in the reverse fixture (though unlike against Villa days earlier), Irwin's placement was precise.

At two-nil up the game seemed won, with United fans revelling at the scoreline. There were no surprises in the target of their gloating as home captain Ince, who had ripped Keane's shirt in disputing the penalty award, was serenaded with: 'Charlie, Charlie, what's the score?'

The earlier spot-kick decision had been clear-cut; the next was anything but. When Patrick Berger turned the ball across goal, Blomqvist slid in to beat Oyvind Leonhardsen and cleared the danger. The Kop appealed, unlike their players, and Elleray gave another penalty. Supposed perpetrator Blomqvist was incredulous; Jamie Redknapp converted from 12 yards.

If that call was harsh on United, the next was harsher. Having been booked for a mistimed tackle, Irwin was shown a second yellow card for kicking the ball away, despite believing that he'd kept it in play and hadn't heard the whistle. 'I deserved the first booking, because I mistimed my tackle,' said the Irishman, who would now miss the FA Cup final through suspension. 'But it was touch and go whether the ball was in or out for the second. What am I supposed to do? Do I stop because I think it might be over the line?'

United's ten men in white did their best to hold on. But, just as at Old Trafford in January's FA Cup tie, there was more late drama. In the 89th minute, Steve McManaman threaded a through pass to Karl-Heinz Riedle; his path was blocked but the ball ran loose and Ince, of all people, stabbed home the equaliser. He revelled in his moment and cupped his ear in the direction of United's fans as he left the pitch, later saying in an interview: 'My message to our fans is, yes, they can get carried away with this result, because it meant so much to everybody stopping Manchester United – and we might have done that.'

Despite the late blow, Alex Ferguson was disappointed but not dejected. 'It looks like it's definitely going to go to the last game of the season,' said the boss. 'We must win all of our three remaining matches. And goal difference might be the deciding thing. Or it might be goals scored. It could come down to that. That's how tight it is.'

Liverpool: Friedel; Song (Berger 57), Babb, Carragher, Staunton (Thompson 79); Matteo, Ince, Redknapp, Leonhardsen; McManaman, Riedle
Subs not used: James, Ferri, Bjornebye

Manchester United: Schmeichel; G.Neville, Johnsen, Stam, Irwin; Beckham, Keane, Scholes, Blomqvist (P.Neville 77); Yorke, Cole (Butt 77)
Subs not used: van der Gouw, May, Sheringham
Booked: Scholes, Keane
Sent-off: Irwin

Man of the Match: Dwight Yorke
Bagged his first league goal since February by converting yet another Beckham cross, and was a nuisance to the Liverpool defence all evening. He made a mockery of talk that tiredness was taking a toll on his game.

Sunday 9 May 1999 | Premiership | Riverside | Attendance: 34,665

MIDDLESBROUGH 0
MANCHESTER UNITED 1 Yorke 45

Still smarting from the perceived injustice of the midweek draw at Anfield, Ferguson's men arrived on Teesside determined to make the most of this game in hand on Arsenal – not just with three points, but also with a boost to the goal difference. A fortnight earlier, Middlesbrough had been thrashed 6-1 by the Gunners; now it was United's turn to try to win in style.

Ryan Giggs was not ready for a return, so Jesper Blomqvist continued on the left flank, meaning there were only two changes from the side that had been controversially held on Merseyside. Teddy Sheringham replaced the rested Andy Cole, while David May stepped in for the injured Ronny Johnsen. The mounting injuries were a worry for the Reds, who were digging deep physically and mentally to drag themselves over the finishing line.

The feeling that fate was conspiring against Alex Ferguson's men continued to build when Roy Keane limped off 25 minutes into the match. Not just because it meant Nicky Butt – the man being wrapped in cotton wool for the Champions League final – had to play, but also because United had been denied a perfectly good goal 11 minutes earlier. Keane's drive had been fumbled by Mark Schwarzer and Sheringham had tucked away the rebound, only for a linesman to raise his flag for offside. TV replays suggested the goal should have stood.

Fans' nerves were frazzled, but the players stayed calm. And on the stroke of half time there was another contentious decision, except this one went the way of the Reds. Collecting possession after a half-cleared corner, Butt lobbed the ball back into the crowded box, Sheringham headed across goal and Dwight Yorke nodded the ball down and into the Middlesbrough net. The home crowd screamed for offside, with good cause according to replays, but the goal stood.

Bryan Robson's side had produced two decent chances of their own in the first half: Mark Summerbell's shot struck the outside of a post and Brian Deane skewed wide from 12 yards. But for the hosts, after the break it was all about keeping out the visitors – which Schwarzer did. Just. The Australian gathered a Paul Scholes shot at the second attempt, blocked another from Gary Neville, and was relieved when the best chance of the second period, for Andy Cole, looped over his head but bounced off the top of the crossbar.

Following his words about the officials earlier in the week, Ferguson sent out his assistant Steve McClaren to summarise events. 'I think we controlled the game from the beginning, played some excellent football and worked very hard. We got the win and we're back on top,' he said. Top indeed, but by the finest of margins, as United and Arsenal were both on 75 points, and had an identical goal difference of +42, but the Reds were ahead thanks only to scoring 78 goals to the Gunners' 58. McClaren made no comment on the goal that should have been, or the one that shouldn't, instead focusing on the job ahead: 'If we win the next two games in the league, I believe we'll win the title.'

Middlesbrough: Schwarzer; Vickers, Gavin (Campbell 71), Pallister; Stockdale, Mustoe, Summerbell, Townsend, Gordon; Deane, Ricard
Subs not used: Beresford, Maddison, Baker, Armstrong
Booked: Mustoe, Townsend

Manchester United: Schmeichel; G.Neville, May, Stam, Irwin; Beckham, Keane (Butt 25), Scholes (P.Neville 90), Blomqvist (Cole 66); Yorke, Sheringham
Subs not used: van der Gouw, Brown
Booked: G.Neville, Scholes, Sheringham

Man of the Match: David May
Sheringham was the freshest and most creative of United's front men, but his display was bettered, just, by the Reds' deputy in defence. Brian Deane and Hamilton Ricard are a handful for any back line, but May used his physical presence and well-timed tackling to keep them at bay.

Wednesday 12 May 1999 | Premiership | Ewood Park | Attendance: 30,436

BLACKBURN ROVERS 0
MANCHESTER UNITED 0

United could have all but secured the title at Ewood Park after a leg-up to the Premiership's summit by the unlikeliest ally, as Leeds beat Arsenal 1-0 at Elland Road the previous night to put the Reds top on goal difference with two games left. But Blackburn were a determined, if unadventurous, side in the death throes of a doomed relegation battle. Meanwhile, United didn't do enough to warrant victory and, rather fittingly in this most dramatic of campaigns, would have to battle for the title on the final day of the league calendar against Tottenham at Old Trafford.

Even the visitors' absent finishing touch couldn't save Rovers from the drop, and while there is little room for compassion and virtually none for charity at this stage of the season, United, and especially the young players who benefited under the tutelage of Blackburn boss Brian Kidd during his time at Old Trafford, would not have wished to be the ones to seal his fate.

The Reds were boosted by the return of Ryan Giggs, who had been out for a month since injuring his ankle amid his heroics against Arsenal in the FA Cup semi-final replay. But there was no Roy Keane, out with a bruised left ankle, and Jaap Stam came off at half time with a sore Achilles. David May stepped in for Stam, while Phil Neville toiled impressively in midfield in Keane's absence.

Hard work wasn't United's problem – finishing was. Giggs hit a post with a header from David Beckham's searching cross, while Andy Cole fired over the rebound. Dwight Yorke's long-range effort forced a good save from John Filan, while Cole's daisy-cutter after Phil Neville's raking 60-yard pass was comfortably saved, and Ronny Johnsen headed wide from Beckham's corner.

Kidd's players showed a feistiness that contradicted his scathing words after their 2-1 weekend loss against already-relegated Nottingham Forest. 'There are a lot of rubber-dinghy men whose attitude is: "The ship is going down, I'll go for help!"' he had said. 'Brave men will have bad games and I can live with that. But there's no courage in the dressing room. People are hiding.'

United responded to Rovers' physical commitment, with Beckham energetic as always, Nicky Butt booked for a crunching tackle on Lee Carsley, while Phil Neville clattered David Dunn in the air. The hosts had a chance on a breakaway attack after 83 minutes, but a beleaguered Ashley Ward couldn't find the target. Neither could Alex Ferguson's men. This United side rarely set a course for plain sailing, and yet a draw here at least meant the Reds could clinch the title on home turf, something Ferguson craved.

Blackburn Rovers: Filan; Croft, Peacock, Henchoz, Davidson; Gillespie (Johnson 81), Dunn, Carsley, Wilcox; Jansen, Ward
Subs not used: Flowers, Broomes, Duff, Davies
Booked: Davidson

Manchester United: Schmeichel; G.Neville, Johnsen, Stam (May h-t), Irwin; Beckham, Butt, P.Neville (Scholes 76), Giggs; Yorke, Cole (Sheringham 71)
Subs not used: van der Gouw, Solskjaer
Booked: Butt, Beckham

Man of the Match: David Beckham
Phil Neville deserves credit for his midfield role but Beckham, whether on the right or drifting more centrally later in the game, tore about with a purpose and energy that was absorbing to watch. He created a handful of scoring chances, sadly not capitalised on.

Sunday 16 May 1999 | Premiership | Old Trafford | Attendance: 55,189

MANCHESTER UNITED 2 Beckham 43, Cole 48
TOTTENHAM HOTSPUR 1 Ferdinand 25

United reclaimed the Premiership crown on an afternoon of high drama, tension and, ultimately, unfettered joy – how else would the

Reds end this epic league campaign? The first of three 'cup finals' in 11 days was a perfect way to get the party started, as Alex Ferguson clinched a fifth Premier League crown as United boss, and crucially it was his first won while on home turf at Old Trafford.

'I have long cherished the ambition of winning the title on our own ground, in front of our own fans and on the last day of the season,' he had said beforehand. 'Now we have the chance of achieving it. And this is the one that really matters. This is going to open the door for the other two trophies, because it puts everyone in the right frame of mind.'

Beating Tottenham and winning the title was vital not just as a stand-alone achievement – a reward for a long, hard season – but because of the momentum it would create in the chase to add the FA Cup and Champions League to the trophy haul. Ferguson opined before kick-off: 'If you had asked me at the start of the season which trophy I wanted most, I would have told you the European Cup. That's because winning the Champions League would elevate this club onto the world stage. But ask me now and there's no doubt in my mind at all. The most important thing is the league championship – and that's how we will approach Sunday's game.'

No doubt with their manager's inspirational words in mind, and the atmosphere buzzing inside Old Trafford, United set out with frenzied purpose from the first whistle and the drama barely waned until the very last. After just four minutes, Dwight Yorke almost opened the scoring when he met Ryan Giggs's cross at the near post, and he inadvertently went even closer when Spurs goalkeeper Ian Walker's clearance hit the United No.19 and rebounded off the post before the relieved shot-stopper pounced on the ball on his goalline.

Yet it was the visitors who scored first after 25 minutes, as Les Ferdinand beat Ronny Johnsen in a sprint to reach Steffen Iversen's flick-on and he lifted the ball back over Peter Schmeichel and into the net. There was now an added edge to the atmosphere. United's response was unequivocally committed. Paul Scholes was twice denied an equaliser in quick succession by Walker, first from the midfielder's thumping 20-yard drive and then again as Teddy Sheringham squared the rebound to United's No.18, whose second attempt was again blocked by Walker, this time from point-blank range.

The Reds were rampant as David Beckham headed Giggs's cross over the bar from close range when a goal seemed a certainty, but there were no doubts about his emphatic strike two minutes before half time to haul United level. Giggs and Scholes worked the ball to Beckham inside the area and he angled a brilliant shot into the top corner past Walker. Old Trafford erupted as the goal the home side's play deserved crashed into the net.

At the break Ferguson replaced Sheringham with Andy Cole – a move that Sheringham was deeply unhappy about, seeing as the game was against his former club, whose fans had rejoiced in his trophyless first season in Manchester. How things were about to change.

The manager's decision was almost immediately vindicated when Cole found the net within three minutes after the restart. Gary Neville's lofted left-foot pass put Cole through on goal and he produced three smart, instinctive touches to find the net. His first plucked the ball out of the air, his second allowed him to readjust his position while simultaneously teeing up his third touch, which lifted the ball brilliantly over Walker's head. His 24th goal of the season was a superb finish and the pent-up pressure was released once again. Now the Reds were in control.

The game was far from over, though, as United had almost a full half to get through. And when chances to further the advantage went begging, and news filtered through in the stands that Arsenal (just one point behind United at the start of the day) led 1-0 against Aston Villa at Highbury, it meant that one slip against Spurs and the title, and Treble, dream would be over.

The two minutes and 42 seconds of stoppage time at the end of the second half felt like an age, but when referee Graham Poll finally blew his whistle, Beckham was one of many players to sink to their knees in jubilation. Ferguson, having celebrated with his coaching staff on the bench, came running onto the pitch and hugged every single one of his newly crowned champions. This feeling of winning the league at Old Trafford was fresh and new, and yet the season still promised so much more. For now, everyone's focus was the league.

Arsenal boss Arsène Wenger was gracious in defeat, saying: 'Finishing one point behind is like losing a marathon by a yard. It's terrible to think that we've picked up seventy-eight points, the same as last year, have a better defensive record and a team that's grown in quality and still we haven't won it. But the difference has been Manchester United. I congratulate them for what they've achieved. They've had a remarkable season, and now I hope they win the Champions League because it is important for English football.'

Perhaps fuelled by the bubbly, Ferguson swooned: 'You can look back at great days and all the rest of it, but they don't compare with this. I am starting to paint my players as Gods of the game. I'm even thinking about a forward line of five strikers against Newcastle in the FA Cup on Saturday. Those thoughts will almost certainly disappear by tomorrow when the champagne has gone. But we're all allowed to dream, aren't we?' United and Ferguson had dared to dream the impossible. Now it was beginning to become reality.

Manchester United: Schmeichel; G.Neville, Johnsen, May, Irwin; Beckham, Keane, Scholes (Butt 70), Giggs (P.Neville 80); Yorke, Sheringham (Cole h-t)
Subs not used: van der Gouw, Solskjaer
Booked: Sheringham

Tottenham Hotspur: Walker; Carr, Scales (Young 71), Campbell, Edinburgh; Anderton, Sherwood, Freund, Ginola (Dominguez 10 (Sinton 78)); Iversen, Ferdinand
Subs not used: Baardsen, Clemence
Booked: Anderton

Man of the Match: Roy Keane

Keane redefined the term captain's performance in this incredible campaign, and this immense display was precisely why. Despite an ankle injury, he hauled his team over the finishing line like a patched-up warrior. 'How fit was he?' said Ferguson. 'He was one hundred and fifty per cent because he wanted to be one hundred and fifty per cent fit.'

Saturday 22 May 1999 | FA Cup final | Wembley | Attendance: 79,101

MANCHESTER UNITED 2 Sheringham 11, Scholes 52
NEWCASTLE UNITED 0

'One down, two to go' read a Wembley banner in the United end and, in truth, the Reds easily racked up a record third domestic Double while basking in glorious Wembley sunshine on the simplest leg of the triple-trophy haul. Newcastle, despite their early aggression, simply couldn't help but succumb to Alex Ferguson's side's inexorable march to glory.

Ferguson was by now well acquainted with juggling his squad, tailoring his team to suit the occasion and the opponent, but even best-laid plans must sometimes be torn up, solutions to specific scenarios improvised upon – not least as several squad members complained of flu in the days leading up to this final. Fortunately, even an enforced early personnel change worked in Ferguson's favour, as it brought about a breakthrough in the match.

With the Champions League final just around the corner, and Paul Scholes and Roy Keane unable to play against Bayern Munich due to suspension, Nicky Butt could not be risked at Wembley. Besides, Scholes and Keane had already been assured of their places at the national stadium and Ferguson kept his word.

Denis Irwin was suspended, so Phil Neville took his place at left-back, and Jaap Stam's Achilles problem meant he wouldn't be jeopardised, although Ferguson felt the Dutchman deserved an FA Cup winner's medal as a substitute. Jesper Blomqvist was rested, with the intention of using him on the left in Barcelona, as Ryan Giggs was earmarked as Butt's central partner, with David Beckham on the right. That was the Nou Camp plan.

But with Newcastle attempting to exert early physical authority, Gary Speed clattered into Keane after just two minutes and United's game plan was thrown in the air. Keane trundled off after nine minutes and, with no central midfielders on the bench, United simply had to go for it. Teddy Sheringham replaced Keane, Ole Gunnar Solskjaer shifted to the right and Beckham shuffled infield. It was an inspired switch.

Within 96 seconds, Sheringham had scored and so good was Beckham in the centre that it forced a rethink for the Champions League final, as the Reds' No.7 would instead partner Butt. However, the Nou Camp was a world away with the scores at 0-0 and influential captain Keane forced from the field of play.

Those concerns were quickly assuaged. David May fizzed a pass into Andy Cole and the United striker turned and aimed the ball at Giggs out on the left. Sheringham was in its path and was in no mood to be bypassed. He controlled the ball with his first touch, nudged it past Rob Lee with his second, slipped a pass inside to Scholes and went for the return ball in the box before incisively steering a shot through Steve Harper's legs. Four touches, all of them pure class. It seemed so simple. 'We were firmly in the driving seat and from then on it was an absolute stroll,' Ferguson later remarked. 'I couldn't believe an FA Cup final could be so easy.'

United's lead never really looked in danger, either, as the Reds' dominance was compounded seven minutes after the restart when Solskjaer intercepted Nikos Dabizas's weak clearance and found Sheringham inside the box with his back to goal. It was then a simple case of laying the ball off for Scholes, who let rip with a low left-footed shot beyond Harper. Roy Collins, of the *People* newspaper, wrote: 'One goal always looked like being enough for Manchester United. But when Scholes scored the second early in the second half, we could all have packed up and gone home. Newcastle knew it, the crowd knew it and United's players certainly knew it.'

Temuri Ketsbaia and Sheringham both hit the woodwork in the second period, but this match was set for only one outcome. At the final whistle, Keane was beckoned from the bench and donned the captain's armband once again as the injured skipper hobbled up the 39 steps to collect the famous trophy. 'Yes, you beauty,' he screamed.

It was another afternoon tinged with personal frustration for United's No.16 in another cruel twist to the Irishman's season. 'I had been struggling with my right ankle before the game and then I twisted my left ankle in the tackle,' Keane explained. 'The team needed someone who was one hundred per cent fit. The substitution made it for us, but the whole squad deserve the credit.'

Sheringham's sizeable impact on the afternoon didn't go unnoticed. 'Teddy was magnificent,' purred Ferguson. 'He has proved a point today. He was the key to victory.' But he wasn't the only player to catch the eye. Beckham continued to impress in his and United's *annus mirabilis*, this time in a controlling central midfield role.

'People say that going to Barcelona without Roy Keane will be a major hurdle, but I don't think so now,' added Ferguson, even if his words were unmistakably designed to boost his No.7's confidence. 'Beckham took over Keane's role and was absolutely magnificent. But I'm so pleased and proud of all the players. It's fantastic – three Doubles in five years. It was a great performance by the team. We played some excellent football.'

Now it was two down, one to go – the toughest yet. But the Treble was on and United were on the crest of a powerful wave. 'I feel great,' added Ferguson at Burnham Beeches as the Reds prepared for the trip to Barcelona. 'The spirit of these players is such that everyone is looking forward to Wednesday. The confidence is very high – it's never say die and they don't want to be beaten.'

Manchester United: Schmeichel; G.Neville, May, Johnsen, P.Neville; Beckham, Keane (Sheringham 9), Scholes (Stam 76), Giggs; Solskjaer, Cole (Yorke 60)
Subs not used: van der Gouw, Blomqvist

Newcastle United: Harper; Griffin, Dabizas, Chavret, Domi; Lee, Hamann (Ferguson 12), Speed, Solano (Maric 68); Ketsbaia (Glass 78), Shearer
Subs not used: Given, Barton
Booked: Hamann

Man of the Match: Teddy Sheringham
The Londoner was fast gaining a reputation to rival Ole Gunnar Solskjaer's ability at making an incisive impact from the bench, and Sheringham's introduction here undoubtedly shaped the course of the game. His goal after less than two minutes on the field was brilliantly worked and he had a hand in the second, too. Few could question his move to Manchester now.

Wednesday 26 May 1999 | Champions League final | Nou Camp |
Attendance: 90,000

BAYERN MUNICH 1 Basler 6
MANCHESTER UNITED 2 Sheringham 90, Solskjaer 90

There have been better European Cup finals, there have been worse finals with better goals, but it's doubtful there has ever been a final with an ending quite as dramatic as this one. Talk about saving the best till the very last.

In injury time of the 63rd match of a gruelling, testing season, Manchester United pulled off the seemingly impossible. Ribbons in Bayern Munich's colours had been tied on to the handles of the over-sized trophy. Lennart Johansson had offered his commiserations to Sir Bobby Charlton on his way to pitchside to present the Cup. Some Reds, like George Best, had given up and headed off into the balmy Barcelona night. But then, in 102 adrenaline-drenched seconds, sub-stitutes Teddy Sheringham and Ole Gunnar Solskjaer struck two never-to-be-forgotten goals to win United a second European Cup and complete a tumultuous trophy Treble.

'Even if you only saw it on TV, you don't like football much and you can't even stand Manchester United, it was a two-minute mira-cle you will tell your grandchildren about,' reported Jonathan Margolis of the *Daily Mail*. Only fully paid-up members of the Anyone But United brigade – or shell-shocked Bayern fans – would beg to differ. It was a climax that transcended football; it was pure sporting theatre.

Heading into the Continent's showpiece match, the similarities between the clubs were obvious. Bayern were chasing a Treble of their own, had dominated their domestic game for the past decade, enjoyed a huge following that came from well beyond their home city and had waited since 1976 to win European football's elite club trophy. On the pitch they were also well matched, the two group games earlier in the season ending 2-2 and 1-1, with United arguably edging both ties.

Despite the parity of the two previous meetings, Bayern boss Ottmar Hitzfeld was confident his side would prevail in the Nou Camp and took the unusual step of naming his side two days before the game. Alex Ferguson was less bold, sticking to his preferred approach of waiting until the big night to reveal his eleven.

Everywhere you looked on the teamsheet were mouth-watering match-ups: Stam against Jancker, Butt facing Effenberg, Beckham battling Jeremies, Cole versus Kuffour. They were the key battles that would help decide who was crowned the kings of European football.

An estimated 50–60,000 United fans invaded Catalonia, with the Germans bringing 40,000 of their own. That combination inside Barcelona's iconic stadium, with the majority of neutral sections seemingly filled by Red Army foot soldiers, created a cacophony of noise. Soon, though, there was silence, at one end of the ground at least, as Bayern struck the game's first goal after just six minutes.

Ronny Johnsen was harshly adjudged to have fouled Carsten Jancker, who appeared to make the most of the slightest contact, presenting Bayern with a free-kick within range. 'Super' Mario Basler stepped forward, feigned to curl the ball over the wall to Peter Schmeichel's right, only to bend it into the net low to the Dane's left.

It was the lead the German champions had been wanting, playing perfectly to their game plan. Even with so long left in the match, it allowed them to sit back, soak up pressure and look to strike on the break. For United, knocking Bayern out of their comfort zone would have been difficult enough at full strength; with the suspension of Roy Keane and Paul Scholes bringing about a reshuffle, the Reds were looking a shadow of a side that was on a 32-game undefeated run. David Beckham buzzed around in the middle of midfield, but with Ryan Giggs switched to the right and Jesper Blomqvist on the left, the supply to the front men was far from fluent. Hitzfeld's side deserved their interval advantage.

Alex Ferguson needed to lift his side and at half time gave a simple yet stirring speech, as later revealed by Sheringham. 'He said to us, "If you lose, you'll have to go up and get your losers' medals,"' explained the striker. '"You'll be six feet away from the European Cup, but you will not be able to touch it. For many of you, that will be the closest you ever get. Don't dare come back in here without giving your all."'

There was a reaction from the Reds in the second half, but only after Bayern had twice gone close: first through Jancker, who drew a save from Schmeichel, then Sammy Kuffour, whose diving header drifted wide. Having been kept quiet for over an hour, United finally produced a move to admire. After a spell of possession play, the ball was worked out wide right to Giggs. He sent over a left-foot cross and Blomqvist stretched out a leg in an attempt to turn the ball home. He got there, just, but sent the ball high over the bar.

Stirred, United pushed forward in search of parity, and on 67 minutes Ferguson took a gamble by throwing on Sheringham for Blomqvist. Beckham shuffled to the right, Giggs to the left, for a now unfamiliar 4-3-3 formation. It increased the Reds' hopes of an equaliser, but left them looking vulnerable to the counter-attack. Stefan Effenberg fizzed a 25-yard shot narrowly wide, then had a volley palmed over by Schmeichel. And when Mehmet Scholl's lob hit the post and bounced out, the United stopper gratefully gathered the loose ball.

With ten minutes remaining, further changes were made by both sides – and for United the replacement of Andy Cole with Solskjaer would prove decisive. Yet before the Norwegian could make an impact, there were two further scares for the Reds: Schmeichel denied Scholl, tipping round his post, and Jancker thumped the crossbar with an overhead kick. Having survived those heart-in-mouth moments, caution was thrown to the wind. Crosses were flashing across goal: Dwight Yorke missed one completely, then Solskjaer tested Oliver Kahn. With the 90 minutes now up, it seemed as though United's efforts had been in vain, but then came the history-making moment that changed it all.

United's big goalkeeper forayed forward for a Beckham corner and caused a suitable distraction as Yorke headed back but away from goal. Giggs skewed his right-footed volley back into the box but it was heading seemingly wide, only for substitute Sheringham to redirect it on target. One-all. Pandemonium on the pitch; scenes mirrored in the stands.

United supporters had barely stopped celebrating, but now their attention was on the Bayern box again. Another corner. Beckham over the ball. Then, within the blink of an eye, the euphoria of the first goal was multiplied. Sheringham flicked on at the near post, Solskjaer stuck out his right leg and the ball hit the back of Kahn's net. Two-one. Promised land reached. The ultimate football high.

Referee Pierluigi Collina dragged the devastated German players to their feet, the ball briefly bounced around in midfield and the final whistle was blown. Emotions poured out. 'It's one of the best feelings in the world,' said Beckham. 'We are the team that never dies,' gushed Gary Neville. 'Obviously you feel sorry for Bayern after being one-nil up for so long. But that is the beauty and cruelty of football,' added Schmeichel.

Bayern and their fans were disconsolate. United players and supporters danced into the early hours, celebrating not just a second European Cup but having achieved the seemingly impossible: the Treble. The mastermind of the triumph, the soon-to-be Sir Alex Ferguson, summed up the feelings of everyone connected with the club when he said: 'I'm proud of my players, proud of my heritage and proud of what my family has given me. This is the greatest moment of my life.'

Manchester United: Schmeichel; G.Neville, Johnsen, Stam, Irwin; Giggs, Beckham, Butt, Blomqvist (Sheringham 67); Yorke, Cole (Solskjaer 81)
Subs not used: van der Gouw, P.Neville, May, Brown, Greening

Bayern Munich: Kahn; Linke, Matthaus (Fink 80), Kuffour; Babbel, Jeremies, Effenberg, Tarnat; Basler (Salihamidzic 88); Jancker, Zickler (Scholl 71)
Subs not used: Scheuer, Kuffour, Tarnat
Booked: Effenberg

Man of the Match: David Beckham
Switched into the centre due to suspension to Keane and Scholes, Beckham was United's star performer in a below-par Reds display. His accurate crossing had been a main contributor to United's Double success, now he made it a Treble with two corners that caused panic in the Bayern box and resulted in two historic goals.

May in statistics

Final Premiership table

	P	W	D	L	F	A	GD	Pts
Manchester United	38	22	13	3	80	37	+43	79
Arsenal	38	22	12	4	59	17	+42	78
Chelsea	38	20	15	3	57	30	+27	75
Leeds United	38	18	13	7	62	34	+28	67
West Ham United	38	16	9	13	46	53	-7	57
Aston Villa	38	15	10	13	51	46	+5	55
Liverpool	38	15	9	14	68	49	+19	54
Derby County	38	13	13	12	40	45	-5	52
Middlesbrough	38	12	15	11	48	54	-6	51
Leicester City	38	12	13	13	40	46	-6	49
Tottenham Hotspur	38	11	14	13	47	50	-3	47
Sheffield Wed	38	13	7	18	41	42	-1	46
Newcastle United	38	11	13	14	48	54	-6	46
Everton	38	11	10	17	42	47	-5	43
Coventry City	38	11	9	18	39	51	-12	42
Wimbledon	38	10	12	16	40	63	-23	42
Southampton	38	11	8	19	37	64	-27	41
Charlton Athletic	38	8	12	18	41	56	-15	36
Blackburn Rovers	38	7	14	17	38	52	-14	35
Nottingham Forest	38	7	9	22	35	69	-34	30

May form (all competitions): WDWDWWW

Goals scored: 11   **Goals conceded:** 5

Most appearances: Peter Schmeichel, Gary Neville, David Beckham 7 each (630 mins)

Players used: 17

May – The Promised Land

Most goals: David Beckham, Dwight Yorke, Teddy Sheringham
2 each

Most assists: Paul Scholes, Teddy Sheringham 3 each

Different goalscorers: 8

Quickest goal: Teddy Sheringham, 11 mins [v Newcastle (n)]

Latest goal: Ole Gunnar Solskjaer, 90 mins [v Bayern Munich (n)]

Watched by: 390,282

Average attendance: 55,754

Chapter 11

The Players

Goalkeepers

1 PETER SCHMEICHEL

It was a season of two halves for the world's best goalkeeper. Prior to being sent for some mid-winter R&R, he was unusually error prone, his confidence low and he appeared anything but the indomitable stopper of the previous eight years. Returning from a Barbados getaway he was rejuvenated, saving his best till last in an impressive final few months of the club's most successful ever season. Against Arsenal in the FA Cup semi-final replay he saved Dennis Bergkamp's late penalty to ensure extra time. Then, in the final game in the Nou Camp, he made an impact at both ends: first keeping Bayern at bay as the Reds chased an equaliser, then helping secure one by causing a 6ft 3in distraction in Munich's box as Teddy Sheringham netted. Having decided to head for pastures new, it felt only right that the acting captain ended his Reds career lifting the European Cup.

Premiership: 34 apps; Champions League: 13 apps; FA Cup: 8 apps; Charity Shield: 1 app; Total: 56 apps

17 RAIMOND VAN DER GOUW

The Reds would have been hard pressed to find a more reliable understudy to Schmeichel than the Dutchman. Not only did he step in whenever required – on eight occasions – but he also doubled up as goalkeeping coach. His calm demeanour helped secure league wins at Southampton and at Old Trafford against Wimbledon, West Ham and Sheffield Wednesday.

Premiership: 4(1) apps; League Cup: 3 apps; Total: 7(1) apps

Defenders

2 GARY NEVILLE

Consistency. That's what the elder Neville brother contributed to the Treble. Even allowing for the odd blip, like the 3-2 home defeat by Middlesbrough, his displays rarely dropped below an eight out of ten. Alex Ferguson knew that by including Gary he'd be assured of a wholehearted, solid display at full back, that he'd shore up the Reds' right flank with his great mate David Beckham, and when pitched at centre-half he'd assist Jaap Stam through his assimilation to English football. In fact, his finest display came in the middle in September when he kept Liverpool livewire Michael Owen quiet in United's 2-0 victory. He also weighed in with a goal, always a rare feat, in the 3-1 home win over Everton. Gary guarantees passion – bags of it – and the Reds' No.2's badge-kissing, chest-thumping celebration on the Stadio Delle Alpi pitch after the Champions League semi-final win was one of the season's iconic images. Gary Neville is a Red – and was at his very best in 1998-99.

Premiership: 34 apps, 1 goal; Champions League: 12 apps; FA Cup: 7 apps; Charity Shield: 1 app; Total: 54 apps, 1 goal

3 DENIS IRWIN

A continual source of stability and strength for Alex Ferguson's teams in the 1990s, the 33-year-old Irishman's experience was now more valuable than ever. Young Phil Neville snapped at his heels for game-time, but Irwin remained a vital cog in defence, particularly in a back four whose central pairing changed frequently, while Ryan Giggs and Jesper Blomqvist interchanged ahead of him. Irwin played in all but one match on United's European odyssey and was outstanding in the semi-final in Turin, where he nearly won the game with a second-half shot that hit the post. Attacking was a natural feature of Irwin's game and, with Gary Neville on the opposite flank, United had two forward-thinking full-backs who relished rapid breakaways. Of Irwin's three goals in 1998-99 – all from the penalty spot – two came against Liverpool; May's encounter, however, was bittersweet as he was harshly sent off by David Elleray and missed the FA Cup final. Regardless, Irwin's contribution on all three fronts was invaluable.

Premiership: 26(3) apps, 2 goals; Champions League: 12 apps; FA Cup: 6 apps, 1 goal; Charity Shield: 1 app; Total: 45(3) apps, 3 goals

4 DAVID MAY

Oldham-born May missed much of the campaign through injury as well as the form of Stam, Berg, Johnsen and Brown. In fact, May had played just twice – in the League Cup – by mid-April, but he helped see out the season, notably when called upon at Leeds after Stam was injured in the warm-up, and played in six of the last seven league games and the FA Cup final.

Premiership: 4(2) apps; FA Cup: 1 app; League Cup: 2 apps; Total: 7(2) apps

5 RONNY JOHNSEN

Started and ended the season as Alex Ferguson's partner of choice for Jaap Stam, linking well with the defensive mainstay in the semi and final of the Champions League triumph. Early teething problems were down to the time when the Dutchman was settling in to English football, Johnsen then missed September to December through injury, but the pair still racked up 20 appearances together, conceding just 18 goals. It proved by far the most consistently strong centre-back pairing; Johnsen providing the silk to Stam's steel. Yet not all of his season highlights came at the back; his youthful past as a striker paid dividends, with Ronny scoring three times (including a brace in United's 3-0 Boxing Day defeat of Nottingham Forest) and his stints in midfield were useful, too. There was a long cast list for this epic Treble season, but Johnsen was one of the central characters and appeared in all three of May's 'cup finals'.

Premiership: 19(3) apps, 3 goals; Champions League: 6(2) apps; FA Cup: 3(2) apps; League Cup: 1 app; Charity Shield: 1 app; Total: 30(7) apps, 3 goals

6 JAAP STAM

The towering Dutchman (briefly) became United's record signing, the most expensive player in Dutch history and the world's costliest defender when he signed for £10.75 million from PSV Eindhoven in summer 1998. It took time to adjust to the cut and thrust of English football and he was initially pilloried in some parts of the press, yet he emerged as a colossal figure, a brick wall of a defender who stood tall all season. His one and only Reds goal came in the 6-2 win over Leicester City, but it was his consistent excellence at the back that made the greatest impact, most notably in the latter stages of the Champions League against Inter Milan and Juventus. In the semi-final second leg, despite United conceding two early Pippo Inzaghi goals – the second deflecting in off Stam's boot – the Dutchman was utterly dominant and drew praise at home and abroad. His power, presence, deceptive pace and uncompromising command proved to be money very well spent indeed.

Premiership: 30 apps, 1 goal; Champions League: 13 apps; FA Cup: 6(1) apps; Charity Shield: 1 app; Total: 50(1) apps, 1 goal

12 PHIL NEVILLE

To describe the younger Neville brother as a valuable squad player suggests that he played merely a supporting role in this most memorable of seasons; he was more than that. In September and October, he was a regular at left-back, filling in for Denis Irwin and scoring his only goal of the season in the 5-0 home defeat of Brondby. He also started the FA Cup final against Newcastle in May. He played some part in two-thirds of United's matches, not bad for someone who turned 22 years of age midway through the campaign. Perhaps the biggest compliment to Phil was that so smoothly did he slip into the team that you barely noticed Irwin was missing. Collecting three winners' medals was certainly not a bad way to recover from being overlooked by England for their final World Cup squad the previous summer. Season 1998-99 really was one of redemption, not just for Beckham.

Premiership: 19(9) apps; Champions League: 4(2) apps, 1 goal; FA Cup: 4(3) apps; League Cup: 2 apps; Charity Shield: 0(1) apps; Total: 29(15) apps, 1 goal

13 JOHN CURTIS

Another youngster who provided support in this fixture-heavy season. The full-back made one start and three substitute appearances in the Premier League and was a regular in the three-game League Cup run that ended at Spurs. He was overshadowed by the emergence of Wes Brown, but he was still a steady understudy at the back.

Premiership: 1(3) apps; League Cup: 3 apps; Total: 4(3) apps

21 HENNING BERG

In the past, injuries had denied United the services of the Norwegian's no-nonsense defending, but when sporadic appearances in the first half of 1998-99 gradually gave way to a regular starting berth at the turn of the year, Berg really came into his own. Aggressive in the tackle, powerful in the air, he performed formidably as Jaap Stam's lieutenant. Berg grew in stature, and his displays at the heart of defence in the Champions League quarter-final against Inter Milan are still revered by fans. Clearances off the line from Francesco Colonnese's shot at Old Trafford and an acrobatic block to deny Ivan Zamorano a certain goal at San Siro were two pivotal moments in the tie. It was all the more disappointing, then, that medial ligament damage in an innocuous incident in the semi-final first leg against Juventus brought Berg's season to a premature end. However, the late drama in the Nou Camp may not have been possible without him.

Premiership: 10(6) apps; Champions League: 3(1) apps; FA Cup: 5 apps; League Cup: 3 apps; Charity Shield: 0(1) apps; Total: 21(8) apps

23 MICHAEL CLEGG

A mainstay of the Worthington Cup run, Clegg was a steady performer the three times he stepped up from Jimmy Ryan's Reserves. A strong tackler, he was nothing less than fully committed across the three ties, but with Gary Neville in such excellent form – plus a host of more senior alternatives – his first team opportunities were limited.

League Cup: 3 apps; Total: 3 apps

24 WES BROWN

The Longsight teenager made an exciting full-season debut, partly possible due to injuries and fluctuating form among his defensive team-mates, but also simply because of his unquestionable talent. His involvement waned when experience was the watchword, but Ferguson was unafraid to use him; Wes started three European games, including the 3-3 draw in Barcelona and the 1-1 tie with Bayern Munich at Old Trafford.

Premiership: 11(3) apps; Champions League: 3(1) apps; FA Cup: 2 apps; League Cup: 0(1) apps; Total: 16(5) apps

30 RONNIE WALLWORK

Mancunian Wallwork replaced David May at half time of the Worthington Cup fourth-round tie against Nottingham Forest and put in a solid 45-minute display alongside Henning Berg. But that was the young Reserve's only outing of the season before moving on loan to Royal Antwerp.

League Cup: 0(1) apps; Total: 0(1) apps

Midfielders

7 DAVID BECKHAM

'A lot of people were writing me off at the start of the season saying I would crack or maybe go abroad, but that never even entered my head,' said David Beckham, fresh from becoming a Treble-winner. Thank goodness he did neither. Spurred on by the boos of opposition fans, he produced the finest football of his career to date, buzzing around from the first kick of the season at Wembley to the last in the Nou Camp. His crossing was pinpoint, his free-kicks stunning, his workrate unrivalled, and his overall contribution a major factor in United's three-trophy haul. In 1998-99 he took his game to a whole new level, and knew exactly who to thank for his inspiration. 'The people booing did me a favour,' he said. 'I just ignored them, got my head down and got on with my game – but I'm sure it improved me as a player.'

Premiership: 33(1) apps, 6 goals; Champions League: 12 apps, 2 goals; FA Cup: 7 apps, 1 goal; League Cup: 0(1) apps; Charity Shield: 1 app; Total: 53(2) apps, 9 goals

8 NICKY BUTT

This gritty son of Gorton played the least of the five main midfielders used in 1998-99, but such was his importance that he still ranked 11th in the list of overall appearances for the campaign. With Roy Keane the first name on the team sheet, Butt and Scholes were rotated alongside their captain – Alex Ferguson basing his selection on which of the two best suited the opposition. Even so, many of Butt's finer displays came when deputising for his absent skipper – among them his shackling of Stefan Effenberg in the Champions League final. Better still was his display in the five-goal thriller against Leeds at Old Trafford, settled by his 78th-minute spectacular drive. The arrival of Jaap Stam, Jesper Blomqvist and Dwight Yorke played a huge part in the triple-trophy triumph, but the backbone for the success was unquestionably the lads from the Class of '92. Butt's contribution to this stunning season was his fierce will to win and unstinting dedication to the cause.

Premiership: 22(9) apps, 2 goals; Champions League: 4(4) apps; FA Cup: 5 apps; League Cup: 2 apps; Charity Shield: 1 app; Total: 34(13) apps, 2 goals

11 RYAN GIGGS

The Welshman scaled heady heights in 1998-99 and was revered across Europe, particularly by the Italians who feared his pace and clever possession play. He was a major threat at home, too. The key for Alex Ferguson was keeping his winged wonder fit and firing; Jesper Blomqvist's arrival allowed Giggs rests at key points – although the Reds' No.11 was still among United's top ten appearance-makers. Injury briefly struck in early winter and a hamstring strain in February brought back painful memories of 1997-98, when Giggs's absence hampered United's challenge to Arsenal's Double success.

This time, the Welshman returned quickly and immediately hit a vital late winner at Coventry. He later bagged a draw-salvaging stoppage-time goal against Juventus, but his indelible mark on this epic season was one of its defining moments: his genius solo winner in the extra-time FA Cup semi-final replay win over Arsenal at Villa Park. Few moments top that for significance and theatre.

Premiership: 20(4) apps, 3 goals; Champions League: 9 apps, 5 goals; FA Cup: 5(1) apps, 2 goals; League Cup: 1 app; Charity Shield: 1 app; Total: 36(5) apps, 10 goals

14 JORDI CRUYFF

He may have been out on loan at Celta Vigo by the time the three silver pots were being collected in May, but the Dutchman did make a contribution to the campaign as a whole. Twice he stepped off the bench to score – at Southampton and Derby – with the latter a crucial, bobbling equaliser that secured a barely deserved Premiership point at Pride Park. As they say, every little counts.

Premiership: 0(5) apps, 2 goals; Champions League: 0(3) apps; League Cup: 2 apps; Charity Shield: 0(1) app; Total: 2(9) apps, 2 goals

15 JESPER BLOMQVIST

The Swedish winger played a crucial role in his debut season for the Reds, not only allowing for Ryan Giggs to be rested but also providing genuine competition on the left-hand side of midfield. He settled quickly, taking to life at United as if he'd been at Old Trafford for years, putting in notable early-season performances against Charlton, Bayern Munich, Southampton and Everton. At Goodison Park he scored his only goal of the season – following up his own half-blocked shot with a headed strike. Dislodging crowd favourite Giggs was never going to be an easy task, and it was whenever the Welshman was out injured that he enjoyed his most prolonged spells in the side: in November and a crucial period between mid-April to mid-May. Possessing a good cross, accurate passing and the ability to beat a man, the Swede played an important role.

Premiership: 20(5) apps, 1 goal; Champions League: 6(1) apps; FA Cup: 3(2) apps; League Cup: 0(1) apps; Total: 29(9) apps, 1 goal

16 ROY KEANE

Of all the factors that contributed to the landing of the seemingly impossible Treble, none was quite as vital as the return of Roy Keane. It was not only the exemplary performances of English football's finest marauding midfielder that were so sorely missed during his injury the previous year, but also his crucial commanding of team-mates. It took a while for those qualities to re-emerge. First came match fitness, next the old sharpness, then finally his authoritative aura of old. By the season's end, he was producing match-defining displays weekly. Ironically, his best 90 minutes of the season were also his worst personally. In the second leg of the Champions League semi-final in Turin he was booked, meaning the heartbreak of suspension from the final should United progress. Rather than sulk, he gave the hallmark performance of his career to lead the Reds to victory – his headed goal launching the fightback, his bossing of Zinedine Zidane and Didier Deschamps nullifying Juventus. He later admitted embarrassment at receiving a medal in the Nou Camp; yet nobody deserved one more.

Premiership: 33(2) apps, 2 goals; Champions League: 12 apps, 3 goals; FA Cup: 7 apps; Charity Shield: 1 app; Total: 53(2) apps, 5 goals

18 PAUL SCHOLES

With Keane and Beckham the two constants in United's midfield, and Ryan Giggs supported on the left by Jesper Blomqvist, Paul Scholes and Nicky Butt shared the last remaining midfield spot beside captain Keane, each playing a similar number of games – Scholes had 38 starts and 13 substitute appearances to Butt's 34 starts and 13 sub outings. Alex Ferguson alternated between Scholes's creativity and Butt's combativeness, depending on the occasion and opponents, but the Reds' No.18's craft going forward was a huge asset – indeed, he was United's fourth-top scorer with 11 goals. In September, Scholes scored three in three games, with goals in the draws with Barcelona and Bayern Munich sandwiching a 79th-minute effort in the 2-0 league win over Liverpool. His late San Siro strike against Inter Milan confirmed United's progress into Europe's last four, and while it was a crying shame Scholes missed the Champions League final through suspension, he scored in the FA Cup final against Newcastle at Wembley to reaffirm his vital contribution.

Premiership: 24(7) apps, 6 goals; Champions League: 10(2) apps, 4 goals; FA Cup: 3(3) apps, 1 goal; League Cup: 0(1) apps; Charity Shield: 1 app; Total: 38(13) apps, 11 goals

28 PHIL MULRYNE

The Northern Irishman was in the same FA Youth Cup-winning side as Phil Neville in 1995 and earned two League Cup starts in 1998-99. He played in the 2-0 third-round win over Bury and the fourth-round 2-1 victory over Nottingham Forest before departing for Norwich City at the end of the season.

League Cup: 2 apps; Total: 2 apps

33 MARK WILSON

The Scunthorpe-born midfielder appeared in two of the Reds' three League Cup ties (against Bury and Nottingham Forest), and stepped off the bench in the Champions League win at Brondby. He displayed all the attributes expected of a youth system graduate – solid technique and bags of industry – but could not break into United's strongest-ever midfield.

Champions League: 0(1) apps; League Cup: 2 apps; Total: 2(1) apps

34 JONATHAN GREENING

In his first full season for the Reds, youngster Greening played in all three League Cup ties and showed flashes of the potential that prompted his signing from York City. So much so that he made three substitute appearances in the Premiership and picked up a Champions League winner's medal as an unused substitute at the Nou Camp.

Premiership: 0(3) apps; FA Cup 0(1) apps; League Cup 3 apps; Total: 3(4) apps

Forwards

9 ANDY COLE

He started the season with a goal against Lodz, briefly lost his place, then burst into life in October as one half of the seemingly telepathic partnership with Dwight Yorke. Cole contributed 24 goals, Yorke 29, as the pair ran defences ragged across the country and continent. Yorke brought the best out of the Reds' No.9, and he the best out of the new arrival. They started in tandem 37 times, from which they scored a combined total of 45 goals, and were together on the same scoresheet on ten occasions. Cole's undoubted season highlight, just pipping his Champions League final-sealing strike at Juventus, was his winner against Tottenham to clinch the first leg of the Treble. On as a substitute, he controlled a Gary Neville pass with his very first touch, before lobbing Ian Walker to seal a 2-1 win and the return of the Premiership title to Old Trafford. An undoubted star of the Treble.

Premiership: 26(6) apps, 17 goals; Champions League: 10 apps, 5 goals; FA Cup: 6(1) apps, 2 goals; Charity Shield: 1 app; Total: 43(7) apps, 24 goals

10 TEDDY SHERINGHAM

He started the season as United fans' whipping boy for the 1997-98 title miss; but he ended it with three shiny medals hanging around his neck. A knee injury twice interrupted his season for sustained spells, and the success of the first-choice Yorke–Cole axis didn't help when he was fit, but he was back when it really mattered. Teddy forged his own secondary partnership with Solskjaer, and the pair produced in injury time on the biggest stage of all. His equaliser against Bayern in the Nou Camp was the highlight of his season, just days after he bagged the FA Cup-clinching second goal at Wembley against Newcastle. Despite watching from the stands for long periods of the season, the Reds' No.10 never lost hope that he'd have a telling impact. 'The boss was very good,' he said. 'He saw in advance that everybody was going to be needed and he was spot on.'

Premiership: 7(10) apps, 2 goals; Champions League: 2(2) apps, 1 goal; FA Cup: 1(3) apps, 1 goal; League Cup: 1 app, 1 goal; Charity Shield: 0(1) app; Total: 11(16) apps, 5 goals

19 DWIGHT YORKE

An indisputable catalyst on and off the pitch during United's Treble success, Yorke made a galvanising impact after a record £12.6 million move from Aston Villa that was likened by team-mates to that of Eric Cantona. His 29 goals were a remarkable first-season contribution, so too were his many assists. His unique understanding with Andy Cole made United's attack the envy of England and Europe, and perhaps just as deadly was his link-up with David Beckham, whose wicked crosses Yorke gleefully capitalised on. Just as important was Yorke's infectious enthusiasm and swaggering belief; he was a breath of fresh air at the Cliff and Old Trafford. Yorke's perma-grin happiness permeated through the squad – even his notorious input to regular squad nights out boosted camaraderie, further fuelling United's Treble drive. His season highlights were many: his equalising goal in Turin, a hat-trick at Leicester, braces against Barcelona, Chelsea and Inter, where his partnership with Beckham was at its most obvious, and important winners against Charlton, Derby and Middlesbrough. His influence cannot be overstated.

Premiership: 32 apps, 18 goals; Champions League: 11 apps, 8 goals; FA Cup 5(3) apps, 3 goals; Total: 48(3) apps, 29 goals

20 OLE GUNNAR SOLSKJAER

The Norwegian's triple-barrelled name will forever be linked to the Reds' incredible Treble. Of the ten months of football, 63 matches and 128 goals, it is the footage of United's No.20 prodding the ball into the Bayern net that will be shown and re-shown in perpetuity. He contributed 17 other goals over the course of the campaign, making vital contributions along the way – like his injury-time winner in the FA Cup against Liverpool and four goals in ten minutes at

Nottingham Forest – but it's that late, late strike in the Nou Camp for which he'll remain synonymous with United's Treble. Yorke and Cole scored more goals, Beckham provided more assists, Keane gave more man-of-the-match displays – but the player that produced the final telling moment of the whole triumph, the man who sealed it, was Ole Gunnar Solskjaer. And to think he almost joined Tottenham at the start of the season. The football gods move in mysterious ways.

Premiership: 9(10) apps, 12 goals; Champions League: 1(5) apps, 2 goals; FA Cup: 4(4) apps, 1 goal; League Cup: 3 apps, 3 goals; Charity Shield: 0(1) apps; Total: 17(20) apps, 18 goals

22 ERIK NEVLAND

The young Norwegian striker appeared just once in 1998-99, as a half-time substitute in the League Cup third-round tie against Bury, where he added to fellow countryman Ole Gunnar Solskjaer's earlier extra-time effort to clinch a 2-0 win. He then joined IFK Gothenburg on loan.

League Cup: 0(1) apps, 1 goal; Total: 0(1) apps, 1 goal

29 ALEX NOTMAN

Made only one appearance all season – the only one of his United career – in the disappointing League Cup exit at White Hart Lane. The Edinburgh-born forward came off the bench for the final 18 minutes of the 1-3 defeat to Tottenham and was full of running and determination to make an impact. He spent the latter half of the season on loan at Aberdeen.

League Cup: 0(1) apps; Total: 0(1) apps

The Coaches

ALEX FERGUSON, Manager

Of all the success enjoyed in his 26 years as Manchester United manager, lifting the seemingly impossible Treble was surely the greatest. Arsenal had raised the bar in 1997-98 and United met that challenge to take it higher still in 1999. Ferguson raised eyebrows by assembling a squad of two players for every position, including four top strikers, and critics sniped that he'd never keep them all happy. He was told that his side conceded too many goals to taste success in Europe. Even when his assistant departed mid-season, he took his time to ensure the right man was found as his replacement when many called for swift action. He rested key men at key times to ensure they'd be ready for when the campaign reached its climax. He proved his doubters wrong at every turn. Yet it wasn't simply the number and stature of the trophies collected; it was how they were won. Attack, attack, attack: it was football played in the finest traditions of the club. It was fitting that his final act of the season should be sending on the two men that would score the goals to land the European Cup and ultimately the Treble. He'd had that kind of season and richly deserved the knighthood that followed his masterminding of the unprecedented trophy haul. Sir Alex Ferguson, the greatest, we thank you.

BRIAN KIDD, Assistant Manager (August to December)

A hugely respected coach at United and the perfect foil to Alex Ferguson's managerial style, Kiddo's December departure to fulfil a long-held desire to dabble in management with Blackburn Rovers was a devastating blow, particularly to the home-grown players who the Collyhurst coach had helped nurture through the ranks. It was a bittersweet moment, therefore, when United's 0-0 draw at Ewood Park in May consigned Kidd and his Rovers team to relegation from the Premiership.

STEVE McCLAREN, Assistant Manager (February to May)

One day he was barking instructions on the Old Trafford touchline to the Derby County players, a few days later he was helping Alex Ferguson plot United's path to the impossible Treble. The boss took his time in locating Brian Kidd's replacement, and after making his choice said: 'No matter who I asked, the name Steve McClaren kept popping up. Quite simply, we wanted to make sure we got the best, and we have.' Bringing a fresh approach, the new assistant manager worked on the players' fitness, produced a programme to increase their stamina, knowing that hard work in winter would bring dividends in spring. An innovative coach, he presented new ideas to his manager and found ways to get more out of players already seemingly at the peak of their powers.

JIMMY RYAN, Coach/Acting Assistant Manager

The Scot filled the role vacated by Brian Kidd while Alex Ferguson embarked on his search for a permanent replacement. Stepping up from coaching the Reserves, he was even manager for a day as Alex Ferguson missed the 3-2 home defeat to Middlesbrough due to a family bereavement. A loyal club servant, Ryan played his part in helping the Reds through December's indifferent form.

Epilogue
by Ole Gunnar Solskjaer

There must have been about a million people in Nou Camp the night we clinched the Treble, because it feels like that many people have come up to me saying: 'I was there, you made my day,' or: 'That was the best day of my life, don't tell my wife. Better than my wedding day, my wedding night, it was the best day of my life.' I always tell them it's a pleasure, but that it was quite nice for me as well!

That whole season was just incredible. So much happened. Even at the very start, all the abuse that Becks was getting after the World Cup only made him more determined to succeed, and it inspired the rest of us too, because he was one of us. The team spirit in that squad was so special, not least because we worked at it. At the end of the season we had parties after winning each trophy, but going out was hardly a rarity for us: social events were important to us as a squad. I think it's very important for a team to have that possibility of going out drinking together. We knew that if there was a week until the next game, we could do it.

We always had parties, because along the way you have got to celebrate the little victories. If it's just: 'can't do it yet, can't do it yet', then that kills the team spirit. I think the parties relaxed us and meant we could be together in a different environment, away from football. We travelled a lot and we were together all the time anyway, and the lads were quite young so we recovered quickly. I think it was part of growing up together for a lot of that squad.

It was key to spend time together, because it helped foster the spirit the manager demanded. We just never gave up. If you wanted to play for Alex Ferguson, you gave everything. If he saw you give up once, that was it. If you're a quitter, you'll always be a quitter. There were never any lost causes. I think what happened in Turin epitomised what we were about that season. It wasn't just a case of dropping back, it was just going for it all the time. It was a proper Manchester United performance, a proper Alex Ferguson performance, and there were a few of those that season.

With that kind of mentality, we always had a chance of doing what we did. There were so many defining moments in the Treble season, but they all went for us. Off the field, we had things like Steve McClaren coming in, and Steve was important because he was a forward thinker who maybe changed our focus. But look at all the examples on the field, too. If Bergkamp scored his penalty against us in the FA Cup, I am sure Arsenal would have won the league and the FA Cup, so they would have had the Double and we would have had nothing, because we could not have changed games the way we did if Peter hadn't saved that penalty. But it's not just Peter's save, it's my goal against Liverpool or Keaney's header against Juventus, Yorkie against Charlton or Coley against Spurs. There were so many defining moments that went for us, and it's because of momentum.

Momentum is a funny thing in football. Momentum and confidence. You can get it for ten minutes in games or you can get it, like we did, for five months. After we lost to Middlesbrough when the manager was away, it just grew in us. From then on, it was just one of those things where we knew we were going to win the game. We just thought to ourselves: 'It'll happen, don't worry.' The best part is that it always did. One way or another, it always happened. That is what made the Treble year so special to so many people.

Season Statistics

The Treble by competition

Premiership

Most starts: Peter Schmeichel, Gary Neville 34

Top scorer: Dwight Yorke 18

Most assists: David Beckham 12

Biggest win: 8-1 v Nottingham Forest (a), 6 February 1999

Longest winning run: 5 matches (West Ham, Leicester, Charlton, Derby County, Nottingham Forest, 10 January – 6 February)

Longest unbeaten run: 20 matches (26 December – 16 May)

Best performance: 8-1 v Nottingham Forest (a); The scoreline says it all, and Ole Gunnar Solskjaer's four goals from the bench was a stunning contribution.

Highest attendance: 55,316 v Southampton (h)

Lowest attendance: 15,251 v Southampton (a)

Average attendance: 55,188 (h), 31,980 (a)

Total league attendance: 1,656,204

Champions League

Most starts: Peter Schmeichel, Jaap Stam 13

Top scorer: Dwight Yorke 8

Most assists: Dwight Yorke 8

Biggest win: 5-0 v Brondby (h), 4 November 1998

Best performance: 3-2 v Juventus (a); At 2-0 down, Keane's astonishing drive and determination hauled United back into the contest, and Yorke and Cole did the rest. Full speed ahead Barcelona.

Highest attendance: 91,000 v Bayern Munich (final)

Lowest attendance: 8,000 v LKS Lodz (a)

Average attendance (total): 54,613

Total Champions League attendance: 709,970

FA Cup

Most starts: Peter Schmeichel 8

Top scorer: Dwight Yorke 3

Most assists: Andy Cole 3

Biggest win: 2-0, Chelsea sixth round replay; Newcastle final

Best performance: 2-1 v Arsenal (n). The FA Cup semi-final replay at Villa Park was the best display all season. Epic in every way, it took guts, gall and one very special goal to win it in extra-time.

Highest attendance: 79,101 v Newcastle (final)

Lowest attendance: 30,223 v Arsenal (semi-final replay)

Average attendance (total): 49,728

Total FA Cup attendance: 397,824

Appearances

Top appearance-makers
(All competitions)

Peter Schmeichel, 56 total

'I said I would do my very best to go out on a high note. I feel privileged to be in this position with this great team and these great players.' – *Peter Schmeichel*

David Beckham 53(2), 55 total

'I've rested most of the players at some stage this season. Not Beckham. He has the best stamina of any player at this club.' – *Alex Ferguson*

Roy Keane, 53(2), 55 total

Keano was so important to us all through the season – he was our leader on the pitch.' – *Dwight Yorke*

Gary Neville, 54 total

'If you trust the players behind you in defence then you can get forward and attack. Gary offers that consistently every week.' – *Alex Ferguson*

Jaap Stam, 50(1), 51 total

'There was the pressure of a new club, a new country, new team-mates – and the fee. But Jaap coasted through it all. He was brilliant.' – *Gary Neville*

Appearance records

Most consecutive matches played: 28 (Gary Neville, 24 January – 26 May)

Games with goals: In six matches from 10 January – 6 February, Dwight Yorke scored 9 goals

Full quota: Peter Schmeichel and Jaap Stam started all 13 Champions League matches

League leader: Roy Keane made most Premiership appearances: 33(2) (35 total)

Super sub: Ole Gunnar Solskjaer made the most substitute appearances (20)

Goals

Scored by competition

Total goals scored: 128

Premiership: 80

Champions League: 31

FA Cup: 12

League Cup: 5

Charity Shield: 0

Conceded by competition

Total goals conceded: 63

Premiership: 37

Champions League: 16

FA Cup: 3

League Cup: 4

Charity Shield: 3

How United scored

Right foot: 73

Left foot: 28

Header: 26

Own goal: 1

Free-kick: 5

Penalty: 3

When the goals came

00-15 mins: 13

16-30 mins: 22

31-45 mins: 16

46-60 mins: 26

61-75 mins: 20

76-89 mins: 19

90+ mins: 12

Where United scored

Inside box: 111

Outside box: 17

Top 5 scorers

Dwight Yorke 29

Andy Cole 24

Ole Gunnar Solskjaer 18

Paul Scholes 11

Ryan Giggs 10

Top 5 assists

Dwight Yorke 20

David Beckham 19

Paul Scholes 12

Andy Cole 8

Teddy Sheringham 6

Scoring combinations

Beckham assist, Yorke goal: 9

Yorke assist, Cole goal: 7

Cole assist, Yorke goal: 6

Yorke assist, Solskjaer goal: 5

United scored three goals direct from set pieces:

Goal quirks

Yorke scored 11 headed goals

Yorke scored 17 first-half goals

Scholes hit 7 of 11 goals on his left foot

Solskjaer scored 8 goals after 80 mins

Yorke v Charlton (Beckham free-kick)

Johnsen v Nottingham Forest (Beckham corner)

Keane v Juventus (Beckham corner)

Acknowledgements

Even with three authors, writing this book has been a monumental effort which has required the assistance of several incredibly helpful people.

At Simon & Schuster, Ian Marshall, Tom Whiting and their team have provided unyielding support and flexibility, while Paul Thomas and James White at Manchester United have been vital figures throughout the copy approval process and at various stages between the book's conception and execution.

MU Media scribe Mark Froggatt has been an invaluable ally throughout the months of interviews and transcripts, while MUTV's Steve Bibby, Laura Kane and Mike Shaw were herculean in their efforts to provide us with footage of every single second of every single game. Craig South at PDI also played a key role in filling in any blanks which arose.

Simon Davies, John Peters and Matt Peters were ultra-accommodating as we trawled through their vault of Treble season imagery, while Karen Shotbolt and John Allen provided assistance in the player recruitment process. For that same reason, the efforts of Maric Priest, Kate Lowe, Claire Robson, Louise Wanless, Andrew Lisgo and Jim Solbakken were central to our drive to arrange interviews.

Sincere thanks go to all the above, but special gratitude must be extended to the players and staff of the 1998-99 vintage. Their generosity of time, spirit and memories has been genuinely staggering and they have done nothing to dispel the notion that they are a truly special group of human beings.